# Two Sisters' Secret

# Diane T. Holmes

Brighton Publishing LLC

435 N. Harris Drive

Mesa, AZ 85203

# Two Sisters' Secret

## Diane T. Holmes

Brighton Publishing LLC
435 N. Harris Drive
Mesa, AZ 85203

www.BrightonPublishing.com

Copyright © 2020 Diane T. Holmes

Printed in the United States of America

ISBN: 978-1-62183-566-0

# First Edition

Cover Design: Tom Rodriguez

# ᑕᔆᕈAcknowledgmentsᕀᘛ

Thanks to Gayle at the Pleasant Hill Library for helping me start this journey - pulling books for me on writing and publishing, to Professor Susan Shapiro, New York University, appreciation for her advice and direction following my first outline, to editors, Betsy Maury, and Judy Hagey for their excellent skills, ideas, and suggestions, and to Mel Hughes for her additions and belief in Grandma Bernadine's story.

A special thanks to the people in St. Benedict, Iowa, for putting together, *The History of St. Benedict Parish 1877-1977*, an invaluable resource for my book.

*Two Sisters' Secret* would not be possible without family. I am grateful for so many who shared their treasured memories: my siblings, Joe and Marilyn, who also verified birth and death dates of older relatives mentioned in my book, my son, Brian, for his critiques, proposals, and ideas, my husband, Lyell, daughters, Julie and Jackie, daughter-in-law, Laila, and son-in-law, Barry, for their collective suggestions and encouragement, and my grandkids Brad, Nate, Benjamin, Daniel, Trevor, Sarah, and Lauren for their interest.

A special recognition and appreciation for my acquisition's editor Don McGuire and Brighton Publishing for their guidance, explanations, and work in making *Two Sisters' Secret* available for readers to enjoy.

And prayers of gratitude to God for giving me patience and persistence.

# Dedication

*I dedicate this novel to Grandma Bernadine.*
*Without her life this story would not be possible.*

# ᴄ↝Chapter One↜ᴏ

"**I** don't want to keep your secret, Elizabeth." Bernadine burst into tears. "I feel so deprived. You are taking advantage of me. I want to tell."

"Hush, you promised me. No more of your outbursts, please. Be quiet and not another word about it. Let's be happy and enjoy our time here before we go to the new country, America."

"I'm going to see my best friend, Judith." Bernadine stomped off slamming the door behind her.

She was with Judith for only a short time when Elizabeth shouted for her. Bernadine grabbed Judith's hand and dragged her into the woods.

"What are you doing?" Judith demanded.

"I don't want to go home," Bernadine replied, stalking forward. "Everything is different. I hate it."

"But she's your—"

"She's my *sister*, and I should obey. But it's not fair, Judith—it's not."

Her friend gazed at her in disbelief.

"Well," Bernadine relented—just a little. "How would *you* like it? I told you what she wants."

"You have to go home sometime. You have no other place to go."

Bernadine gave her a wistful look. "We could stay here in the forest forever …"

"And eat nuts and mushrooms for every meal? I don't think so, Bernadine."

Bernadine sighed. "Fine, I'll go home. But I won't like it."

Judith took her hand. "I know. We'll walk back together."

"It's not going to be my home much longer anyway." Bernadine wailed. "I don't want to leave this place, Judith. You're my best friend—how can I leave you? How can I leave these woods and green pastures? How can I leave my church? Or the cemetery I walk past each day where my ancestors are buried? Everything and everyone I've ever known is here, and she … Elizabeth … wants me to forget, and go with her to a strange land. What if there are no pastures, no churches? I've heard it's all cowboys and Indians and uncivilized."

"It's not that strange," Judith observed. "And while there may be cowboys and Indians, they say the Indians are leaving, and the cowboys … maybe they're handsome, who knows? They say there are churches, woods, and pastures in the United States of America, too. You would be leaving me, yes. But we can write to each other. Who knows, maybe someday I will even come to your new home myself. And other than that, you are leaving your ancestors, but even though we have different faiths, we both believe our ancestors will not stay sleeping in their graves. Our God can resurrect the dead."

Judith was so levelheaded. Sometimes Bernadine thought Judith was even older than Elizabeth instead of eleven, like Bernadine herself. She nodded. "You make me feel better. Better than Elizabeth does, anyway. All right, let's go."

Elizabeth beckoned when the pair came into sight of the house. "Didn't you hear me calling? We must begin packing." She glanced at Judith. "Thanks for bringing her home, Judith. I'm sure she would have ignored me if not for you."

Judith blushed, but made no reply. She waved and trotted back to the rutted dirt road.

Elizabeth gave Bernadine a stern look. "There's not much time, and you haven't begun to pack. I've already gone through your things and removed everything you've outgrown …" she smiled. "You are growing like a weed, you know. Anyway, we can't take much with us, so you must pick out your favorite clothes."

She pulled the smaller girl into the house and avoided the pile of cartons and bags littering the floor as the two made their way back to the narrow room they had always shared.

"I can at least take all my books, can't I?" There was a pleading note in Bernadine's voice that made Elizabeth want to change her mind and cancel all her plans. But she could not do that; this was her last chance at a decent life for both of them. Bernadine might not understand it now, but she was young. Elizabeth was older; almost twenty-five and she knew how the world worked.

She made her way back to the heap of cartons and found an old leather satchel. "You can take as many books as you can fit in this bag."

"But I can't even get one shelf full into that."

"I'm paring my entire closet to whatever fits in the smallest trunk. Does that sound fair, Dena?"

Bernadine nodded, but there were tears in her eyes. "I still don't understand why we have to do this."

"We need a fresh start," Elizabeth said. "Now, please don't ask again."

It took half a day for Bernadine to pick her books. She would put one in the satchel, only to replace it with another. Then, instead of choosing the next book, she would look at the one she had taken out—and put it back in again. She rearranged the books again and again, trying to fit more in the satchel. When she finally filled it, it was too heavy for her to lift, and she still had to take some out.

When Elizabeth was grading papers at the *Grundschule*, Judith came to the house.

"I can't take all my books," Bernadine said. "These are all the ones I can't take. Would you like them?"

Judith lit up like a candelabra. "Could I really? Which one?"

"All of them. Elizabeth says I can't take them with me."

"There are so many …" Judith's eyes filled with tears. "I can't pay you for them."

"Nobody is paying for them." Bernadine tossed her head so hard her long hair bounced. "Elizabeth sold our house, so whoever bought it is coming in and keeping everything we leave behind. But I don't want them to have my books; I want you to have them. Come on, load up your arms, and I'll load mine, and we'll take them over to your house. If we hurry, we can finish before she gets home."

It took four trips to transfer all the books to Judith's house, and Judith's mother was frowning when they came in with the last load. "Are you *sure* you can do this?"

"My *mother* is dead," Bernadine said with a scowl. "And so is my *father*. That's why we are moving. I don't want to move; I love Germany and I want to stay here, but my sister doesn't care. And those books were mine and no one else's, and I can give them to anyone I wish. I wish Judith to have them."

She climbed the ladder up to Judith's attic room, and Judith gave her disbelieving mother a shrug and followed.

Bernadine was giggling. "It's going to be crowded."

Judith looked around the room. "It was already crowded. Now it's going to be stuffed like a goose neck. But I don't care. When Shifra gets married next month, I'll have the whole attic to myself, plenty of room for books then." She sniffed. "Funny, I thought you would be here for the party."

"I thought so too. I'm sorry. You know I'll miss you."

"And I will miss you. You're my best friend in the world. Promise you will write, Bernadine."

"I will. And you had better write back."

They smiled through tears then and hugged.

Bernadine watched as the carriage approached. She swallowed and bit her lip.

"*Guten morgen, mädchen.*" The driver extended a hand to Elizabeth. Gathering her skirts, she stepped up and into the carriage and settled on the padded leather seat. She patted the spot beside her as Bernadine hesitated, shyly eyeing the driver. She put a hand up to her short, light-brown hair, feeling self-conscious. Elizabeth had insisted on cutting it the night before, and Bernadine had cried, thinking she could not even take her hair to this new country.

"Come on," Elizabeth laughed. "He won't hurt you."

"I'm not worried about him," Bernadine whispered. "I'm nervous about … everything."

"Don't be. We're starting a new life. It'll be our grand adventure—America. Perhaps we'll be regaled someday like one of those famous explorers—Columbus, or Ponce de Leon."

Bernadine managed a weak smile. She took a deep breath to calm her nerves, and then put a foot on the step. Not as tall as her sister, she had to bounce on one foot three or four times before she could clamber aboard. While she settled herself, the driver threw their trunks and valises into the back of the carriage. Bernadine twisted around to watch him, and then looked back at her sister.

"When do we have to start speaking English?"

"We'll practice a little every day, maybe with our sessions getting longer each day. By the time we leave the ship I want us both able to speak English comfortably all the time. You'll do fine." Elizabeth sounded pleased, the way she did when one of her slow students finally understood a long division problem. Bernadine gritted her teeth and looked away as the driver jumped aboard and clucked to the horses.

They passed the cemetery where Mama and Papa were buried. Bernadine remembered them and the love they had given her when she was just a small child. She recalled how Papa had died, and then Mama only a few months after. Did she remember right ...had Mama really said "Child, you must start over" before she died? Was this what Elizabeth was always talking about? What did "starting over" mean, and why was it so important to Elizabeth that they had to move all the way to America to do it? Hadn't they already moved once?

The carriage rolled past Friedrich's General Store with the colorful handbill in the window. America: Land of Opportunity—Book passage today on the SS Trave. The sign that had started it all, Bernadine remembered. From that day to this, Elizabeth never shut her mouth about America and that magic word, "opportunity."

They drove past Schloss Varlar in Rosendahl. The castle looked as clean and white as a set of freshly laundered sheets. Bernadine and Judith had always thought it would be the best thing in the world just to peek through one of those dozens of huge windows, but nobody could get that close. A deep moat surrounded the palace.

Around them, the gently rolling countryside was a lush patchwork of woods and pastures. A sob caught in Bernadine's throat as she thought of Judith, and she took out the packet her friend had given her. "Don't look at it until you are well away from Coesfeld," Judith had warned her, her stern voice at war with the merriment in her eyes.

"How far are we from home?" Bernadine asked.

Elizabeth gave her an annoyed look, "About four thousand miles."

"I mean, from our *former* home." Bernadine bit her bottom lip.

"Almost five miles and you know it. You and Judith used to walk around that silly castle all the time."

Bernadine did not reply. She caressed the package again. "Five miles is good enough." She opened the envelope. There was a note in Judith's thin, spidery handwriting, and a photograph, a real photograph, in stark black and white and shades of gray. She looked at the picture; it was a castle she had never seen before—or rather, the great ruins of a castle. The huge, round tower was the only part of the castle still intact, and it was so big it made the nearby trees look like children. A majestic church stood adjacent to the castle ruins, and below, running down the side of a craggy hill, ran the neat rows of grapevines, tied to upright sticks like wooden soldiers.

She sniffed once, and then looked at the note.

*My dear Bernadine,*

*This is Bischofstein Castle on the Moselle River. I received it in yesterday's post with a letter from my brother Levi who has gone to be a winemaker's apprentice. Levi purchased the picture at a shop and had to spend two whole pfennigs for it. He sent it to me because he knows I love to look at castles, but I am giving it to you. After all, there may not be any castles in the United States of America, and you can look at this and remember the castles here in Prussia. Besides, I don't have a photograph of myself, so when you look at this, you can remember me as well. I will always be ...*

*Your friend,*

*Judith*

Tears filling her eyes, Bernadine replaced the note and the photograph in the torn envelope, and then returned it to her reticule.

"Don't cry, little sister," Elizabeth said, giving her a quick hug. "We're not running away from anything."

"No—we are being chased." Bernadine couldn't keep the bitterness from her voice.

Elizabeth sighed. "We are running *to* something, Dena. We are running to a new home in a wonderful land of opportunity."

Bernadine looked into the distance, and too softly for Elizabeth to hear, she murmured, "I'll come back someday."

From Münster they took the train all the way to Bremerhaven. Neither girl had ever traveled so fast before. The unheard of speed of thirty miles per hour, which they reached several times, was dizzying. Twice they had to change trains, and once they had to stop while a farmer moved his cows across the track on their way to another pasture.

Bernadine did not speak to her sister for most of the trip. Elizabeth was convinced that everything would be wonderful, but as they chugged through the bright green fields and past the heavy, dark forests, all Bernadine could think was that she would never see her home again, never see green pastures so bright or forests so deep. Never see a castle. Everything she knew and loved was lost to her and Elizabeth … their whole relationship had changed in the last year. Bernadine hated it, but there was nothing to be done for it.

At Bremerhaven, they hired a cab, and the driver maneuvered the two-wheeled Hansom through the traffic at the port of Bremerhaven, drawing as close to the loading area as possible. Two muscular men appeared as soon as the driver reined the horse to a stop, ready to unload the trunks and bags. Elizabeth took Bernadine by the hand and led her through the crowd to the emigration authorities. Their papers in order, the agent approved the Vornholdt sisters for passage.

*"Dort drüben."* The agent stabbed a thumb over his shoulder. "You must go through the medical building before you can board."

"This way, Dena," Elizabeth gathered their belongings. They fell in line behind a family with four young children. A man in an official-looking uniform walked back and forth beside the line intoning, "Here you will be given minor physicals. Your throats will be checked for tonsillitis and strep throat, and your chests and lungs for congestion and pneumonia. In a separate area, your eyes will be examined for trachoma, a contagious, chronic eye disease. Please be patient as you wait your turn. If all goes well, you will receive a health certificate that allows you to board the steamship. Don't lose it. It will take two days to process your papers, and the steamship company will provide lodging for you while you wait."

Bernadine snickered. "He sounds bored."

"Maybe he is. How would you like to have to repeat the same thing again and again? I didn't always enjoy repeating myself to my students," Elizabeth said, "but they usually listened after the second or third time I said something."

"I miss school," Bernadine muttered.

"I'm sure there will be one in our new home town."

"What if I don't speak English well enough? Or what if I'm too old?"

Elizabeth laughed. "I am a good teacher. Don't worry; you'll be perfect. And twelve years old is young enough to stay in school, even in the United States."

While waiting for their medical papers, Elizabeth and Bernadine listened to a briefing on the rules and regulations aboard ship and what to expect when they arrived at Ellis Island. Then they walked around the bustling town of Bremerhaven. Bernadine scuffed her feet on the cobblestones and looked in the shop windows. Everyone seemed to sell umbrellas.

"It rains here all the time, they told me," Elizabeth said. "That's why there are so many umbrella vendors."

"This place stinks," Bernadine said.

"Don't be rude."

"I'm not—it does stink. Ever since we've been here I've smelled nothing but fish."

"Bremerhaven is a fishing town. Did you expect to smell flowers?"

That night at the *bakerei* across from their boarding house, Elizabeth purchased a small *berliner ballen* for each of them. "I have to be careful with our money," she said. "But tonight, we will celebrate."

Bernadine tasted the fat jellied doughnut. "Mmmm, I haven't had anything this good since—"

"Bernadine ..." Elizabeth's voice carried a warning.

Bernadine wanted to throw the pastry at her then, but she only looked down and mumbled, "I was going to say, since Mama was alive."

"I remember. I used to help her make these." Elizabeth swallowed. "But I really don't want to talk about the past anymore. I've told you this already."

"Do you want to forget ... Mama and Papa?" Suddenly, the berliner seemed to taste like sawdust.

11

"No, of course not, but ... you don't remember everything that happened in those days, little sister. And there are things I'd rather forget. I'd rather concentrate on the future."

"It isn't fair." Bernadine could barely hear her own voice.

"No, it isn't," Elizabeth agreed. "But it is *best*. Please do not speak of it again. It will be our secret."

That night Elizabeth had almost drifted into a doze when she heard Bernadine crying softly. She sighed and went to her sister's little bed, sitting down and pulling the girl into her arms.

"What has you so upset, sweet Dena?"

"I'm scared ..." Bernadine choked and began to sob. "I don't care if some people didn't like us back home. At least it was home. I had a friend. And you were different. Everything now is unlike it was, and I hate it. I don't want to go to America."

Elizabeth stroked her back. "It's true, little one—things are different now. But I think they will be better. You need to believe it, too. Dena, this is what life's all about. People grow and change. They get married, they move from place to place. The important thing is never to stop learning. America is a new country, and full of new things. To you it's frightening, but I find it exciting. You may think so too, in time. You're very young now, you know. But keep growing, keep learning. Love the people you meet. Life is wonderful, baby, but you must live it."

The next day, it rained from morning to night. The sisters did not venture out since Elizabeth didn't want to spend the money on an umbrella.

A new morning found them waiting, Elizabeth impatiently shifting from one foot to another, as the clerk wrote "April 9, 1892" on the line marked DEPARTURE DATE and smashed a rubber stamp down on the "APPROVED" section. "Good luck," he blurted out and handed over the papers.

"We made it." Bernadine waved their certificates over her head as they made their way up the gangplank.

"I can't believe we're finally on this ship," Elizabeth chuckled, stopping and dropping her bags; just carrying those up the gangway made her arms sore. She rubbed her arms for a moment. "Let's get going. I can't wait to see our quarters."

She again picked up a bag in each hand and almost skipped down the narrow passageway. Starting a new life in America meant freedom and excitement for her. Bernadine still had her doubts, but she grabbed the bag with her books and followed struggling to keep up.

In their cabin, Elizabeth hummed Mendelssohn's *Spinning Song* and danced around as she sized up their temporary home. It wasn't spacious—not like a first-class cabin but not like steerage, either. She breathed a prayer of thanks that her savings and the sale of the farm had been enough to buy tickets for a second-class cabin. She opened the top drawer on the small three-drawer chest and told Bernadine, "I'll take the top drawer and half of the middle one. You can share the middle one with me and have the bottom one." Elizabeth began unpacking while Bernadine sat quietly on one of the single beds, trying to stay out of her sister's way.

"Do you like the room, Dena?"

"I don't know. I've only just got here."

Elizabeth sighed. "I know it's not very big, and we have to share bathrooms down the hallway with many other people—it's not very private. But ..." she grinned. "We do have two single beds."

Bernadine grinned back, "With very firm, thin mattresses."

"That should feel like home, at least." Elizabeth agreed.

"Except that they're nailed to the floor." Bernadine pointed.

"That's so we don't slide back and forth when the ocean is rough."

"And I suppose that's why there are railings on each side, to keep us from falling out of bed. It was kind of them to do that for us."

"Woolen blankets, too," Elizabeth said. "This will be a nice little home for the next couple of weeks."

"As long as we follow the rules," Bernadine picked up the long list, and Elizabeth read it over and sighed.

"It says we get fresh linens in a bundle at our door every four days, and we need to strip our beds and place the sheets, pillowcases, and towels outside our room. Help me remember that, will you, Dena?" Before Bernadine could nod, Elizabeth was reading the next line.

"We use the pitcher and basin here on the washstand for cleaning up, sponge bathing, and washing hair. It says here that large tubs of hot water are placed on stands in the hallways each morning and evening. We should get our water right away before it gets cool."

"I remember the tubs," Bernadine said. "You can't miss the signs around them: Use Water Sparingly. Do Not Waste. Supplies are Limited."

"All right, it won't be like home, but I think we will be comfortable." Elizabeth shrugged, "For a couple of weeks, anyway."

"It really takes two weeks to cross the ocean?"

"I think I read twelve to fourteen days."

Bernadine whistled. "It took Columbus several months."

"Four months—and do not whistle; it's not ladylike."

Bernadine's face reddened. "You're not my mother. You can't tell me what to do."

Elizabeth fixed her eyes on the girl. "Don't start that again."

The two glared at each other, but Bernadine looked down first, as always.

Elizabeth huffed. "It's going to be a long voyage, after all."

Bernadine tried to share Elizabeth's enthusiasm for their journey, but ocean travel was decidedly not to her liking. She spent the first two days throwing up; she had never known of such a thing as "seasickness," and reflected that if she had known about it before they left, she would have stayed behind, even if she had to live in the woods forever and eat nothing but Judith's much-feared nuts and mushrooms. "This is worse than death," she muttered after losing the little amount of breakfast she'd managed to eat.

Elizabeth was nauseous too, but she tolerated it better. "They say it stops after a few days."

"You always say, 'They say,' but you never say who says it."

"Dena, be reasonable."

She became more reasonable when her stomach stopped heaving, but by then it was raining. And when it wasn't raining, a foggy mist shrouded the ship, and the heavy scent of burning coal hung over them and she found herself complaining again. "I'm tired of being cooped up in our cabin. I want some fresh air."

"Then we'll go and walk on deck," Elizabeth suggested, trying to be agreeable. But the wind was fierce and the waves high; the deck was wet and slippery, and it was still difficult to walk on a moving ship. They returned after only a few minutes.

Bernadine looked at her. "Don't you worry about losing your balance or the ship being wrecked, Elizabeth?"

"A little," Elizabeth admitted. "I'd be foolish not to recognize the risk. But this is not a little fishing boat—it's a large steamer, built to withstand turbulence. And the storms will pass eventually."

"I hope so." Bernadine sighed. "I don't think I was made to be a great explorer. I get scared when the ship rolls, and I'm ready to be back on solid ground."

"Well, we still need fresh air. We've smelled little but coal and vomit for the last three days."

That night a baby was born just two cabins away, and everyone's spirits improved. "Did you see that tiny baby?" Elizabeth asked Bernadine.

"I did, a baby boy. He looked healthy, but he certainly was tiny. It's a good thing there are doctors on board for emergencies like that. What a story the parents have to tell their son when he gets older. 'You were born in the middle of the ocean.'"

Bernadine and Elizabeth even went to see the family, and the newborn, a lusty, loud baby boy, waved his fists and made strange noises, almost like a duck quacking, when they held him.

"Oh, he's wonderful ... better even than a puppy." Bernadine rhapsodized as they returned to their own cabin. "Elizabeth, do you think we'll ever have children?"

Elizabeth chuckled. "I will settle for finding a husband. Children are easy to find. Husbands are not. Let's both get married first."

"I'm eleven. How can I get married?"

"I mean—let's just let the days take care of themselves. Eventually, you'll grow up, and you'll want to marry and have children. Just make sure that you get married first. Girls who don't marry first often have problems later."

"Humph. Mama certainly warned us about it enough."

Elizabeth paused a while, thinking. "I hear there will be a wedding here in a few days. I'd like to see it."

Bernadine nodded. "What will a wedding be like aboard a ship in the middle of the ocean?"

"We'll have to go if we want to find out."

"I can't stand this inactivity," Elizabeth moaned. "Bernadine, I have to get out and walk a while. Will you come with me?"

Bernadine looked up from *Treasure Island* and shook her head. "I don't like the top deck. It's too easy to fall."

"I see you're reading about someone else's adventure," she said gesturing toward the book Bernadine held. Elizabeth had given it to Bernadine on her last birthday. She hoped Bernadine would adopt some of Jim Hawkin's adventurous spirit and courage while realizing their own adventure was far less fraught with danger.

"Don't fall," Bernadine warned.

"I'll be careful—but I'm going. You can read about someone else's adventures, or you can have one of your own. I'm going to have one of my own."

Bernadine watched as she grabbed her big straw hat, tied it on, and headed for the door. "Don't fall overboard."

Elizabeth snorted and let the door bang shut as she headed out. Bernadine was such a … child. "Was I ever that young?" she murmured as she climbed the steps to the top deck.

She walked to the promenade. Rough seas made it difficult. She staggered from side to side, trying to keep her balance. Her feet tripped faster and faster, and she stumbled across the deck. Then the ship swayed the other way, and she stumbled backward; she tried again, tripping, almost falling, tripping again, and finally standing still, gripping a nailed-down deck chair. Suddenly, a huge wave rocked the ship. She lost control and tumbled forward and a pair of arms shot out and caught her just before she could land on her face.

Struggling up, she turned to face a tall, young man with chestnut hair and twinkling blue eyes. He grinned at her. "You are ... well?" he asked in hesitant English.

Her cheeks flushed, she stuttered back in German, "Oh, I am sorry, but it is hard to walk with the ship rocking back and forth."

"*Ach*," he said and laughed. "Thank God you are also German. There are a dozen Englanders on board, and two dozen Poles and Russians. This much English I speak—" he spread his hands about a foot apart— "and THIS much Polish." He moved his index finger and thumb about an inch apart, "And no Russian at all. Yet I keep running into only Englanders and Poles and Russians. And, now, God be praised, I've run into another German and a beautiful one at that."

Elizabeth felt her cheeks flaming with embarrassed delight. "You are a flatterer, sir."

"Not in your case." He chuckled and extended his right hand. "I'm Hans Hartmann."

Elizabeth responded with a smile and a handshake. "Elizabeth Vornholdt."

"Have you had breakfast yet? I was just going to the ship's mess—"

"I would like to have breakfast with you, Hans."

Smiling, he took her arm and led her down to the dining room. "You know, I had a cousin in the Navy. What was I thinking to say the ship's mess? I'm glad you knew what I meant."

Elizabeth barely registered his words. She was looking at his navy blazer and well-pressed flannel trousers. She wondered if he was in first class. He was far too well-dressed for steerage. She was still marveling over his clothes when he pulled out a chair for her.

"Now you must tell me all about yourself, *Fräulein*."

"What would you like to know?"

"Everything," he said his eyes warm and locked on hers. "I want to know you like my favorite book. Tell me, where in the United States are you going?"

"We're going to Iowa."

"Not alone, then. Do you have family traveling with you?"

"Just a sister. You may have seen her."

"And you left no family behind in Germany—no parents or siblings?" Hans asked.

"No relatives at all. First, Papa passed away, and within a year Mama died. I think she died of a broken heart. She and Papa were close. Papa was an only child, and Mama's sisters died young, so we had no relatives to take us in. I was devastated, but a couple of good neighbors helped with chores and the harvest. After Mama died, people from Coesfeld helped me sell the land, machinery, and livestock. I can't believe I made it through all that work, teaching, and caring for Bernadine as well. She and I are the only ones left in our family …" Her voice trailed off, and she looked up at him. "I'm sorry. I hope I didn't bore you."

"It would be impossible for you to bore me. Do you know, I've noticed you before, Miss Elizabeth," Hans said. "I wanted to meet you, but could not contrive an introduction." He grinned. "Now I must give thanks to the mighty god Neptune for his help."

She laughed, feeling shy.

"And the young lady you are usually with? This is your sister?"

"Hmmm? Oh, Bernadine. Yes. She's twelve."

"That's quite an age gap. Forgive me, but are you not at least twenty?"

"Flatterer," she said and blushed. "I'm twenty-four."

"*Mein Gott*—I am but twenty-eight myself. You carry yourself well for a woman of such *advanced* age."

At this, she laughed aloud. "That's why Bernadine is usually with me—she acts as my cane."

"Well, her loss is my gain, for I shall be your cane today, lovely Elizabeth. You will walk with me again, yes?"

"Oh, yes."

Bernadine looked up to see Elizabeth all but floating into the room. "What happened to you?"

"Oh, Bernadine, I met a young man—the most handsome, nicest young man on this ship. Perhaps in the whole world. I lost my balance when the ship started rocking, and I literally fell into his arms. He saved me from hitting the deck. Then we talked a while and ate breakfast together."

"We already had breakfast." Bernadine rubbed her eyes and yawned.

"Being with him made me hungry all over again," Elizabeth confessed.

Bernadine looked up as if praying for patience. "This is not the first young man you've ever met. Why are you acting so silly?"

"Don't be cruel, Dena. This is the nicest young man, and he likes me. He wants to meet you, too. He's seen us before and thinks we are lovely people. Please don't spoil his impression of us."

"What did you tell him?"

"Just the usual things—that our parents are dead, that I'm twenty-four, and that you are twelve, and that we are bound for America."

"But that's not—"

Elizabeth's brows came down. "You asked what I told him. That is what I told him. We are having dinner with him today, you and I, and tomorrow we will accompany him to the wedding. I will ask you to be polite and not contradict me. This is only common courtesy."

Elizabeth opened a trunk and pulled out one skirt after another. "I wonder if I should wear something dressier."

Bernadine watched as she pulled one outfit after another out of the trunk, looked each over carefully and laid it aside before finally settling on a navy-blue skirt and white shirt with a ruffled bib and mutton chop sleeves.

"This Hans must be something exceptional for all the time you're putting into choosing what to wear," Bernadine said.

"Bernadine, just wait till you see him. He's very handsome." Elizabeth adjusted her skirt and repinned her hair. I'm ready now. Let's go."

Hans, Elizabeth, and Bernadine celebrated the wedding with other guests. By this time, Bernadine was, in her own shy way, trying to be friendly to the young man. And his smiling and teasing seemed to put her at ease.

The bride wore a pale green suit and a brimmed, green felt hat. The groom had chosen a simple, dark suit.

"Isn't everything tasty, Bernadine? Look at these tiny sandwiches. And the wedding cake is delicious. It's all so lovely for a reception aboard ship," Elizabeth smiled.

Bernadine, her mouth full, just looked at the other people in the room.

Hans cocked his head. "I hear music in the next room. Let's see what is happening."

On the dance floor, guests moved in time to the music. The band consisted of a violin player, someone on a harmonica, and few others with makeshift instruments.

"Let's dance, Bernadine." Elizabeth twirled her sister onto the floor.

"I'm just a clumsy beginner," Bernadine protested. "You can dance with Hans."

Hans, hearing Bernadine, joined the two. "You can both dance with me. Who goes first?"

Bernadine cleared her throat, and Elizabeth said, "I'll go first, Hans. We'll show my sister how it's done."

The two polkaed and did the *landler* together, and Bernadine watched in apprehension. After five dances with Elizabeth, Hans approached Bernadine and gently waltzed her around the room. Bernadine, flushed and a little breathless, curtseyed to Hans and turned to Elizabeth. "I'm tired. I'm going to bed."

"But we only just got here." Hans cried.

23

Elizabeth chuckled. "I'm exhausted too. I'm sorry, Hans—will you excuse us?"

"Now I shall have to dance the *Zwiefacher* with the fat Bavarians," Hans said with a pout. "Good night, lovely ladies. Shall I see you to your room?"

Bernadine giggled. "No, no, Hans—you can't keep the Bavarians waiting."

Elizabeth sighed as they walked back to their cabin. "Wasn't it fun? Now we've seen a birth and a wedding on a ship. What's next, I wonder."

"I'm not sure I want to find out," Bernadine said. "I like Hans. Even when I try not to like him, I have to. You're right that he's nice. But he's coming between us—and it frightens me."

Bernadine found Elizabeth was spending more and more time in the company of Hans Hartmann and less time in the company of her only family. *Well*, she thought, *perhaps he is nicer than I have been. And certainly, he seems to look forward to America. Not like me. I have not been nice lately, and I don't look forward to America. It scares me.*

Meanwhile, Elizabeth was telling Hans some of the same information. "There's such a difference in our ages, and it's hard to remember what I was like then. The children I taught in school were younger than she is. It makes it difficult to talk to her; I'm always talking as if she's too young or too old. And she's afraid of the whole notion of change. America will be different from Germany; therefore, she thinks it is to be feared."

"She should talk to some of the other people," Hans told her. "So many passengers on this very boat have put all their hopes and dreams into this change. Maybe if she hears it from them, she'll look forward to it more."

"You are a born older brother, Hans," Elizabeth said. "I'll try that."

"You may think of me as an older brother for little Bernadine. But I'll be disappointed if *you* think that way of me."

Elizabeth blushed. She found herself doing that a lot lately.

Back in their cabin, she asked Bernadine if she was still worried about America.

"I'm trying to read more about it," Bernadine said slowly. "There are some books and magazines in the ship's library. And much of what I read is fascinating, I admit. But that is nothing like seeing it firsthand. I'm more anxious each day to get there."

"Hans and I were talking about it. He says there's nothing to be anxious about."

Bernadine tossed her head, and her too-short hair bobbed. "He's being met by a priest when he gets to the United States."

"We're being met by our own sponsor."

"Is he a priest?"

"No, but I'm sure he's a nice man."

"But we don't know this. We don't know if he'll help us or sell us into slavery."

Elizabeth burst out laughing. "There is no slavery in the United States now. I told you about the war they fought some thirty years ago. The war ended slavery."

"Yes, but people still get shanghaied there."

"I know the article you're speaking of, I saw it too. But that's in San Francisco, which is in California—on the Pacific Ocean. We're going to Iowa, which is nowhere near that area. Dear Dena, stop being so determined to hate your new home."

"I just hope people treat us well, that's all."

That afternoon, when the winds calmed, and the sun shone, Elizabeth studied her sister as she sat on the upper deck pretending to read a book.

*In personality and form, she is so different than I was at that age*, Elizabeth mused. Bernadine's almost-twelve-year-old body showed little interest in maturing. The short haircut Elizabeth had insisted on for the long journey suited Bernadine's face and her inattention to her physical appearance. Of course, it also lessened their resemblance. Now only their straight-edge noses and fair skin suggested they were siblings.

"Are you reading or daydreaming? I haven't seen you turn a page in some time." Elizabeth smiled, rumpling the girl's hair.

Bernadine closed the book. "I can't concentrate. I wonder what it will be like in America. Will people like us? Will we be happy?"

"Why don't we talk to some of the other passengers and find out why they left Germany, and what they expect to find in America," Elizabeth said. "That might answer some of your concerns."

Elizabeth held Bernadine's hand as they walked around the upper deck together, looking for likely interview subjects.

"I'm going to get a herd of dairy cattle," said a man in a green hat and matching plaid jacket. "Then I'll sell milk and cream to the creamery where they make cheese. I'll be able to make my own butter. My brother in Wisconsin said he'd help me get started."

As they left the man, Bernadine shook her head. "He has relatives in America and a place to go. He's one lucky person. I wish we had relatives there."

"We did have Uncle Walter. He's the one who asked Mr. Herman to help us, so we do have a representative from Iowa meeting us," Elizabeth reminded her.

"He's a stranger." Bernadine stuck her bottom lip out. "And Uncle Walter died. It was the last letter you got before we sailed, remember? Mr. Herman said—"

"He said he'd still meet us, and he will. We will be fine."

# Chapter Two

An older gentleman in dark pants and a blue flannel shirt told them, "I am going to Iowa to stay with a younger brother who is already established. He will get me started farming, raising cattle and hogs. I'll work for him for my room and board until I am ready to go on my own."

And as they walked away, Bernadine observed, "Again, here is someone who has relatives to give him a start. We're on our own. Do you think he is going close to where we're going in Iowa?"

"I hope so. Maybe he'll be on our train, and we'll recognize a familiar face. I'll admit I envy people who have relatives to show them the way and help them get started. I wish Uncle Walter had lived longer. But at least we have a sponsor and a place to stay for as long as we need.

"Look, Bernadine. Some passengers are writing letters—probably to family or friends left behind. We don't even have anyone back in Germany to write to, but we have each other." She gave her sister a quick squeeze.

Bernadine pulled away. "I will write to Judith."

"Yes, I forgot about her. Well, you can write her. But I'm still your sister, and I'll take care of you."

Bernadine fixed her with a cold stare. Then she looked away. "I see quite a few immigrants play cards. Do you know any card games?"

"Not really, but I'm willing to learn. I noticed some board games too."

"It's time to eat."

"I'm ready." Elizabeth gave her a bright smile.

Bernadine sighed. "Don't tell me we have to eat with Hans again."

The smile evaporated, and Elizabeth's patience along with it. "You don't have to eat with Hans if you don't want to. I, however, plan to eat with him."

"I'm not hungry. We only eat beans, beef and rice every day anyhow."

"Then read. You know, a good girl would be thankful we have something to eat. Think of the people in the world who go to bed hungry every night."

"Well, I'm not such a good girl, then. But I'm still your sister, so you can't get rid of me … yet." There were tears in her eyes as she ran back toward their cabin.

In the dining room, Hans pulled out her assigned seat and Elizabeth slipped into it. Sure enough, Bernadine had been right. It's sliced beef, with beans and rice on the side.

"Ugh," Hans muttered. "It is good the company is so excellent. The food leaves much to be desired."

"Maybe tomorrow the food will be different." Elizabeth managed a weak smile.

"My little optimist," He cocked his head. "But you are sad. What has happened?"

"I tried having Bernadine talk to the other passengers. Now she's even more frightened. She's so angry. Have I made the right decision, uprooting us from our home?"

He patted her hand. "I can only speak for myself, *Liebchen*. I am very happy you are here."

With Hans, the days seemed to pass quicker. Elizabeth looked forward to getting up in the morning and dreaded the evenings when they had to part. They roamed the deck, watched the ocean together, taught each other songs and dances, and of course, ate together. Elizabeth made it plain to Bernadine that she was welcome to join them, but not obligated. Sometimes the girl did join them, and Hans always quizzed her about the books she was reading. He always seemed surprised by the level and range of material she read.

"Why do you look surprised?" Bernadine asked him, blinking. "Elizabeth taught me to read before I was five years old. She let me bring along one bag of my favorite books, and I found some aboard the ship, too. I like reading on any subject. I've learned a lot about ancient religion, history, geography, art, and much more. And of course, I read everything I can find about America."

"What do you anticipate?" Hans tapped his fingertips together.

"The English language, for one, Elizabeth helped me learn English. I just hope I know enough to manage, especially if I'm able to go to school."

"Bernadine, you are a smart young lady to educate yourself through all your reading and so well-spoken. You have a great future ahead of you, I'm sure."

Elizabeth watched them talking, and at times like these, she felt hopeful.

More often than not, though, Bernadine remained behind, and Elizabeth spent her days with Hans. One day as they walked on deck together, she said, "I just realized, we always talk about me or about Bernadine. I know nothing about you, Hans and that's wrong. As you said, I want to know you like a favorite book, too. So ... tell me. What about you? Did you leave parents, siblings, or other relatives behind?"

"No, my situation is much like yours. Papa and Mama are deceased, and my only brother died young of pneumonia. Father Emmanuel, who immigrated to America from our town—"

"What town are you from? I don't remember you saying before."

"Duisburg. Have you heard of it?"

Elizabeth clapped her hands together in surprise. "Of course I've heard of it, you goose. It's only fifty miles from where we lived. But it's hardly a 'town.' Duisburg is a big city in the Ruhr Valley ... and full of mines?"

"Well, yes ..." Hans looked off toward the eastern horizon. "It is pretty big, at that, and it's a mining area. My family owned mines there. Anyway, Father Emmanuel made several trips to our parish during their sickness and deaths and helped me through the sad times. I managed the family's coal mining operations alone for five years. Finally, Father Emmanuel persuaded me to sell everything and make the move to America."

"Had you been to America before?" Elizabeth asked.

"No, this will be my first experience, and I'm excited to venture to a new country and see what's there. But this is your first trip too, no?"

"Yes, and I'm just as eager and anxious to see what the future brings. I hope I can get a teaching position. I enjoy seeing children mature as they develop new skills."

"You speak English so well, even teaching it to your little sister. Where did you learn the language?"

"I learned it in school, while I was getting my teaching credentials. It was required."

"That's a real benefit, and I'm sure you will have no problem getting hired as a teacher. You know, I thought this voyage across the ocean was going to be dull, but you make it so enjoyable, I don't want it to end. Let's just keep sailing and sailing."

"I feel the same way, Hans. I think I could go on and on with you," Elizabeth laughed. "Thank you for treating Bernadine so well. That means a great deal to me. Who knows, maybe we'll end up in the same community or nearby each other."

His handsome face clouded. "I think not, Elizabeth. Have you not examined the maps? Iowa is a great distance from where I will be going. Remember, I will be traveling to West Virginia, where there are coal mines."

"Oh." She swallowed and looked down. "I had heard that Iowa had coal, too."

"Not like in West Virginia. Why are you going to Iowa, anyway? Do you have a job waiting or some tie that binds you there?"

"We used to have an uncle who had settled there. He persuaded a friend to help us. But our uncle died not long before we sailed. So no, we have no one there, just us and our hopes."

He cleared his throat. "I'm sorry. Is anyone meeting you and Bernadine at Ellis Island?"

"Mr. Herman from Iowa is to be there for us."

"Ah. And Father Emmanuel is meeting me. He lives in West Virginia near the coal mining areas. He's the one who persuaded me to immigrate to that part of the country. 'You'll be in America, Hans,' Father said to me. 'And with your education, background, and keen business mind, especially about mining operations, I assure you, there are many opportunities for you. There are rich coal fields in the area, many businesses starting, and more needed to meet the needs of the people settling there.'"

She hesitated before replying. "Well, I'm sure you will help a lot of people."

"Possibly make some money too," he said with a grin. "But it will be a very lonely life without you, Elizabeth."

"And for me without you, too," Elizabeth replied.

They went back to their cabins then, and each spent a sleepless night.

"I'm losing you," Bernadine whispered. "I knew Hans would come between us, and he has."

Elizabeth pulled out a handkerchief and handed it to her sister.

"I'm not crying."

"Well, you look like you're about to."

"I'm not. I'm just worried. You're in love with that man."

"*Liebchen*, people do fall in love. It's been happening for thousands of years. That doesn't mean you lose someone as a result. Think of it as a math problem—instead of subtracting me, you simply add Hans. If he and I should happen to get married, you would gain a brother."

"Yes." Bernadine's voice was muffled under the handkerchief. "But I think I understand our situation better than you do—you never talk about it, and it's all I think about. Hans is going to West Virginia. He's in coal mining. He won't give that up to come to Iowa with us. He'll expect you to give up teaching instead and go with him. You won't want me anymore. You're taking me to a country where I know no one, but you're going to leave me so you can be with him. Why did you make me leave home? If you wanted to leave me, you could have done it back there, and I would at least have been in a familiar place."

"No one is leaving anyone, Dena." Elizabeth's voice was firm. "Do you think I would marry someone I've known only two weeks? I think I love Hans, yes, but it's easy to fall in love. Making a life together, that's different. It takes a lot of planning and preparation. If Hans and I were to marry, it would not be immediate, or even soon. You and I will go to Iowa just as I have said."

"But …" Bernadine gulped. "Mama said you were flighty and didn't think—"

"Maybe there was a time when I would have put less thought into the future than I would now, Dena, but that time is gone. I have learned from my mistakes. Mama has forgiven me. Why can't you?"

"There was never anything to forgive from me. I just don't understand why everything had to change."

"Because I had to make a new start, now before the sun rises, let's try to get a little sleep."

With the cross-Atlantic trip nearing an end, Hans and Elizabeth's conversations grew more sober. "We have only a couple of days remaining before we reach Ellis Island," Hans said, "and we'll go our separate ways. My heart is heavy, Elizabeth."

Elizabeth began to cry. Hans put his arms around her. "We need to find a way to keep in touch. Let's try to exchange postal addresses with help from our sponsors, Father Emmanuel and Mr. Herman. I'm certain that's our answer."

"We have just a short time together before we dock. Let's make the most of it. I don't want to be sad. I want to enjoy you, and I will. I'll always remember how we met, me falling into your arms when that big wave rocked the ship."

Hans chuckled. "What a great beginning for us," he said. "I'm glad I was there to catch you."

The night before docking at Ellis Island, Elizabeth rolled over and over in her narrow bunk, unable to sleep. She slipped out of bed, dressed, and tiptoed through the passageways to the upper deck. Stars twinkled in the sky. The full moon shined on smooth ocean waters, and the steamship charged full speed ahead. She breathed deeply taking in the fresh night air. The gentle lapping of the waves soothed her. When she turned to return to the berth, she noticed a still form standing on the opposite side of the deck. She stopped, and the shadowy shape turned and spotted her. It was Hans.

"I couldn't sleep."

"I couldn't either. Elizabeth, I'm in love with you." He took her in his arms, held her tightly and pressed his lips to hers. "I want you to be a part of my life always. I want you with me. I'm dreading our separation. What can we do?"

Tears spilled from her eyes. Hans wiped them away.

"I know I am in love with you, Hans. I don't want to be separated either, but while it won't be easy, it is necessary." She kissed him. "We'll have to plan visits through our letters. Can we?"

"We must."

Elizabeth shivered in the night air. Hans put his jacket around her and kissed her again.

As the ship steamed into New York Harbor, Bernadine, Elizabeth, and Hans crowded to the railing to catch their first glimpses of the Statue of Liberty and sprawling city beyond. The colossal lady representing the United States stood tall in the harbor, welcoming people just like them who were looking to make a fresh start in a new land.

A few minutes after passing Liberty Island, the ship docked at Ellis Island. Once again, tears rolled down Elizabeth's cheeks as the three said their good-byes. Hans held her close and whispered, "I'm going to miss you. I love you, and remember, we will see each other again."

"We will, I promise. I love you, Hans."

Bernadine watched her sister say good-bye to the man who had been so kind to them both. She swallowed and turned away.

"You don't get away that easily," said Hans. "I thought you were my friend too, little Dena."

Bernadine flushed. "Friends do not call me 'Dena.' Only Elizabeth has that privilege."

"*Ach, es tut mir leidt*," Hans cried, and laughed. "I'm so sorry. I'll have to come up with another name for you, more suited to your dignity. Next time I see you, I'll know how to address you."

"Do you think there'll be a next time?" Bernadine smiled her voice soft as a kitten's fur.

"You can count on it," Hans replied. "But we can't say goodbye just yet. Let's meet once more at the entrance after I find Father Emmanuel. He said he would be holding a large sign."

Bernadine bit her lip. Tears were in her eyes, but they did not fall. She turned away from the others and rubbed her eyes.

Drying her own eyes and speaking around the lump in her throat, Elizabeth said, "Yes. Mr. Herman will also meet us with a sign. We'll meet you at the entrance."

"I don't think we should," Bernadine said.

"Why ever not," Elizabeth asked?

"Elizabeth, you're crying already. You have to stop so we can go through immigration. But you'll start if we see Hans again. Why not let this be a clean break?"

"I don't want a clean break," Elizabeth retorted. "I want his address, and he doesn't know yet what it will be. So I have to meet Father Emmanuel."

"All right—but I bet you'll cry again."

"I will not."

Relief flooded Elizabeth when she spotted a man in a dark jacket and bowler hat holding high a sign that read Elizabeth and Bernadine Vornholdt.

"I see him, Bernadine, over there. Take my hand." Elizabeth pushed her way through the crowd until she was standing in front of the man. She caught her breath and held out her hand. "I'm Elizabeth Vornholdt, and this is my sister, Bernadine. You're Mr. Herman? I'm so glad we found you. What a lot of people."

Mr. Herman shook Elizabeth's hand and greeted Bernadine with a pat on the shoulder. "I'm here to help in every way I can to get you safely to St. Benedict."

"It's in Iowa," Bernadine said with the grave concern common to anxious adolescents. "Do you know of it?"

Mr. Herman gave her an amused smile. "Yes, my dear, it's in north-central Iowa. In fact, I live about twelve miles from there."

Elizabeth blushed, embarrassed. "We appreciate all your help."

"My pleasure, ma'am, I consider it a privilege to help folks like you find their way in America and get settled. We're happy to welcome you to Iowa, but first we must navigate Ellis Island, and I only understand the basics of the process myself. It's new, and it's congested, as you can see. Stay close together. We don't want to get separated." Mr. Herman turned toward a long, brick building and began jostling his way through the crowd. Elizabeth clutched Bernadine's hand and followed Mr. Herman. Bernadine wanted to look at all the different people, some she recognized from the ship, others she had not seen before, but she was afraid to take her eyes off Mr. Herman's back. Around her she heard snatches of German, but what were those other languages? Fresh air mixed with remnants of vomit and unwashed bodies.

As they came closer to the building they would need to pass through before continuing their journey west, Mr. Herman's pace slowed further. "It'll take us a while to get to the front of the line. We need to be patient."

"We understand, Mr. Herman." Elizabeth touched his arm. "After all, we are Germans—one thing we are used to is waiting in lines."

Finally, they reached a kiosk where they received the first set of paperwork. Mr. Herman directed them to a sitting area where they completed the form, including their names and destination.

"Now, we must wait in another line while officials review the forms. If everything is in order, they will stamp them and approve you to enter the United States."

"This is like the process we went through before we entered the ship at Bremerhaven," Elizabeth said.

Mr. Herman left them to wait in line while he went to do something else. It was more than an hour and a half later that they reached the desk where the immigration clerk would stamp their papers.

"V-O-R-N-H-O-L-D, Vornhold. Elizabeth—E-L-I—" the immigration clerk wrote. Elizabeth, watching his hand make the letters (which appeared upside-down to her), put her hand over his.

"Forgive me, but you've left off the 'T'."

The clerk looked at her through bloodshot eyes. "What 'T'?"

"Our surname is 'Vornholdt,' with a 'T' on the end."

"It's close enough, lady, don't make a fuss."

"I make 'fusses' over very few things, sir. But my name is worth a fuss."

The clerk muttered something unintelligible. Then he raised his voice. "Why can't you foreigners have proper names?"

"Our name is quite proper," Bernadine piped up. "And wouldn't you be mad if someone left the 'O' off 'O'Hara'?"

The clerk, whose name was clearly listed as "O'Hara," tightened his jaw, stamped the immigration forms, and turned to Elizabeth. "You need to teach your kid some manners, lady."

Elizabeth lifted her head. "My sister is a child, not a kid. A kid is a goat." She snatched the papers from his hand. "And so are you, Mr.—Mr. *Hara.*"

And the two sisters—now legally known as "Vornhold," stepped away from his desk.

Elizabeth looked at Bernadine. "What an awful man."

"And he was the first person we met." Bernadine looked at the papers. "We've lost our name. We're no longer Vornholdts. How much more will we lose here?"

"I, for one, do not intend to lose anything more. Come on, let's find Hans. And Mr. Herman, I'm ready now for only good things to happen."

# ⚛Chapter Three⚛

With the documents stamped, Elizabeth and Bernadine Vornhold were approved for entry. "These are important papers," Mr. Herman warned, "so please keep them with you at all times while you travel."

"We will," Elizabeth replied, but her eyes were distracted. She was looking everywhere for Hans. Suddenly he was there, but it was all wrong. He dashed to her.

"Our carriage driver wants to get underway. We have a ferry to catch. This is the address for Father Emmanuel."

"I'll write as soon as we arrive, Hans."

"I love you. I have to go. Goodbye." He gave her a fast peck on the cheek and ducked back into the crowd and Elizabeth burst into tears. Bernadine wished she could hide somewhere, but in the huge crowds of people, many of whom were crying as they separated, Elizabeth was just one red-eyed person in a sea of tear-stained faces.

Mr. Herman cleared his throat, looking away. "We should go, ladies."

Bernadine was thinking, "I told you it would be better to make a clean break," but she was too wise to say it aloud. She took the sign Mr. Herman had been carrying. He had been about to throw it away, but she took it, saying, "No, I want at least one thing with my own name on it."

Elizabeth blew her nose. "I'm so sorry, Mr. Herman. I'm not normally so undisciplined. But ..."

"Don't worry," the big man said, patting her shoulder. "I understand. It's hard to say goodbye to a friend when you don't know anyone where you're going. But it will get better. Come with me, please. And from now on we should speak English. It will help to get used to it."

"We speak English already," Bernadine said, but Elizabeth gave her a warning look and took her hand to follow Mr. Herman.

Herman called over his shoulder, "You have to undergo physicals, but you came second class, didn't you?"

"We did."

"Well, physicals are pretty brief for the first and second-class passengers. I think the idea is that if you have sufficient money for a good ticket, you have sufficient money to stay clean."

After physicals, which mostly consisted of eye inspections, the next stop was the ticket booth for the train. Again Mr. Herman led the Vornhold sisters through the chaos to purchase train tickets and exchange their gold marks for U.S. currency.

"Our train is on the mainland. Trains in New York City run mostly underground. We have a brief ferry ride, and then we'll take a carriage to the station. But first I must get your luggage."

Elizabeth handed Mr. Herman the paperwork he would need to pick up their trunks from the dock where they had been offloaded. He left to arrange everything and was back within the hour. With their luggage secured, Mr. Herman weaved through the crowds back to Elizabeth and Bernadine and ushered them onto the ferry.

Settling into her seat with a sigh, Elizabeth said, "Thank God for your help, Mr. Herman. We never could have made it this far without you."

Mr. Herman smiled and nodded. "You're welcome. I know how exhausting the immigration process is. I made the trip myself a few years ago. My sponsor was so helpful to me that I decided I wanted to return the favor for other immigrants. Now that Ellis Island is open, perhaps the system will be refined, and the process will be easier for those who follow us."

From the ferry, they entered a small, squashed Hansom cab that looked unsteady but rode well. Mr. Herman took his hat off, twisted it between his big-knuckled hands, and leaned forward, resting his elbows on his knees. Elizabeth saw kindness in his brown eyes. His voice was soft but sure. "Wait until we reach the train. Then we can relax."

She gazed out the window of the cab, taking in all the new sights. She remembered reading that the population of New York City was around a million and a half people. That explained all the carriages. She made out the silhouette of the Brooklyn Bridge. She had read about the engineering feat it was. Seeing it, even from a distance, confirmed it.

Elizabeth took a deep breath and let it out slowly. With Mr. Herman in charge, she could finally relax. Bernadine tugged on her sleeve, "Oh Elizabeth, look." Pointing, "Look how tall the buildings are. Some are twenty stories high. I've read about New York City, and it's known as Sky Scraper City. I can see why. There's St. Patrick's Cathedral. See the twin spires? Those were only completed three years ago. And they're three hundred feet tall."

It came to Elizabeth to remind the girl that the spires of the cathedral in Köln were almost twice that high. Even Münster had an impressive cathedral and that those cathedrals were *real* Gothic architecture, not this "neo-gothic" American fad. But just then, Bernadine gasped. "Elizabeth, have you ever seen such a beautiful country?"

*Thank you, God for an answer to prayer,* Elizabeth thought, sitting up. But now that she tried to get interested in her surroundings, her thoughts kept returning to Hans. He'd promised to write, but would he? Would she ever see him again?

Mr. Herman looked up from his newspaper to see Elizabeth pull a handkerchief from her bag and blow her nose. "You're in love with that young man." He gave her an encouraging smile.

"Yes, I am. I have never met anyone who treated me with such respect. He is a special man. We will be far away from each other. I gave him the address for General Delivery in St. Benedict. Do you think he will write?"

"I'm sure he will," Mr. Herman answered.

Bernadine turned her attention to her sister. "Hans will write."

"I'm still wondering," Elizabeth pleaded. "Will we see each other again? He will be so far away. Will he find work? Will he invest in something that is of interest to him? Maybe he'll move even farther away than West Virginia, someplace where there are larger deposits of coal. Will he find another woman?" With that, her sobs returned.

Mr. Herman patted her knee and offered his own handkerchief. "I saw the way that young man looked at you. I'm sure he will write. Why, I have a feeling he'll even find a way to get to St. Benedict to see you, Elizabeth."

"I hope you are right, Mr. Herman. I pray it happens."

"For now, though, let's take the future a little at a time," Mr. Herman suggested. "First, I congratulate you both. You speak far better English than I did when I came here."

"Elizabeth taught me," Bernadine replied.

"Well then, she's a good teacher. Now, let me tell you about the place you're going."

"St. Benedict," Bernadine prompted. "I couldn't find much written about it."

"Ah, but it's there, young lady. St. Benedict is booming. Many new businesses are coming in, buildings are going up, and new families move in monthly. Many of the settlers in the area come from different states in the German Empire. Many immigrated to Wisconsin first and later made their way to Iowa. They will make you feel welcome."

"What about our host family?" Elizabeth asked, interested in spite of herself.

"That's Mr. and Mrs. Leonard. They'll help you get settled and find your way around."

"Do they have any children?" Bernadine demanded.

"Not living at home," Mr. Herman replied.

"Is there a school?" Elizabeth asked.

"More than one," Herman replied, smiling. "At least three, I believe. The Leonards can tell you more."

"Three schools," Elizabeth murmured, "A surfeit of riches."

Bernadine raised an eyebrow but did not comment.

"I saw that," Elizabeth warned, and gave a light swat to Bernadine's arm. "It's just that I'll be looking for a position as a teacher, Mr. Herman. Three schools, if there are so many I'm sure to find a job at one of them. I feel less like one of the *huddled masses* all the time."

"Eh?" Herman's dark eyebrows went down. "What does that mean?"

"It's a poem." Bernadine pointed to a magazine with a drawing of the Statue of Liberty on the cover. "The poet calls immigrants by some rather unflattering names."

By then they had arrived at the train station, swarming with people. They had to wait again while Mr. Herman had their bags taken aboard, and then they boarded the train. This was not a typical train, Herman told them. Most immigrants had to ride bare-boned trains with uncomfortable wooden seats, but he had managed to secure tickets on a train with Pullman cars for at least part of the way. Their Pullman car was dark green, richly decorated, with heavily padded seats.

"It will take us three-and-a-half to four days to get to Iowa. First we must go to Hoboken, where we change trains. The rest of the trip will probably be a little less comfortable, though."

"Will we stop anywhere after that?" Bernadine asked.

"There may be a couple of stops, but the biggest will be in Chicago, where we have to change trains again. Then on to Iowa we go."

Bernadine nodded. Mr. Herman saw her shoulders relax. He patted her knee. "Try to get some sleep, if you can."

Bernadine knew Mr. Herman was right. She should rest, but the events of recent months kept spinning through her mind, and her eyes refused to close for a while. But then the train went underground, and there was nothing else to see. Finally, it was the deep green seats that accomplished what

Mr. Herman could not. The soft, warm velvet cushions rendered both girls drowsy. An hour after leaving Manhattan, both were sound asleep.

At Hoboken, they awoke again, and the second phase of the trip began. Just as the girls had to get used to being on a ship, they now had to get used to being on a train. It swayed, jounced, and made a lot of racket. They had to stop once to clear the tracks after a rockslide had blocked the way. For the better part of three days this went on, and they arrived in Chicago, exhausted and sweaty. The hotel they stayed in was next to the stockyards and stank to the heavens, and between that and the bawling of the hundreds of cattle and hogs milling about, they got no sleep that night. The next morning they had to make do with wooden benches all the way to Iowa City.

Their last change of trains was the worst. By now the hard wooden benches looked good since this train was much like the one they had ridden on from Münster to Bremerhaven, frequently stopping to get the livestock out of the way. Unfortunately, those hard wooden benches were filled with other passengers and Mr. Herman and the two girls had to stand for half of the last two hundred miles, a seven-hour ride, glaring at several burly men who refused to surrender their seats to the ladies.

"We're here," Herman announced with forced enthusiasm as the train chugged into Wesley at a snail's pace, brakes shrieking and squealing. "Wesley is only seven miles from St. Benedict."

"Now I'm nervous," Elizabeth admitted. "But it's a good nervous. Anticipation, I suppose. How do you feel, Dena?"

"I'm not nervous at all," Bernadine told her. "I'd settle for a haystack to sleep in. I just want to sit down."

"You will, soon. I've arranged for a coach to pick us up." Herman gave them an encouraging smile. He went to the dingy window and pointed to a carriage with the number "74" on its rear fender. "When we stop, ladies, please go to that carriage and seat yourselves comfortably. I'll make sure your luggage is loaded, and then we'll be on our way to the Leonard home."

"What does the future hold for us?" Elizabeth murmured, taking Bernadine's hand as they walked stiffly toward the door. One of the burly fellows who would not surrender his bench leaped up suddenly and shoved past the girls.

"Hey." Mr. Herman shouted, "Apologize to the ladies."

The big man didn't even turn, but he shouted over his shoulder "*Es tut mir leidt*" in a tone that let them know he was not sorry at all. He jumped to the station platform and dashed to a man waiting in the crowd.

"Some of us may be huddled masses," Bernadine told Elizabeth, "but I am certain that man was *wretched refuse*."

Elizabeth began giggling, and they were both grinning broadly by the time they mounted the steps of their carriage.

The coach ride to the Leonards belied Mr. Herman's earlier assurances. It was not exactly a bustling village on the prairie. There were about twenty buildings up, with one abnormally sized building under construction on the edge of the town. "What is it?" Bernadine asked.

"It's called a grain elevator," Herman said. "I think so, at least. I've seen them in the eastern states. I'm sure the Leonards can tell you more. And look, there's one of the schools. From here it's only a little farther to your hosts."

Five minutes later they pulled up in front of a white clapboard house, and Bernadine felt her hand sneaking into Elizabeth's hand, almost of its own volition. The two exchanged weak smiles as Mr. Herman jumped out of the carriage and turned to help them down.

Mr. and Mrs. Leonard greeted them with warm handshakes and hugs, while Mr. Herman unloaded their trunks. "Please, Herr Herman," Mr. Leonard said in German, "my wife prepared a meal to celebrate the arrival of these young ladies. We would be honored if you would stay and partake."

"Your generosity is wonderful, but I really must be on my way back to my own family," Mr. Herman said in his careful English. "I've been away for three weeks now."

Elizabeth followed him. "Thank you for all you've done, Mr. Herman. We want to repay you for all you did for us."

"I was just happy to help you in every way I could," Herman replied with a smile. "But it's thirteen more miles to my own home, and I must leave at once if I hope to be there by nightfall."

He waved and jumped back into the carriage; the coachman tapped the horses with his whip, and they were gone.

"He's a kind man," Mr. Leonard remarked, switching back to English. "He has settled probably a dozen people here in the last three years. Now, Miss Elizabeth, Miss Bernadine, please come inside. Welcome to our home."

Mrs. Leonard, a tall, big-boned lady with a ruddy face and graying hair, showed Elizabeth and Bernadine their rooms. "I have warm water in the basins and soap for you to freshen up a bit. Take your time, change clothes if you want, and unpack some things that you might need right away. We'll have something to eat after you've had time to relax. We look forward to you living with us."

"These rooms are so spacious and large," Elizabeth exclaimed. "And look, Bernadine, *schranks* and chests of drawers for our clothes. Thank you, Mrs. Leonard. You are very kind."

Mrs. Leonard smiled. "You must say 'wardrobe' now, Miss Elizabeth. We are in America!"

"I forgot, but only for a moment," Elizabeth replied with a nervous giggle. "It's such a very German wardrobe, Bavarian, perhaps?"

"Very good, Miss Elizabeth, yes, we brought it over from Erlangen with us in 1862. But we can talk about our family histories and our trips to the New World later. For now, wash up and relax."

She bustled out and down the long stairway.

The girls' doors stood opposite each other at the top of the sturdy staircase. Elizabeth crossed over into Bernadine's room and looked around again. "This is as nice as our old home and even bigger. We've been fortunate."

Bernadine stayed silent for a moment. Then, her voice very small, she said, "I would be more comfortable sister, if I could sleep with you in your bed."

"Don't be silly, Dena," Elizabeth said. "These are single beds; we wouldn't have room to turn around if we were both in one."

For a moment, the younger girl looked as if she might cry.

"And don't be childish, either." Elizabeth tapped her on the chin. "You're nearly twelve. That's almost the age at which a girl becomes a woman. Dena, we are blessed. These people are more than kind. These rooms are beautiful and airy. We could not have prayed to God for anything nicer than this."

"I know," Bernadine said softly. She turned back to the pitcher and ewer that sat on the washstand and busily began soaping her face and hands.

"We feel like new people. What a wonderful feeling to have all that traveling behind us," Elizabeth announced as she and Bernadine trooped back downstairs."

"Excellent. Let's have something to eat," Mrs. Leonard motioned for them to sit at the table. "We're going to have a light meal tonight, but don't worry, there's plenty of everything."

"It all smells delicious. We're hungry." Elizabeth followed them to the table, pulling Bernadine by the hand.

Mrs. Leonard called it a light meal, but after two weeks of shipboard fare and three days of tinned train fare, the ham sandwiches, fresh green beans, and chocolate pudding made a veritable feast. As the girls finished their meals, Elizabeth once again offered an effusive thanks to their hosts. "Mrs. Leonard, this is the best food we've had in a long time."

"How kind of you to say so."

"It isn't kind," Bernadine insisted. "If you saw what we had to eat on that steamer."

"Dena, manners," Elizabeth warned, but she smiled to take the edge off it. "She has a point, though, Mrs. Leonard.

51

The food on the ship got a little monotonous. But you must let us wash your dishes, ma'am. Bernadine and I want to help wherever you need us for letting us stay with you. I know canning, and my sister is good at baking. My—our mother taught us both the ways of the kitchen."

"I would be glad for your help," Mrs. Leonard added. "And Mr. Herman told us that you were a teacher, back in Germany."

"This is true, and once we're settled, I would like to get a job teaching here if I can."

"And I hope I can attend school in St. Benedict," Bernadine put in.

"Well, you should both be happy then," Mr. Leonard announced. "There are three schools here, and what with the teachers in two of them always getting married, they have a lot of vacancies. At the Catholic school, they have nuns as teachers."

Their bellies full, the girls helped clear the table; then Elizabeth motioned Mrs. Leonard back and grabbed the huge kettle of steaming water to fill the dishpan. "I insist. I'll wash, Mrs. Leonard. Bernadine will dry. You may sit down and supervise."

Mrs. Leonard grinned. "I will enjoy supervising from a chair."

Once the kitchen was sparkling, the three headed into the parlor. "Does either of you girls play the piano?"

"I play a little," Elizabeth said, her voice hesitant. "It's been a long time, though."

"That's all right. I will play for us all tonight," Mrs. Leonard offered. "I love music, and it's so relaxing. And, while you live here, you can play whenever you want,

Elizabeth." She looked at Bernadine. "Do you think you might like to learn? I can teach you."

Bernadine blushed. "I would like that very much."

"Let's go into the parlor now that the kitchen is clean, and I'll play some music on the piano. I love to play, and it helps you relax before bedtime."

"Oooh," Elizabeth and Bernadine exclaimed in unison. "*Komm lieber Mai und mache.*" They began clapping their hands and singing along with the piano. But the sudden decompression of arrival, followed by the good food and fellowship, had already begun to take their toll. By the time Mrs. Leonard moved from another lively folk tune to a lullaby, Bernadine had laid her head on Elizabeth's shoulder, and Elizabeth was stifling yawns.

"It looks like we're relaxed and ready to turn in for the night," Elizabeth admitted. She roused Bernadine and steered her toward their room. "We'll see you in the morning, and thanks for all you are doing for us."

"Get a good night's sleep and sweet dreams."

Elizabeth woke to sunshine streaming through the windows. She crossed the hall to Bernadine's room and walked in, finding the girl still sound asleep. "Come on, sleepyhead," she teased. "Don't you remember what a farm is like? I'll bet the Leonards have been up a couple of hours already."

Bernadine sat up, yawning. "I haven't had a good night's sleep like this in a long time."

"Smell that fresh, clean air, Bernadine. I've opened the windows so the cool breeze can freshen up the rooms. Let's go downstairs and tell Mr. and Mrs. Leonard how well we slept. Besides, I think I smell bacon."

They found a large skillet of *Bauernfrühstück* on the big stove, but no one else was in sight. A note in spidery English words made in German cursive said, "Help yourselves, we are in the barn."

Elizabeth grinned in delight. "I haven't had a real farmer's breakfast since, well, forever."

"I don't think I've ever had it." Bernadine looked cautiously at the heaping skillet. "What is it?"

Already spooning the mix onto a plate, Elizabeth said, "Can't you tell? Potatoes, bacon, eggs, ham, and onions, all fried together. It's heavenly. Mother used to fix it when I was little. Dena, grab two glasses and pour the milk while I fix your plate."

"It's still warm," Bernadine said. "She must have brought it in fresh from the cow. The fat is floating around."

"I haven't had fresh milk in forever, either. This is even a better feast than last night."

They dug in with their forks and had their plates clean and glasses empty in ten minutes. They made a hasty job of washing up, and then ran outside to find Mrs. Leonard in the barn, looking into the stall beyond.

"Breakfast was heavenly," Elizabeth began her announcement, but she fell silent as she looked past the older woman. A black and white heifer was lying on her side in the stall, groaning.

"How small are her hands?" Mr. Leonard demanded, pointing at Bernadine.

Mrs. Leonard grasped Bernadine's hands. "They're small enough. Bernadine, we need you."

"To do what," Bernadine asked, in a tiny, fear-tinged voice.

"She's having a calf." Mrs. Leonard pointed at the heifer. "But it's not coming out."

Elizabeth put her hands on Bernadine's shoulders. "She's too young for this. I will help you."

"Your hands are as big as mine," Mrs. Leonard replied. "And there is no such thing as 'too young' on a farm. We must all do what we can."

The heifer bawled, lashing her tail. Straw and something wet flew toward Bernadine, who felt the blood leaving her face. "I can't touch that cow. I'm afraid of cows. I—"

Mrs. Leonard took her by the arms. "Bernadine, if this calf dies inside the mother, the mother will die also. And that cannot happen. We only have two cows. If this one dies, we won't have enough milk for us all. Now, time is short."

Swallowing, the girl went into the stall. "What must I do?"

Mr. Leonard had her kneel by the cow's hindquarters. "When a calf is born, it comes out there—" he pointed. "And it comes out with its hooves first, and its nose between them. This one has its legs bent, so it can't come out." He handed her a long piece of string. "My hands are too big. You have to put one hand in and find the calf's hoof. Try to pull it forward. If you can't pull it all the way out, wrap this string around the hoof instead and knot it, so …" He wrapped the end around his finger and made a one-handed knot.

Bernadine swallowed again. Timidly, she touched the cow's bottom, and again it groaned. The girl jumped back with a squeal.

"Hurry," Mr. Leonard kept his voice low, but his urgency was plain to hear.

Bernadine tried again, this time managing to put her hand inside the cow. She reached further in and made a horrible face. "It's hot in there, and slimy—ewwwwww. She's squishing my arm."

"Just look for the hoof, girl."

"I've got it."

"Pull it forward."

Bernadine pulled and made another face. "It's stuck."

"Then wrap the string."

She brought her arm out, covered with mucus and blood, took the string, and tried again. "I have it."

Leonard took the string and began to pull, slowly. The cow's head came up, and Mrs. Leonard went into the stall and knelt by her head, pulling it back down. "Easy, Bessie, it will be over soon."

A small, cloven hoof appeared. Bernadine now engrossed in the event, reached back inside, looking for the other hoof. "I've got it—and I think I can get this one out." She pulled slowly, and another hoof appeared.

"Ah," Leonard grasped the calf's forelegs and began to pull; sweat broke out on his forehead, and his large arms strained with the effort. A minute later, the entire calf slid out and onto Bernadine's lap, covering them both in goop and bloody discharge.

The calf did not move.

"It's dead," Bernadine whispered, making a little choking sound.

Leonard grabbed an empty burlap sack and began rubbing the calf's body hard and fast. A minute later he dropped the sack and with a frustrated curse, he grabbed the calf's snout, put his mouth over one nostril, and blew. He blew twice more—and the calf heaved, shuddered, and began to struggle against him.

Mrs. Leonard cheered, and Elizabeth laughed. Bernadine jumped back to avoid a flailing leg, and Mr. Leonard grabbed her and pulled her away from the calf as Mrs. Leonard let the mother loose so it could stand. Ignoring them, the mother began licking the calf all over.

An hour later they had cleaned themselves up, and the newborn calf was swishing its tail and nursing eagerly. The humans were still talking about the birth. Bernadine was the hero of the day, and both Mr. and Mrs. Leonard boasted that she was a born farmer. "You will be the mother-goddess of all the cows," Mr. Leonard told her with a merry laugh.

For Bernadine's part, she was walking taller, proud of herself for doing something she never would have thought she could do. And not only that, she had succeeded. Reaching into the cow had been horrible, but she had saved the lives of both mother and baby. The new calf, another heifer, had been dubbed "Bovine Dena" by Mrs. Leonard adding; "Now her very existence will be in your honor."

Elizabeth had given Bernadine a big hug. "I'm so proud of you."

By dinnertime, the Leonards were back to being hospitable as well as informative hosts. At every opportunity, they offered tidbits about St. Benedict's history and plans for its future.

"We farmers are fortunate to have found some of the most fertile, rich, black soil in the world," Mr. Leonard boasted. "They say that many years ago, glaciers passed over the area. All the material they carried along and left behind rotted and produced our good, black soil.

"The climate brings an ideal growing season with consistent production most years. Rarely do we have drought, hail, or too much rain, only once in a while. Then the farmers struggle to find feed for the livestock and raise enough crops to sell to buy food for the table. They pray to God that the following year will bring adequate rain, sunshine, and everything needed to allow them a bountiful harvest."

"This is so interesting," Elizabeth said. "You're a walking history lesson on Iowa farming!"

"I was one of the first settlers to arrive in the area," Mr. Leonard replied. "I was born in Bayern, that is Bavaria and I came with my family to America in 1862. At that time, we settled in Beaver Dam, Wisconsin. Many families from Germany migrated to Wisconsin and later made their way to this part of Iowa. Some came here by rail directly from Ellis Island like you two. When I first came, I worked in various jobs to earn money. One of my jobs was working on the tracks of the Milwaukee Railroad. I helped with harvesting during that season, and I accepted work wherever I could to make enough money to live on. I became involved in everything. Then in 1870, I came here and purchased a tract of farmland."

"It sounds like you were a real leader in the area," Elizabeth noted.

"I tried to get others involved in developing plans to make this a workable community that satisfied the needs of all." He shrugged. "I listened to their ideas and recommendations, so the town was for the people, not just my opinions. We made plans for a bank, lumber and coal yards, and other businesses that might get started. I've enjoyed seeing this little town take shape. All this time I also farmed and raised crops and livestock—my favorite interests."

"I want to know about Bessie," Bernadine cut in. "I've seen cows like her back in Germany, but I don't know what they are."

"Over here, Bessie's breed is called a Holstein."

"Like Schleswig-Holstein, the state?"

"Exactly, do you know, Bernadine, that little calf you delivered this morning? She weighed ninety pounds."

"No wonder her mama was squishing me," Bernadine realized. "There wasn't much room in there to start with, but that calf was huge."

"Um ..." Elizabeth, blushing, cleared her throat. "I'd like to know more about the schools in this area."

Leonard thought for a moment. "The first one opened in 1875—"

"No, husband, it was 1876," Mrs. Leonard interrupted. "Would anyone like pie?"

Mr. Leonard chuckled. "You're right, *Liebchen*, it was 1876. Then a second opened in 1883. These were known as township schools, and children of the area attended them. They had no distinction between grades. All the children sat together. They all learned the ABC's, arithmetic, reading, writing, and spelling, just the basics. Later, as the children grasped the things they needed to know grades became more defined and students were separated into groups by age."

"I think it would be difficult to teach all ages the same subjects," Elizabeth said, "But maybe not if they were all learning the subject matter for the first time."

"I had not thought of that before. You will be a good teacher." Leonard took his pie plate and sniffed, the corners of his lips curling in appreciation. "Correct me if I'm wrong, *Liebchen*... in 1889 the first Catholic school opened. Two ladies taught in that school for a short time. Then the Sisters of St. Francis from Dubuque took charge."

Elizabeth sighed. "Do you think perhaps I'd be able to get a teaching job at one of these township schools or the Catholic school?"

"It's very possible," Mrs. Leonard responded.

"I'll need to learn more about the teaching requirements and availability of jobs in these schools. Everything sounds promising. Can you direct me to someone with whom I can speak about getting a teaching position in one of these schools?"

Mrs. Leonard nodded. "Surely, teachers with your education and experience who are fluent in both German and English are always in demand. I know there will be a place for you."

"Can I attend one of the schools?" Bernadine asked. "Or is twelve too old to go to school here?"

"We'll check into that for you, Bernadine," Mrs. Leonard replied, "And we'll let you know."

"I will go elsewhere if there is need," Elizabeth began, but at Bernadine's frightened look, continued, "but of course I'd prefer to stay in St. Benedict. I don't want to leave Bernadine alone."

"I can help," Bernadine announced. "I love caring for little ones—newborn babies, toddlers, and older children. I can cook and prepare a few meals, and I'm good at baking. I can even do general housework like cleaning, washing clothes, and ironing. Do you think I could find a family who would provide meals in exchange for my help?" Bernadine asked.

"We'll look into that too," Mrs. Leonard assured her.

"You are arriving at a good time," remarked Mr. Leonard. "Some of St. Benedict is already developed, but plans are in the making for all kinds of work, especially construction jobs as we anticipate new businesses.

"We have a small church and plans for a bank, hardware store, general store, lumberyard, and more to be built. You saw the grain elevator they're building on the way into town, yes?"

Both girls nodded, remembering.

"You see? Elizabeth and Bernadine, you are here to witness our entire community unfold right before your eyes."

Over the next few weeks, Mr. Leonard continued sharing his knowledge of their new home with Elizabeth and Bernadine. Kossuth County, in which St. Benedict was located, had been organized in the 1850s. By the time Elizabeth and Bernadine arrived, the state census listed 3,350 people within its boundaries, attracted by reports of excellent grazing lands, timber, and large herds of elk and buffalo. The terrain was slightly rolling with the Ridge, a range of small hills, separating the high lands on the one side from the lowlands on the other. The United States government sent army expeditions through the area as early as 1820 to set up forts to protect the frontier settlers, who were essential to the fur industry. Lured by glowing reports from the army and the desire for cheap land, more and more adventurous immigrants made north-central Iowa their home.

As Elizabeth and Bernadine learned more about the area and the Leonards, they relaxed and felt more confident about getting established in the town, though Elizabeth often grew quiet and distracted. This let Bernadine know that Hans and their promise to stay in touch was never far from Elizabeth's mind.

One evening after supper, Elizabeth told the Leonards about Hans. "I met a nice young man on the boat coming here. He was so kind to Bernadine and me. We spent a lot of time together and discovered that we have much in common. He was involved with his family's coal mining operations in the Ruhr Valley in Germany. We exchanged addresses and plan to keep in touch by letter. Can you help me get my letters to the post office?" Elizabeth asked.

"Yes, of course, dear, I can see by the way you speak of him that Hans is more than a friend," Mrs. Leonard offered.

Elizabeth blushed. "He is special."

It soon became apparent that much of life in St. Benedict revolved around the Catholic Church. The church was the center of the community's social life as well as its religious observances. After the first time they walked by it, Elizabeth remarked on the way it was built.

"It's a frame structure with no foundation. Ordinary benches serve as pews," Mrs. Leonard informed her.

"Some of our first churches in Germany didn't have a foundation either. But they served us well," Elizabeth responded.

"Ah, I remember the Gothic churches all over the old country," Mrs. Leonard remarked. "But Father Erdman—I'll introduce you next week—has purchased new land for a new building. And it's going to be in the Gothic style."

"That will cost a lot."

"The Catholic church is hardly poor," Mrs. Leonard huffed. "They should send a bishop down to help us."

"The church is supported by pew rent," Mr. Leonard explained. "It is an important source of income for this parish. Each pew is numbered and every family is assigned a number corresponding to the pew they occupy when they attend services. They pay monthly rent for the use of the pew."

"What an interesting way to support the church," Elizabeth stated. "I'm not familiar with that method. But we were baptized and raised Catholic in Germany. We will want to be a part of the congregation and help out in the parish."

"As long as you're here," Bernadine whispered. Only Elizabeth heard her.

"I'm sorry, Mr. and Mrs. Leonard, I think it's getting late. Let's go to bed, Dena."

"You're not my—" but before the words left Bernadine's mouth, Elizabeth had grabbed her hand and yanked her out of the room.

Mrs. Leonard turned to her husband. "What do you suppose that was all about?"

"*Ach*, that little Bernadine is a fireball, that's what it's about." Mr. Leonard lit his pipe, grinning.

In Bernadine's bedroom, there were no grins.

"Don't start with me again," Elizabeth warned. "We're here, we're in the new country, and we're doing well. Why must you always start with the mopes and the challenges?"

"You play the game so well," Bernadine muttered. "You want to be a part of the community, you want to pay pew rent and support the church. Oh, you're such an exemplary citizen, Miss Vornholdt."

"Vornhold."

"I hate that."

"It doesn't matter, get used to it."

"And *that's* what you say about everything!" Bernadine was squeezing her eyelids together, but the tears behind them were leaking out anyway.

"No, no, Bernadine. This was to be a great adventure, remember?"

"For *you*, this was the great adventure. For me, it meant leaving my home. But you said it didn't matter; I could get used to a new home. For you, you had no friends back home. I had a friend. I loved her like a ..." she choked a little. "Like a sister. She was a better sister than you are. But you said it didn't matter because I could make new friends. Never mind that I'm shy and quiet, I should go into the midst of strangers and make brand new friends."

"Dena ... I'm sorry, but I needed this."

"Yes, I know perfectly well. *I* didn't need any of this, I didn't *want* any of it. But *you* needed it, and forced it on me. For you, this is a fresh start. You were running off and leaving all your dirty secrets behind, weren't you? Only you didn't leave them all behind, because I came with you, and I know the truth that you'll never let me tell. You should have left me in Coesfeld. Do you think Hans will marry you if he learns? Do you think the Leonards will let us stay here? And so now you want to be a pillar of the community... while you are here. But we both know you won't be here long. You're getting away from me as fast as you can before I happen to mention something you'd rather not have said. You're leaving me behind like the furniture in our old house. You didn't want it, so you left it all behind. And you don't want me, so you're leaving me."

She was sobbing now. Elizabeth managed not to roll her eyes. If Bernadine saw, she would only cry more. Elizabeth slid onto the bed next to her, took her in her arms, and stroked her back.

"You're so grown-up, Dena," she said in soft, soothing tones. "I keep forgetting you're only a child of twelve."

"I'm still eleven. You keep saying I'm twelve, but it's two months yet to my birthday."

"I'm sorry. I forgot."

"Yes," Bernadine pulled away, her voice calm now, but dull and resigned. "You forget a lot about me. I think you forget anything that is inconvenient. And I'm expected to act as if all is well. But all is *not* well, Elizabeth. I don't want to be left behind like our old house. I know you are going to do it though. You'll marry Hans and never look back."

"It's true I love Hans, but I would not leave you amid strangers Dena. Don't you see? I promised Mother I would take care of you before I thought of myself, and that's what I'm doing. I'm trying to help you already. If we get involved in church activities, you'll meet lots of new people and make lots of new friends. That way, if Hans and I get married—and I hope we do, someday—it won't happen until you are well integrated into the community and have plenty of friends of your own, and you'll never even miss me then."

"It doesn't matter whether I'll miss you or not. You never think of me and West Virginia in the same sentence." Bernadine blew her nose. "And it's still true, what I said about Hans."

Elizabeth tipped up the child's chin and looked her in the eye. "I don't know whether he would or not. Are you planning to tell him? Because you gave me your word that you would not speak of it."

"You *made* me give my word. That's not—"

"Please don't tell me again that it isn't fair, Dena." Elizabeth's sigh was tired and defeated. "Life never promises fairness. I'm sorry if I have failed you. Truly, I am. But when I said I wanted a new start and a better life, I hoped it would be new and better for both of us. There are things I gave up to come here too, it wasn't as easy for me as you make it sound. When you are a little more grown up, you may find out that nothing is as easy as people think it will be." She forced herself to smile. "Cheer up, Dena. Perhaps by now, Hans has met someone else. Maybe you'll have your way after all. I'll never leave you, and we'll grow old together as sisters do. Will that make you happy?"

"No," Bernadine whispered.

"Well then, I don't know what you want from me. I do know that I can't go on this way. Either you keep the secret, freely and with joy or you get up in church on Sunday and tell the whole town. Find Hans wherever he has gone, and tell him too. But don't keep threatening me every time you feel frightened because you are frightened of everything. When you helped that cow give birth the other day, I thought it was a great miracle. You were overcoming your fear. You were growing up. You could be like that all the time if you wanted."

"I ... could?" Bernadine shivered a little. "I can't imagine going through life without fear."

"Yes, you think fear is your old friend. Well, it's not. It's the thing that will keep you from living. Bad as I am, I've learned that much."

"I never said you were bad, Elizabeth. I said the secret was bad. But you're not. And I love you more than anyone in the world. You're ... you're my ..." She began to cry again.

"Shhh, baby, it's all right. I love you too." And Elizabeth put her arms around the girl again, and rocked her to sleep just like a sister should do.

# ☙Chapter Four❧

The sisters lived with the Leonards for a full month, and although Elizabeth sent letters to Hans every week and went to the post office every day, she never got a letter from Hans. She dared not cry around Bernadine, but in private she sometimes went off to see the little calf named Dena, so she could tell her of her hopes and dreams. At least this Dena would not worry about losing her love. But privately, Elizabeth was also getting worried. What was Hans up to, anyway? Surely, he wasn't waiting until he was a millionaire before writing her. She didn't want him to be a millionaire anyway. She only wanted him as sweet and amiable as he'd been on the ship.

As the weeks went by, though, her other doubts came back. Perhaps he had found someone he liked better. Perhaps he had come to believe two weeks was not long enough to know someone before falling in love with them. On days when those doubts worked their way into her mind, she would rush off to cry on the little calf's shoulder. And this little Dena found the taste of tears fascinating. The calf enjoyed licking her face. She mentioned this to Mr. Leonard, who had a good laugh about it and then thought for a minute. "Must be the salt," he finally said. "Cows love the taste of salt. We keep a little block of salt in their stalls so they can lick it."

By the end of the second month, Elizabeth was certain he had died. Coal mines caved in sometimes, didn't they? What if he was underground when a mine caved in?

It was Bernadine who came to her one day with a peculiar smile on her face and a small packet in her hand. "At least I had you two whole months without interruption," she said and handed the package to her sister. Elizabeth squealed and jumped into the air, then sped away, running out to the barn, her solace these days, and read the lengthy letter to Bovine Dena, who did not comment on the occasional misspellings or grammar errors as the real Dena would.

*My dearest Elizabeth,*

*I am beginning this letter on the train as Father Emmanuel and I make the long trip to West Virginia. Father E says it will take two days. We travel on the Baltimore & Ohio Railroad to a little town called Bramwell. Father E says it will not be little for much longer, as the region around Bramwell has begun to grow in bounds und leaps as a coal mining center with several coal camps operating in the area. Soon one of them will be mine!*

"Hans ..." Elizabeth murmured, tears coming to her eyes. "I am so glad to hear from you, but if you started the letter on the train, why am I only just now getting it?"

*I will live with Father E until I can build my own house for us, my darling. I have enough money to invest in the land that geology scientists surveyed as potential coalfields for my mines, and he says I should also invest in land for railroads. (Everyone is coming here since some of the mines in Pennsylvania have played out.) Then is the cost of getting the men to get at that black rock. I'll have to save the profits to build a house und bring you to join me. But be not afraid, for I will do it faster than you think.*

Three days later. *I had planned to mail this as soon as I got to Bramwell, but I have to tell you some of the things Father E said to me. He believes someday the railroads will be loading West Virginia coal and transporting it to ports as far away as Lake Erie. (I don't know where that is, but I remember hearing it mentioned many times when we went through New York, Pennsilvana and Ohio.) Right now are not many railroads in this area. I can see why. It is hilly and mountainus (did I spell this right my love?) and they will have to use much dynamite to make tunnels through it. Almost I could invest in the railway too, but I have not the knowledge of railroads that I do of mining, so I will stick to what I know, the better to make more money now so I can quickly be joined to you again. Father E will introduce me to people who can help me. He is such a good friend. I told him about you of course. He is happy for us and glad to help.*

*I walked through this area today. Some of it reminds me of the Ruhr Valley, but more it is like the more southern areas in Bayern. There are a few streams and hills that could make me a little homesick if I let them, but I have left the old world behind and the new I embrace.*

One week later. *I lost these pages the day before I planned to mail them! I was so angry. But now that I have found them again I have more news. I lived, as I said, with Father E for several days, but then rented a house close to the church. It is also near the rail line that runs to the coal field. It is a comfortable house but not extravagant, it does not cost much. That was when I found I had lost the pages for my letter. Father E's putzfrau found them where they fell off my bed and landed between the bed and the wall.*

"Wonderful," Elizabeth muttered. "I bet this priest and his putzfrau read the pages, too. The only bright side is this letter might as well be written to one of Hans' pals back in the

Ruhr. Where is the 'I will love you forever'? Where is the 'I long to kiss you'? Is this a love letter or a trip report?"

Next day. *I have today met Mr. Meyer, who took me to the region the geology scientists have surveyed for potential coal fields. Do not let it trouble you, Elizabet, that I don't spell their name correctly. Even in German my spelling leaves much to be desired. The important part is I know what I am doing. Remember I am a trained engineer with coal in my blood. Anyway, a few coal mines are already operating here. It is hard, no, it is backbreaking work whether it is here or home in the Ruhr. Miners must use weapons like pickaxes, hand drills, and dynamite to shatter the huge coal stones and shovel them into carts to haul to weighing stations and then railroad cars. It's a job only done with brute force, and the men who do it are like great, noble beasts of burden. They load the broken pieces onto wagons by hand (more hard work). They live in cheap housing provided by the companies they work for, and they buy their food from company-run stores. It sounds good, but because the housing rent is deducted from their pay, and the food they buy is overpriced, the men never make as much money as they should. But I see a mine where it WILL NOT BE SO, my love, and that mine will have my name on it.*

*I missed you from the moment we parted—no, I missed you even before you left, because I knew how soon the moments would pass. I wish you were here with me every minute. I'd love to hold you in my arms and kiss you again. After I get settled and started with my investments in land, coal mining operations and the railroads, I'd like to visit you in Iowa. I will write more to you soon, and keep you informed as to the progress I am making. How are you doing, and do you miss me? I hope to hear from you soon. Keep busy and make the time go fast, and then soon we will be together forever.*

Five days later. *I am so angry. I lost these pages again. I was writing them down at a loading dock where they called my name, and I like a fool, walked away with my pen in my pocket and the pages left on the table. A man remembered I had been writing, and when I came back today he asked if the pages were mine. So I decided, my love, that from now on I will write KURT letters—I don't remember the English word. Is it shirt? I will write shirt letters und male them immiedatl very fast. So now I am in the post office and will send it to you.*

*All my love to you my dearest Elizabeth.*

*Your Hans*

She kissed the signature but did not allow the calf to look at or lick the paper, though it seemed to want to. "Here," she told Bovine Dena, "Lick my face instead because I'm about to cry."

Three months after their arrival, Elizabeth learned that a teaching job was opening at the Catholic school.

"They are looking for someone who has mastered the English language as you have," Mrs. Leonard announced. "Are you interested, Elizabeth?"

"Of course," she smiled. "I'm eager to get back in the classroom."

"You can stay on with us, even so," Mrs. Leonard assured her.

"Thank, you, but if I really get this job, I'll expect to pay for room and board now that I'll be making some money. And, of course, I'm always happy to help you around the house. Oh, it will be so good to be teaching again. I must let Hans know right away."

Correspondence flowed regularly between the two. Hans kept Elizabeth up to date with the progress of his coal mine operation and assured her he'd be coming to see her as soon as he could. In his letters, Hans always asked Elizabeth to give his regards to Bernadine, and Bernadine returned the greetings. Still, she felt like an intruder in their relationship.

Within a few weeks of their arrival in St. Benedict, Bernadine had established herself as an in-demand domestic helper, with regular duties with two local families. Mary Wagner and Katherine Schmidt were the best of friends. Both had emigrated from Germany with their families, met, and married their husbands in Wisconsin before settling in St. Benedict. Mary had three children, two sons and one daughter ranging in ages from eight months to five years. Katherine had two daughters and one son ranging in age from one to six years. Their husbands farmed adjacent land. The friendship that had developed between them as young girls continued as married women and neighbors. Mary lived a short walk uphill from Katherine. The two women confided in one another and shared tips on childrearing, gardening, and their husband's farming concerns.

Katherine was an excellent seamstress. Others often called on her for special sewing projects, especially wedding gowns.

Bernadine split her time between the two families and received a sleeping room and meals in exchange for her work. When September came, she was able to attend school and continue working for both families. Her homework, caring for the little ones, and helping with housework kept her busy. Although she no longer lived with the Leonards, she saw Elizabeth every day at school. They spent weekends together at the Leonard's house and attended church together on Sundays. Now and then she still found herself wondering if

Hans would marry Elizabeth if he knew her secret. Well, maybe Elizabeth would be brave someday and tell him herself. One thing was sure, Bernadine would keep her word. Forced or not, she had agreed. "I will keep it 'til my dying day," she promised. "And if Elizabeth can start over, so can I. No more being fearful. No more crying like a child. I'm twelve now. I'm almost a woman."

November arrived. With harvest complete, talk in the Leonard household turned to Thanksgiving Day.

"What is Thanksgiving like?" Elizabeth asked.

"It's the all-American holiday," Mrs. Leonard said proudly. "We always have plenty of tasty food. Families celebrate with other families and friends. We prepare menus for large Thanksgiving dinners and assign dishes to individuals and families to bring for the big dinner. We'll have turkey and stuffing, although some of the more recent German immigrants prefer roast goose. And there will be potatoes, sweet potatoes, pumpkin pies, and more."

"I'm looking forward to this," Elizabeth replied, "And I will help you prepare as much of the food as I can. I can't wait to tell Bernadine about Thanksgiving dinner and the big celebration. She'll be as excited as I am."

"I'll do the turkey, goose, stuffing for both birds, and pumpkin pies," Mrs. Leonard said. "Our guests will bring the rest of the meal."

Mrs. Leonard rose early on Thanksgiving morning. Elizabeth and Bernadine joined her. "First," she said, "we'll do the pies. We'll make the piecrust and then the pumpkin filling. You've made pies before, Elizabeth, haven't you?"

"Yes, we both have but we have never worked with pumpkins. I can roll out the crust, and Bernadine can fit it in the tins. We've done that before."

"Good, that will help a lot."

Before long the pies were in the oven baking. Bernadine watched with interest and didn't miss a thing. The women kept the oven hot with cobs and wood chopped from dead trees in the Leonard's grove.

"Next we'll do the birds." They all worked together stuffing the turkey, buttering the breast so it browned, and preparing the goose to put in the oven.

"Pies are done," said Mrs. Leonard. "Now the turkey and goose go into the oven."

Soon the aroma from the pies and roasting turkey and goose filled the house.

"The scents are making my stomach smile," Elizabeth laughed. "By the smell of things, we'll have a great meal."

Relatives and friends arrived with more food. Mr. Leonard asked a couple of men to help him extend the dining table. Soon it was filled with platters of hot, steaming food and all the chairs around the table were full. Father Henry, the parish priest, said grace and blessed the food. Those without seats filled their plates and sat on chairs wherever there was room.

When everyone had eaten their fill, some recalled previous Thanksgiving dinners.

"I liked the roast goose and all the trimmings we used to have at Thanksgiving in our home," remarked Simon. "What a feast. The skin on the breast of the goose was brown and crisp, and the meat was tender and juicy. It was delicious and tasted just like this one. Our goose was caught and dressed right from the yard. The gander was mean and chased us, and to think, I fed and watered that bird."

"Our homemade ice cream was the best. We made it at Thanksgiving to go with our pumpkin pie," added Christina, Mrs. Leonard's cousin. "We had our own milk and cream. Dad chopped ice from the tank or bought it from the icehouse. We used that old ice cream freezer, and everyone took turns cranking the handle. You put salt on the ice to make it freeze quicker, and you added more ice once in a while. When the handle was so ... hard ... to ... turn," Christina made a fist and grimaced as she mimicked turning the handle, "that you almost couldn't push it anymore, it was ready.

"Then Mama got the big platter for the dasher, pulled it out of the canister, and scraped some of the ice cream off, but not too much because we were all standing around with spoons to clean it off and sample the ice cream that was coming later. The ice cream stayed in the canister, and we packed more ice around it and let it sit for about thirty minutes. The homemade ice cream never froze completely, so when you put a couple of spoons full on top of a warm piece of pumpkin pie it melted and ran down the sides of the pie. Ach, was that good. With each mouthful you ate, you thought you were in heaven."

Mr. Leonard pushed his chair back from the table and cleared his throat. "President Lincoln called for a national holiday in 1861, a day to give thanks. I think we should hear what we're all thankful for."

Elizabeth offered, "Bernadine and I are most grateful for all your kindness and the ways you've welcomed us to St. Benedict. We are so happy to be with you."

The Leonard's other guests, in turn, shared their reasons for gratitude, but Bernadine said nothing, and Elizabeth wondered if the girl would ever be grateful for anything. Then Bernadine looked outside and saw Bovine Dena ambling past the window.

"I'm very glad we're not eating veal today," she said, and everyone laughed.

Four days after Thanksgiving, a new letter arrived from Hans. Unlike the others, this one was only one page, and Elizabeth's first horrified thought was that he was writing to say he had found someone else and goodbye.

Her fears were groundless.

*Meine geliebte Elizabeth,*

*I'm planning to come to see you over the Christmas holidays. You'll be on vacation from school Elizabeth and I hope you will have some time to spend with me. I am lonesome for you. I can't wait to see you again and give you a big hug. Say it is all right, please.*

Elizabeth hurried to the kitchen to find Mrs. Leonard cutting potatoes. Waving Hans's letter, she shouted, "Hans wants to come for Christmas. I'm still thinking about how wonderful Thanksgiving was. Now there are two more big things to look forward to, Christmas and Hans. But the big one is Hans."

"What does he like to eat, your young man?" Mrs. Leonard asked, dumping the cut-up potatoes into a saucepan and pouring water over them. "I'll make something special for his visit."

Elizabeth colored and went silent. She had no idea what his favorite foods were.

"What's wrong, my dear?"

"Mrs. Leonard, it's all so strange. I love him. I want to live my whole life with him but I have no idea whether he prefers spaetzle or kartoffelkloesse. I don't know if he'd prefer goose to turkey. I don't even know if he's ever had turkey. How can I want to marry him, knowing so little of him?"

Mrs. Leonard shrugged a little and smiled. "Next time you see him, spend more time listening than talking, and more time talking than kissing."

Elizabeth responded to his letter the same day.

*I'll have all vacation to spend with you for as long as you can stay. You should certainly make plans to come. I want to see you. It seems forever since we last saw each other. I love you, love you, and love you.*

The first snow fell early in December, followed by colder weather and more snow. Farmers used their sleighs to travel along snow-packed roads and trails.

Excitement ran high in the school among students and teachers alike. In addition to the usual anticipation of Christmas gifts and goodies, the entire community shared Elizabeth and Bernadine's eagerness for Hans' arrival. Everyone looked forward to meeting the young man Elizabeth wrote to so faithfully and spoke of so often. The Leonards even planned a party to introduce Hans to the community.

Elizabeth's stomach took turns fluttering in excitement and churning in anxiety as the day of Hans' arrival neared. It had been a long time since they'd seen each other. Would they still find one another attractive? Would Hans again speak of marriage?

And if he did, she knew Mrs. Leonard was right. Too many girls back home had not bothered to learn about the men they wanted to marry. Hans had been cheerful and sweet and kind on the ship but what was he like in ordinary, day-to-day life? Did he prefer coffee or tea? Did he eat with his left hand, German-style, or his right, like an American? Did he want to be a U.S. citizen, as she did? Did he want children?

And was Bernadine right about the past, would he forgive her?

All her questions flew away like butterflies on that special day, when Hans stepped off the Wesley train and spotted Elizabeth. He raced from the train to the platform, grabbed Elizabeth in a bear hug as he twirled around, and then planted a kiss on her lips before setting her down. The crowd gathered at the station cheered as Hans whispered in Elizabeth's ear, "Liebchen, how I love you. How I've missed you."

But there was little time for endearing phrases. She had to introduce him to all the people who had come to meet him. "Elizabeth is such a part of our community," one woman insisted. "When she leaves us, it will be impossible to replace her. So we have to be sure she's leaving us for the right man."

Hans bent double, laughing. "Madam, I will do everything in my power to be the right man, you can rest assured of that."

The Leonards were waiting at their carriage to take them home, but Bernadine was not there. Elizabeth wondered if her young sister was still upset about the man who had "come between them" and what she might do about it. But when they arrived at the Leonard's house, Bernadine was busy making a huge meal for them, complete with an unbelievable dessert.

"Mein Gott, it's Schwarzwälder Kirschtorte." he cried. "Where on earth did you get cherries at this time of year?"

"These were the last cherries to be harvested this season," Bernadine announced. "We froze them, just for you."

"Well ..." Mr. Leonard added, "just for you and all the Bavarians in town, anyway."

This led to the story of how many of the settlers of Iowa had been from southern Germany, so each year they would have a "Bayern Tag," or "Bavaria Day." They had celebrated the previous week, but Bernadine had insisted on keeping some of the cherries frozen for Hans' arrival.

Finally, the last slice of cake had been eaten and the last guest had departed. Hans and Elizabeth sat alone on the sofa in the Leonard's living room, hand in hand.

"It seems like a century since we said good-bye at Ellis Island," Hans remarked. "Being together again is good, even if it is for only a few days."

"Don't remind me of Ellis Island," Elizabeth told him. "I cried so much that day. I thought I'd never see you again."

"Never see me again? Liebchen, you must know you can't rid yourself of me so easily. I intend to become a human burr and stick to you all my days."

Elizabeth allowed herself to laugh, just for a moment. "Tomorrow we'll tour the town. I want everyone to see my fine young man."

The next few days passed quickly. Mr. Leonard loaned them the sleigh to see the town. Elizabeth introduced Hans to all the people she and Bernadine had come to know.

CUTTER AND HORSE SIMILAR TO WHAT ELIZABETH AND HANS
RODE IN WHEN HE VISITED AT CHRISTMAS

"It looks like a thriving town," Hans remarked. "Show me your school, too, Elizabeth."

Rounding the corner, she pointed to the white, wooden two-story building. "There's St. Benedict School, where I teach. It has four classrooms and a chapel on the first floor. On the second floor are a stage, dressing rooms, and a large sitting room with chairs for parents and guests to view plays in which their children participate."

"What subjects do you teach?"

"Well, all the standard ones, but lately I've taught a brief course on Hans-ology." Elizabeth giggled. "My students now know all about you."

He smiled and kissed her.

When she could breathe again, she hurried into a short presentation about life in St. Benedict. "Many of my students come from farm families. Most of the farmers around here plant corn. Many have dairy cattle for the milk they use in the home and sell what they don't need to the creamery for butter and cheese. Some farmers make their own butter. They also raise hogs for market and butcher some for their own meat."

Hans laughed. "You've learned a lot about your new home in a short time."

While Hans spent most of his time and interest on Elizabeth, he was careful to show interest in Bernadine as well. Meeting her one day as she trudged from one job to another, he gave her a peck on the cheek.

"How is school going for you, Bernadine, and what is new in your life?"

She gave him a blank look. "I'm doing well. I love school and the little ones I care for. Their mothers, Mary and Katherine, are like mothers to me."

"But that's wonderful! Why, then, do you look so downcast?"

She looked away. "I don't know."

It was harder to resent Hans and the time he spent with Elizabeth when he paid attention to Bernadine like that. She could also see that their love for each other was genuine. Alone in her room, though, listening to Hans and Elizabeth talk quietly and laugh together, old resentments resurfaced to trouble her. It made her angry sometimes that Elizabeth could begin her new life in America and seem to completely forget the scandal they had left behind.

"It's not fair," she told herself. "I'm the miserable one. She's the happy one. I want to marry someday, too. Maybe have children, but there's this thing hanging over my head and I don't know if I'll ever get rid of it."

For Elizabeth, the days flew. Each one ended too soon. And in the same manner, all too soon it was time for Hans to return home.

As he prepared to leave, he said, "I want to know, Elizabeth, if the two of us can make plans for our future. I love you, and I want you to visit me in West Virginia after the school year ends in the spring. I will get you, so you will not have to travel by yourself, and I'll travel with you when you are ready to go back. Please say you will come."

"I will come, Hans," Elizabeth said, and she kissed him. "I want to see where you live and work. And having that to look forward to will make our time apart go faster."

"You know, you bring out the best in me. I know I'm doing good work in West Virginia, meaningful work, but it's not nearly as important to me as you are. Come and visit me soon, my love. I will derive strength and purpose in life just knowing that you are waiting for me."

Somehow, she kept from sobbing in front of him. She gave him a brave smile instead, and she climbed into the sleigh to sit with him while Mr. Leonard drove them down to Wesley for the eastbound train.

"Maybe when you come back, the St. Benedict railroad spur will be complete, and you can ride all the way here," she announced.

"Don't expect me to wait for it," he replied with a grin. "I'll walk to you if I have to."

"Oh, Hans," This time she did cry, and he held her tightly until she got herself under control again.

In Iowa, January's cold, sunless days and long nights seemed to drag by. For Elizabeth, the days were interminable because she missed Hans. For Bernadine, though, the darkest month brought news. But was it good news or bad news? That was the question Bernadine would wrestle with for weeks.

The letter was in German in which Bernadine was natively fluent. But she had not heard it for so long that it felt odd to be reading in that language. The surname on the envelope was unknown to her, as was the address but she would have recognized the handwriting anywhere. She had written Judith twice a month since arriving in America but this was the first reply she had received, a full eight months later.

*My dear friend Bernadine,*

*I'm sorry it has taken so long for me to write. I began a letter to you months ago, but things seldom happen here, and I found there was little to tell you especially after your exciting letters of delivering calves, hiring out to other families, and attending school. I hope you are still doing well and going to school.*

*My father did not let me return to school this fall, and I hired out to a family as you did but the results were not as pleasant. I am glad your employers are also your friends. I was not that fortunate. I worked from dawn to nighttime for a family with ten children, doing laundry all day long. The children do not help with any of the chores; they are all spoiled and cruel. I only stopped doing laundry when I cooked for them. It was horrible, and they treated me in a vile manner, worse than a slave.*

*When my brother came to visit, he found me, my arms red and chapped from all the hot water and soap, my feet half-*

*frozen because I had outgrown my shoes, but no one would buy me a replacement pair. He took me away from them and set out looking for a husband for me instead. I was married last week.*

*My husband's name is David, and he is pleasant looking, with curly black hair and large brown eyes. He is a kind man, kind to everyone. But we will live far from Coesfeld now, far from everywhere I've ever known. David took all his savings and bought a small farm near Bergen. We are to have five cows and a small dairy. I'm told one of our cows has been bred, so someday I may help deliver a calf just as you did!*

*Please keep writing to me, Bernadine. I am fond of David, but we have not many friends, and I think of you often.*

*Always your friend,*

*Judith*

Dazed and shaken, Bernadine put the letter down.

"What is it?" Elizabeth asked.

"Judith is married," Bernadine whispered.

"Judith? But she's what, your age, isn't she?"

"She turned thirteen two weeks ago."

Elizabeth thought it over. "Well, stranger things have happened. They say Romeo and Juliet were about that age, and they're now immortal."

It took Bernadine a while to find the appropriate words to congratulate her friend, but she finally managed, although rereading the letter, she thought it sounded a little stiff and formal. Not because it was in German, but because of what it said.

*Judith, barely older than I am is married. Elizabeth says nothing, but I'm certain she is engaged. I wonder what will happen to me. Will I go back to Germany? I still don't feel Iowa is home. And wherever I am will I ever find someone who loves me—and who won't leave me?*

February brought bitter winds and more snow. Thankful for the hay he had set aside, Mr. Leonard kept his cows, horses and pigs fed. One of his hens escaped the coop, though, and was last seen being dragged away by a coyote.

With March came a brief thaw, but in the middle of the month there was another hard freeze. The melted snow became a thick layer of glass-like ice so slippery that it was dangerous to leave the house. When Bernadine's employer Mary tried to go out and feed her chickens, she broke her leg, and Bernadine's workload was doubled.

Finally, it was May. Bovine Dena turned a year old and was weighed. At 762 pounds, she was pronounced ready to be bred. By the time the Leonards took care of that, both the end of the school year and Hans' return were in sight.

Sixteen-year-old Joseph Rahm noticed Elizabeth's impatience one day and within moments, her students burst into a chorus of "Beautiful Dreamer." Elizabeth couldn't reprimand them. "I should, though," she said. "But, really, boys and girls, you have all seen Hans. Can you blame me if I'm excited?"

"I don't blame you a bit," shouted fourteen-year-old Nancy Weber. At that, all the students were giggling and Elizabeth with them.

Hans arrived the day after school dismissed for summer. As he stepped from the Wesley train, Elizabeth squealed and ran to him. Bernadine had come to the train this time, but she wisely waited for the happy couple to come to her. When they did, Hans had his arms wrapped around

Elizabeth, and Elizabeth was proudly announcing that she was already packed.

"And here's my favorite young friend, Bernadine," Hans proclaimed, hugging the girl, who blushed and mumbled something unintelligible.

The drive back to the Leonard's house was noisy. Hans and Elizabeth were both talking at once, filling in all the details of their separation. Mr. Leonard drove the team in silence, and Bernadine was also thoughtful and quiet.

"She's so happy ..."

"What?" Mr. Leonard asked.

Bernadine blushed. "I'm sorry, I didn't mean to say anything out loud. I just realized, well, my sister is happy."

"And that's a good thing," Leonard nodded. "I've seen a few couples about to get married and already they couldn't stand each other."

Behind them, Elizabeth was saying, "I didn't think school was ever going to end."

They had dinner that night together with the Wagners and Schmidts after which Mary and Katherine fell to joking about how inconvenient it was to be invited to a dinner hosted by their babysitter since they had to look elsewhere for childcare. Bernadine laughed along with them, but while the women laughed, Mr. Leonard tapped Hans on the shoulder and made a discreet motion toward the door, where Ralph Schmidt and Herbert Wagner waited.

Hans followed him, and all four men went outside to sit on the front porch.

Mr. Leonard lit his pipe, but his gaze never left Hans.

"I must say something to you, young man."

87

Hans eyed him, and then looked at the other two men. "And it takes three of you to say it?"

"Maybe," Leonard shook out his match and tossed it into the moist earth. "The point is, Elizabeth lives with my family. Her sister Bernadine lives with these gentlemen's families. This means these two girls are our family. We think of them as daughters. You understand this."

"I believe I do."

"Then you can understand how we feel about her going off to spend a couple of weeks with you and unchaperoned, at that. She's not even bringing her sister along."

"Now wait just a minute."

"No, you wait, young man." Ralph Schmidt had been leaning against the porch column, but now he stood up straight and reached a long arm, pointing his finger at Hans. "You wait. We want that girl comin' back here either married or unsullied and in good condition."

"Gentlemen, please," Hans said. "My intentions toward Elizabeth—"

"And in our presence, you can call her Miss Elizabeth." Herbert Wagner joined Schmidt.

"—have always been honorable."

"Then why are you taking her on a four-day journey with stops in Chicago and Pittsburgh?" Leonard demanded.

"That's the only way to get to Bramwell unless you think I should take a horse and buggy and then it would take a month."

"Never mind the wise talk, young man," said Schmidt. "Just remember, any dishonor falling on this family will be handled ...in the appropriate manner."

Hans was almost quaking by now, but he managed to control his nerves and keep his tone level. "I have listened with patience to you. Now you can all listen to me. I have never touched Miss Elizabeth in an inappropriate manner, and if I had wanted to, I could have done it on the ship, where no one was watching. I want to marry that young lady, and I want to do it properly. She will have her own room in each hotel, and her own berth on the train. While in Bramwell, she will reside with my friends the Neumanns, not at my house. Do you think I would dishonor the one I plan to marry? No, gentlemen, I swear to you, until she has a ring on her finger, Elizabeth will be my sister and my friend, in Chicago, in Pittsburgh, and in Bramwell alike. All right?"

"We have an understanding," Mr. Leonard said. "Let's go inside now."

"Yes, let's," Hans replied. "I don't like the climate out here."

That night, Elizabeth did not sleep. Bernadine had thrown down the gauntlet all those months ago when she had sobbed, "Do you think Hans will marry you if he learns?"

Elizabeth had no idea whether the girl was right. If she was, Hans would discard her like yesterday's newspaper. And even if she was wrong, Hans would know the only thing that still had the power to hurt Elizabeth. That kind of vulnerability would give Hans a weapon. But then, since that night when Mrs. Leonard had urged her to get to know Hans, Elizabeth had done a lot of thinking. Perhaps love was handing someone a weapon and trusting them not to use it.

As they boarded the train, Elizabeth threw a kiss to Bernadine, who grinned and waved to them both. Hans waved back to her.

"She's a special child," he said. "I'm glad she's your sister."

At that, a troubled look crossed Elizabeth's face. She took his hand and led him into their private compartment. "Hans, I need to talk to you. By the time we reach Des Moines, you may not want me to accompany you the rest of the way; if that happens, I'll go back to St. Benedict. But there are things you don't know about me, and it's important for me to tell you."

"Goodness, Elizabeth, you can be frightening at times. But I warn you, I don't scare easily."

She gave him a weak smile and shut the compartment door. "Hans, there are things about me and my past I haven't told you, painful things. But things you need to know before making any more plans for our future." A tear rolled down her cheek.

"What is it?" He caressed her shoulder.

"It's … it's just so hard."

"I don't understand."

"But you have to know."

"Know what?"

"I wasn't born in Coesfeld." She looked up at him. "And, Hans, you're not the first man I've been in love with."

He said nothing, but his eyes never left her face.

"I was born in a little town called Füssen in Bavaria. Only about ten thousand people live there; it's very near to Austria. When I was younger, much younger, I lost my heart to a man there. It shouldn't have happened, and with the hindsight of years, I can see every misstep I made. Because you see, nobody ever makes one big mistake. They make a lot of little missteps that culminate in a big mistake. But anyway, at the time I was so young—barely a woman—and I thought I knew it all."

She watched his eyes as they closed. "Oh," was all he said.

"Perhaps I was taken advantage of, I don't know. But the shame was mine. Is mine."

He his blue eyes again and fixed her with his piercing blue gaze. "How long ago was this?"

"I was thirteen." She looked down. "Hans, you lived in a big city in Germany, so you can't understand. No, you live in a small town now, so maybe you can see what it's like. Everyone in Füssen knew everyone else. There was a great scandal. People called me the witch girl and pelted me with stones. People even called Bernadine horrible names. I was thrown out of school. I was forbidden to take communion unless I confessed and I wouldn't confess. I couldn't, because the man was married."

He was looking at the floor now, but she continued on, willing her voice not to tremble. "I wanted to be a teacher, but being thrown out of school and ruined, well, you can see how the family was affected. My parents couldn't even look at me, they were so heartbroken and ashamed. They sold their farm and bought another much smaller farm in Coesfeld, and we moved away that same year. Nobody knew us there. It was far to the north."

"What happened to the man?"

"My father wanted to kill him, but he was wealthy and my father was not. We moved instead, hundreds of miles to the north. I heard that later, the same man ruined another girl, and that girl's father did kill him." A shrug. "None of it changed our situation, though. Eventually, my parents forgave me. I went to a different school and became a teacher. Hans, now that our parents are dead, Bernadine is the only one who knows my story, who remembers the way things used to be. Well, almost. After I began teaching in Coesfeld, a man came into town, and he had known our family in Füssen. He saw that my father's farm was doing well, and I was teaching and making money and he threatened us with exposure if we didn't pay him. My father died of a heart attack that night, and the man returned to Füssen with no money. Within the year my mother died too. The last thing she said was that Bernadine and I should get a fresh start. So we sold what little we had and came to America."

"Dear God, Elizabeth," Hans whispered.

"Hans, I'm so sorry I let you believe a lie. I should have told you the minute things became serious, but I couldn't. I loved you even then, and I was so afraid of losing you."

"No, no, that could not happen, Liebchen. I told you I would stick to you, remember? I am your own little burr, and I will stick to you till death." He crushed her into his chest and held her there. "And I will hear no more of this. It was long before you knew me. You were different, I was different. It's none of my business."

"But—"

"No. We will speak no more of it. There's nothing I need to hear. I know you now, and now you are my angel. There is no past."

"Hans ..." Her muffled voice came from his coat. She managed to extricate her face and look up at him. "Did you know that you're the most wonderful man in the world?"

He smiled and stroked her hair. "No. But if you tell me this every single day for the rest of my life, I might just believe it."

# ◈Chapter Five◈

The wedding was set for the following May.

"I'd rather not wait that long," Hans said on the train back to Iowa. "You might change your mind and find someone better-looking."

"There's no one better looking than you," Elizabeth smirked. "You've blinded me to all other men."

"And I'm glad to hear it," Hans told her. "Well, I'll use the time wisely, as the Bible says. I'll build our house and get my business better established. And you will have the Leonards to help with the wedding details. All this is good."

"But Bernadine ..."

"Yes, I wonder how she will take the news."

"I've thought about that too." Elizabeth looked away. "She suffered as much as I did because of the scandal, you know. And she and I have never been apart before. She will probably be sad and afraid, but when she's sad, she keeps it inside. And that's when she resents me, I think. Hans ... is there any way she could come with us?"

Hans' brow furrowed. "I was afraid you might ask that."

"Why? She doesn't take up much space. She's quiet and well-behaved, and she works hard."

"Elizabeth, I'm not marrying you to gain a servant. I want a wife. I want us to have a life together, and all the things that entails. Children, and time alone too. But if your sister is there, we will never be alone. And my mother always said two women should not live in the same house, or there would be no peace. Besides, I remember Bernadine's worries about being uprooted once. Would you want to put her through that again, now that she's finally settling in at St. Benedict?" At her stricken look, he bit his lip. Finally, he pleaded, "Look, give us a couple of years, at least, to be alone together; to begin our own family. And let's see what Bernadine does with her own life. But she needs a chance to have one before we say she can't make it on her own. If she can't find someone to marry and becomes an unhappy old maid, we'll bring her to us then."

Elizabeth nodded. "I guess that's fair."

"I think you underestimate her, though. She'll want her own life too, Elizabeth, just as you want yours."

A small crowd had gathered at the train station in Wesley. Elizabeth scanned the group, looking for Mr. Leonard.

"Hans, look. It's Bernadine with Mr. Leonard." Elizabeth shoved past passengers retrieving their bags, hurried down the steps to the platform, and rushed to embrace Bernadine.

"What a surprise, Bernadine. I'm so happy to see you. Hans and I have important news to tell you."

Mr. Leonard gave Hans a searching look, but Hans shook the outstretched hand and walked over to join the women. Both Bernadine and Elizabeth were talking at once so neither had a prayer of answering the other.

"How was your trip? What did you think of West Virginia?"

"What's new in St. Benedict? How are Mary and Katherine?"

Their questions spilled over one another until Hans raised a hand and motioned for them to quiet. "We can catch up on all that soon enough. First, Elizabeth and I have an announcement to make. We're getting married."

Bernadine squealed. "I knew it. I could see it in your eyes that you had a surprise."

Mr. Leonard clapped Hans on the back. "You've made a wise choice, young man. Elizabeth will make you an excellent wife."

Another barrage of questions: "When is the wedding? Where?"

"We won't get married until next year. Elizabeth will teach another year. Then we'll get married here and go to live in West Virginia."

"Well, at least I'll have you nearby for another year," Bernadine declared, her expression resigned.

"Yes, you will have a whole year together before Elizabeth moves away," Hans promised. "Enjoy your time during this year and think positively. In another year, you'll be older and know more people here in St. Benedict. Before long, you will probably find your own sweetheart, and you'll understand why Elizabeth and I want to spend the rest of our lives together."

His words were tender and his touch gentle. Elizabeth breathed a prayer of thanks as Bernadine gave a brave smile.

"Come on," Mr. Leonard said. "Let's get your bags into the coach and hurry home to tell Mrs. Leonard your news."

Bernadine turned thirteen in July. The rest of the summer passed quickly. Tending the extensive gardens that most families depended on for food took much of the women's time. Elizabeth helped Mrs. Leonard with weeding, harvesting, and canning the vegetables and fruits their garden produced. In addition to gardening and preserving, Bernadine became an expert on many domestic duties along with caring for the children. She loved the little ones, and they returned her love.

Letters continued to pass between St. Benedict and Bramwell. Elizabeth wrote Hans about her students, while Hans wrote about his burgeoning coal mining business.

When the calendar turned to the New Year, Mrs. Leonard suggested, "Elizabeth, we need to begin thinking about your wedding. I've made several wedding dresses and would like to make yours if you allow it. I love to sew."

Elizabeth's eyes sparkled. "That would be great," she beamed. "It will all start to feel real when there's a dress. What should we do to get started?"

"Do you have a preference for color?"

"Yes." Elizabeth smiled. "I want to be like the English queen, Victoria. She made a whole new tradition when she married in a white gown."

"Ah, my mother told me all about that." Mrs. Leonard nodded. "No one had ever thought of doing such a thing before. It's become quite the thing since then, though. We'll work on it together. I've worked with ivory satin before. It handles well and will make a lovely gown. You will be a beautiful bride with your long, dark hair and slender waist."

"When can we start?"

Mrs. Leonard smiled at Elizabeth's childlike excitement. "We'll need to make a trip to Rahm's General Store for fabric and supplies. I'll ask Mr. Leonard if he can take us Saturday."

The Leonards treated the upcoming wedding as if Elizabeth were their daughter. They helped her set a date and time. "Father Henry can perform the ceremony in the parish church in the morning. And we'll host a reception here in our home afterward."

With Elizabeth's gown and veil finished and fitted, Mrs. Leonard started the dress for Bernadine. Her green satin sheath required only one fitting.

"Bernadine, that dress is perfect for you," Elizabeth remarked. "It looks beautiful against your fair skin and light brown hair. You might draw more attention than I do," she teased.

The smile on Bernadine's face faded. "I am happy for you and Hans," she offered. "I can see how happy he makes you, and he's kind to me. But ... will I ever see you again?"

"Bernadine, you have your own life here now with people who care about you. I'm sure we'll come to visit when we can, and I hope you will be able to come visit us in West Virginia. Things will be fine, you'll see."

Bovine Dena, with little effort, gave birth to a heifer in early April. Bernadine was there to cheer her on, and the new calf, at eighty-five pounds, looked like she would be a healthy milk producer herself.

A second letter arrived from Judith, this one announcing the birth of her son Jacob, who had David's curly black hair and brown eyes, but Judith's nose and chin. Bernadine longed to see Judith again and to meet her baby.

"Do you think I could go back to Germany?" she asked Elizabeth.

"Why would you want to?"

"I want to see Judith again."

Elizabeth sighed. "Bernadine, let's suppose you went. And you had a wonderful visit. What would happen then? You can't visit people forever. What would you do?"

"Maybe I could marry."

"You can do that right here."

"Maybe I could marry a relative of Judith or David. Then I'd have a family."

"You must not remember the facts," Elizabeth said with a frown. "Judith is a lovely girl, and I suppose David is a nice man, but they are Jews, and Jews marry other Jews. Very seldom does a Jew marry a German."

"But Judith is a German, she told me so."

"She may think of herself that way, and I'm glad if she does. But ask her, and see if David isn't a Jew, too. I'll be shocked if he's not. It's some kind of tradition, or rule, or something. Jews marry other Jews. Better to look here if you want a husband."

"Maybe I'll never get married," Bernadine replied. "Maybe I'll buy a bicycle and ride it around the world like that girl is doing now. Annie Londonderry."

"I read about her. Her real name is Annie Kopchovsky, and she left her husband and three children so she could make this ride. But around the world, my foot. She's gone from Boston to Chicago, and last I heard, she was on a train going back to Boston." Elizabeth shook her head. "I think she is another insane suffragette who believes women should do anything men do, no matter how silly it is."

"Why can't women do anything men do?"

"Dena, we can do anything men do. But the danger is that if men find out we can, they won't want to marry us anymore, and then we shall have to do all the things they do. Now get these silly ideas out of your head. Finish school and get married."

Hans arrived two days before the wedding, almost a year since they had last seen each other. Absence had made their hearts fonder. Neither could erase the broad smiles from their faces. At dinner that night he announced that he had built a lovely house for his bride, and showed the assembled families the sketches. "Oooh, it's beautiful," Elizabeth breathed. "Hans, I always dreamed of living in a palace, but I never knew it would really happen."

But while the house may have been the shining star of the evening, Elizabeth was the undisputed shining star of the following morning.

Mrs. Leonard adjusted the tulle veil over Elizabeth's shoulders and stepped back to admire her handiwork. The ivory satin fell in soft folds from Elizabeth's trim waist.

"You are ready, Elizabeth." Mrs. Leonard squeezed her hands. "And you are just gorgeous." Next Mrs. Leonard checked Bernadine's dress and headpiece and smiled her approval. "You're both lovely," she observed. "Let's get to the church before it begins to rain."

They had not been at the church more than a few minutes before Mr. Leonard nudged his wife. "And look who's arrived."

Hans stepped from the carriage, handsome in a dark gray wool suit and well-starched white shirt. He wore a green silk tie a shade darker than Bernadine's dress. The three women stood side-by-side, smiling and holding back tears at the same time.

"He's so handsome," Bernadine whispered. Elizabeth pursed her lips and nodded.

"Isn't he?"

Then the organist began to play.

"I now pronounce you husband and wife," Father Henry said. "Hans, you may kiss your bride."

Bernadine forced a smile through her tears and joined the guests in applauding the newlyweds. It's not that she wasn't happy for Elizabeth. She was. She loved Elizabeth. She knew Elizabeth had been through great pain, and she had come out on the other side. Her "trials brought about perseverance," as the Bible states. She could envy her. But now Elizabeth would be leaving, and there was no one to fill the hole in Bernadine's heart.

Hans' eyes focused on Elizabeth they walked from the church to the carriage. "You are so beautiful, Elizabeth. And I love you so dearly."

Elizabeth smiled, looking down. "You're very handsome yourself. And if you don't know by now how I feel about you, I will have to think every letter I wrote you was mis-sent."

Turning to Bernadine, Hans smiled, "You look lovely too, Bernadine. Thank you for being Elizabeth's attendant." He squeezed her waist and kissed her on the cheek. Then he stepped into the carriage, leaving her on the dirt road. The driver flicked the whip above the horses' backs.

The wedding ceremony had been short, but the reception was shorter still. Even the guest list was short. Only the Leonards, Wagners, Schmidts, and the few close friends Elizabeth had made in the two years they'd lived in St. Benedict were invited. Additional guests would have made Bernadine more nervous than she was already. She was glad she hadn't eaten much for breakfast. Her stomach churned, a mixture of excitement for Hans and Elizabeth and anxiety for her own future. But she could hold herself together for a couple more hours. How long could a reception be, anyway?

Bernadine and Katherine had made the wedding cake together, and it was a beauty. White, of course, but the white frosting had tiny, light-blue flowers that Bernadine had spent hours working on. Elizabeth exclaimed over the flowers. "Bernadine, however did you manage such intricate work? And thank you for making them my favorite color."

Bernadine smiled bravely. "For my favorite sister, it was easy."

But when Elizabeth came downstairs in the green traveling suit Mrs. Leonard had made for her, the lump in Bernadine's throat nearly choked her, and she burst into noisy sobs and flung herself at her sister.

"Don't leave me alone," she choked out between tears. "I need you. You've always been my compass, my guide. I can't do this without you."

Elizabeth patted her back and smiled over her sister's shoulder at Hans. "You're all grown up now. You'll do fine. Remember, I taught you and I'm a good teacher."

"I'll be so lonely without you."

"We'll bring you out for a visit next year, Bernadine," Hans promised, offering her his handkerchief. "The time will pass so fast you'll hardly know we're gone."

At that, Bernadine stopped crying, but not for the reason Hans supposed. She said nothing more, and she plastered on a fake smile.

*I'll hardly know you were gone, to be sure. But there will never be a minute that I won't miss Elizabeth that I won't want her back with me. You're such an idiot, Hans.*

"We'll write to you often. You'll write to us as well, won't you?" Hans asked, with a reassuring pat to her arm.

She blew her nose and returned the sodden handkerchief to Hans without a word. She kissed Elizabeth's cheek and stepped back. "Go. Have a wonderful life. I'll be fine."

With Elizabeth gone, and no letters coming from her whether due to Elizabeth's new life or the summer-long railroad strike which impeded mail delivery for four months,

Bernadine didn't know. There was no point in waiting for exciting things to happen. Bernadine began to venture out to church socials with the Wagners and Schmidts. Card games were popular, and with a bit of coaching, Bernadine found herself adept at several. She had a knack both for Einwerfen and Pedro—trick-taking games—as well as Beggar-My-Neighbor. The real shock came when she discovered she had a cutthroat instinct for Cutthroat Pinochle. "Well, Pinochle was invented by German immigrants anyway," Ralph told her once as he dealt the cards. "So we ought to be good at it."

One day in late September, they were getting ready to return home from an afternoon card tournament. While Ralph hitched the horses, Bernadine told Katherine about a new mail-order catalog called Sears and Roebuck that was selling everything from farming supplies to silk blouses. "I'd love to have a silk blouse, wouldn't you?"

Ralph looked up from the horses. "The sky's looking strange out there. There's heaviness in the air that I don't like."

Just after their arrival that morning, a thunderstorm had begun that had ended only a few minutes before, giving them an opportunity to get home dry. Now the sky was dark with a greenish tint, and thick black clouds were roiling in the east.

"You don't want to leave?" Katherine asked.

"I don't know." Ralph looked grim. "Home would be the safest place, but that's two miles off."

Bernadine looked out at the sky and back to the couple. "Why is home the safest place? And why would we risk going out in another big thunderstorm?"

"It's not a thunderstorm I'm afraid of," said Ralph, but he finished hitching the horses all the same. "Get on. We're going."

Other families were also leaving, and far from their earlier merriment, now they all wore the same worried expressions. Without saying their goodbyes, everyone was leaving; many were whipping up their horses to run.

"What's going on?" Bernadine asked Katherine. "Why is everyone so worried?"

"Things happen sometimes in this part of the country, bad things," Katherine declared. Just then a wagon ripped past them, the horses running flat-out. The driver, Rheinhard Siefert, whose land bordered theirs on the south and who had been dealing cards from his own illustrated deck and cracking jokes an hour ago was cracking his whip over them and shouting, "Outta the way, Schmidt, we gotta get home."

Already nervous, Ralph Schmidt waved his own whip, and his two gray Percherons lumbered along faster.

A strange, oppressive feeling was constricting Bernadine's throat, and the air felt heavy and solid, pressing on her chest and making it hard to breathe. She gripped the wooden seat beneath her and twisted to look backward, feeling as if something was following, no, chasing them.

Off toward Algona in the west, a black wall of crud and debris hung in the sky. Was it her imagination, or was it really getting closer?

Bernadine looked to the front again, a wordless terror creeping over her as the horses galloped and the wagon rattled behind them. She leaned forward, willing the horses to run faster.

A few moments later they dashed into their own yard, scattering the roving chickens. "Grab all the food you can and get down to the cellar," Ralph shouted as he began to unhitch the horses.

Katherine looked at Bernadine. "Do it, and fast. I'll help my husband."

Bernadine ran toward the house as huge balls of hail began to drop. "It isn't even raining."

Inside, she filled the biggest picnic baskets with canned goods—most of their vegetables and meats were already in the cellar. She ran back to the door as the two Percherons, their ears pinned back to their heads in fright, were galloping away. Ralph and Katherine were running toward the barn. She watched as they opened the doors and went inside. Moments later the two riding horses and three milk cows emerged, wild-eyed, helter-skelter following the Percherons. Ralph and Katherine dashed back toward the heavy cellar doors. "Hurry up," Ralph shouted, and Bernadine ran toward him. Katherine had one door up; Ralph had the other. Bernadine ran down the narrow steps and the other two followed, closing the doors and letting darkness settle over them. Overhead they heard the hailstones banging on the wooden doors.

Ralph somehow found a lantern and lit it.

"The children ..." Katherine whispered, tears running down her cheeks.

Ralph put his arm around her. "Don't worry. Mary's no fool. I'll bet they've been down in her cellar for a good half-hour now."

"What's happening?" Bernadine asked again. "I know it's bad, but... "

In the distance, she heard a sound like a train roaring through. But there were no trains closer than Wesley.

"They're called tornados," Katherine moaned. She seemed to think explaining the problem would settle everyone down. "A strong whirlwind picks up everything in its path and destroys it. I've heard about them as long as I've been here, but this is the first one I've seen."

Something slammed against the doors, bounced off them, slammed again, and whirled off. Bernadine began to shiver. What if the whirlwind picked her up?

"Are we going to die?" she whispered to Katherine. "Shouldn't we pray?"

"Pray like your life depends on it," Katherine replied, gripping her around the shoulders with one arm and putting her other arm around her husband.

The roaring grew louder, filling their ears, and the ground seemed to shake all around them. "My new cultivator," Ralph shouted, "Oh, God, not the cultivator." He leaped up.

"Don't you dare," Katherine grabbed him. Out of some instinct, Bernadine also jumped to her feet and took him by the arm.

"Ralph, no," Katherine shouted again. "The cultivator doesn't need you and I do."

"But I need that cultivator." Ralph struggled against them. "Oh, God, why didn't I cover it up better?"

"Hang the cultivator," Katherine screamed. "Now sit down, you old fool, before I take a belt to you."

Cultivators, silk blouses, how little they meant right now.

As suddenly as the hubbub had begun, now all was silent.

"It's done." Ralph rushed to the cellar doors and flung them open.

"What if it comes back?" Bernadine whispered.

Katherine looked at her, shrugged, and followed her husband.

They emerged to see a wasteland. The barn lay in splinters. The new corral fence had been picked up and carried away. Ralph's prized cultivator was nowhere in sight. A dead chicken battered almost beyond recognition, lay in a heap next to the cellar door.

"Next time we should take the chickens down with us," Ralph concluded.

"Next time," Katherine repeated, with a horrified look. "God save us from a 'next time'."

Mary had taken her own three and Katherine's three children, and all were safely ensconced in the cellar, but her house had been pulverized. Herbert had been out in the field when the storm came, and no one knew what had happened to him. The boys, all of whom were at least eight, went out with Ralph to see if they could find him. It was long past dark before they returned, dragging Herbert on a makeshift travois of tied-together coats. He was bruised and banged-up, bleeding from scrapes and scratches and had at least a couple of cracked ribs and a broken leg. But he was alive, and Mary nearly suffocated him with hugs and kisses.

"It isn't that the wind is blowing," he told them as he sipped hot beef broth. "It's what the wind is blowing. I was near a lilac bush when the twister came—well-named, those things. It was like a crazed demon from the pits of hell. I dived into the bushes and held on with both hands, learned how it felt to fly and I'm glad now that God didn't make me a bird. Even when the wind picked me up and stretched me out, I held on, and I would've been just fine except that something else the wind had picked up glanced off me. Dashed if it didn't look like your cultivator, Ralph. My broken bones came from that thing."

"You should've held onto it for me," Ralph said with a grin. "I still can't find the thing."

Bernadine wrote a letter to Judith a couple of days later.

*...I don't know and can't understand how Katherine's house was undamaged but the barn next to it was smashed. And in Mary's case, her house was destroyed, along with the windmill, but her barn was fine. Most of the horses and cows lived, but the chickens were blown away and likewise most of the pigs. Herbert lived, although terribly battered and poor Rheinhard Seifert was found at the eastern edge of Kossuth County, unrecognizable. They only identified him because he had a deck of illustrated cards in his pocket, and it was the same deck we played Pinochle with a couple of hours earlier. Fortunately, he had no family, but that also means no one mourns his loss. So every Monday Katherine, Mary and I take the children to the cemetery and put a handful of wildflowers on his grave. Ralph made a cross for him. It's pretty.*

*They say a great many crops were destroyed. I heard that over in Plum City, the schoolhouse was blown to no more than a stack of toothpicks. And a horse got picked up and blown on top of another man's house. I never did find out how they got him down.*

*One good thing happened to me. In that cellar, I started thinking about the things that are important. I used to think I wanted to be rich and live in Schloss Varlar. But I came to see it wasn't where you live or what you wear or how much money you have that's important. What's important is love. Love of God, love of family, love of friends. That's all you have when you die.*

*Aside from my own epiphany, the best thing about any of this is how people have worked together; those whose homes were not damaged have opened their homes to those whose houses were destroyed. They are all getting together on weekends to rebuild houses and barns, and we are all sharing food. My friend Nancy had her house destroyed, and she is living with Katherine and Ralph and me now while her younger siblings are with the Leonards in town. The Weber house and Herbert and Mary's house are the first scheduled to be completed.*

*It's been a blessing to me to see the community come together like this.*

*The families who had lost loved ones had little time to mourn. All the homes and barns were replaced before Christmas. Ralph Schmidt put in a bid on the forty acres that Rheinhard Seifert had owned. When it was approved, he said a prayer of thanks to Rheinhard, and he planted corn on the whole forty acres. Corn was wonderful food for the hogs.*

The twister made national news, everyone said but somehow Elizabeth didn't seem to hear about it. Her letters never mentioned anything but parties, teaching, and how Hans was the smartest man ever to look at coal.

And when the time came to write Elizabeth, Bernadine somehow could not find the words again to describe the deadly tornado or the damage it had done. Or the things she had come to realize as a result. She mentioned that there had been a great windstorm and that a couple of chickens had died. But mostly, she wrote how she was learning to sew with Katherine or about learning to play cards and how much fun all the social events were.

After all, that was what Elizabeth wanted to hear.

# ☾Chapter Six☽

O ccasionally there were dances, but Bernadine was nervous about them. She asked Katherine for help one day. "I've noticed you and Ralph are fine dancers. Can you teach me?"

"Give me a pair of extra-long boots to protect my toes, and I could teach the Kaiser himself," Katherine declared with a grin.

"I don't know," Bernadine said. "I went to a dance on the ship with Elizabeth and Hans. He tried to waltz with me but I think I was hopeless."

"Nonsense, you were just nervous. I'll get your feet moving."

For the next couple of weeks, she took Bernadine outside and danced her around the cattle pen while Bernard, Katherine's son, played the accordion. By the time school had begun again, Bernadine knew the polka and mazurka, even the Zwiefacher Hans had talked about back in their days aboard ship. Once she was proficient and comfortable, she learned the Schottische which was German but meant "Scottish." All these were fast, high-energy dances that left Bernadine panting for air at the end, but laughing and pink-cheeked all the same. After dances like those, a waltz seemed pretty tame, so waltzing no longer made her nervous. And as her self-confidence improved, she began looking forward to the social events and getting to know other young people. The next year passed quickly, with school, hard work, and church activities; harvest brought a spate of invitations from friends to dinners and dances.

At fifteen, there was little left of the gangly almost-twelve-year-old of three years prior. Her hair had grown out again, and she wore it in a fashionable bun, atop her head with wispy side curls for special occasions or in a tight knot when busy with children and chores. Her legs had lengthened, and Elizabeth had always encouraged her posture, so she stood straight-backed and head-up, giving her an air of self-confidence. The little remaining baby fat disappeared, and she learned from her new teachers that a smile was the best way to win friends and confuse enemies.

In her last year of formal schooling, Bernadine had an admirer. His name was Robert. He followed her at a distance, looked for excuses to stay when he delivered groceries to the Schmidt's and drew pictures of Bernadine when he thought she didn't know he was around. Bernadine thought he was adorable in the way that a baby brother or a puppy might be adorable, but she did not consider him "admirer" material, and he eventually found another girl to follow.

There were two boys she did consider "admirer" material. Their names were Henry Seimer and Joseph Rahm. Both were at the top of their class (and two years ahead of Bernadine's). Both were tall and well-formed. Both had beautiful smiles.

And neither knew she existed.

Perhaps they knew—Joseph Rahm, at least, had attended the same school she did. Elizabeth had been his teacher. And both saw Bernadine at church and social events. But they were always talking to someone else, looking at someone else, doing something else. She could never attract their notice until the church bake sale.

About five weeks before, Alberta, Mary Wagner's barn cat, had six kittens.

"Suppose we use the sale as an opportunity to give the kittens away," Bernadine suggested. "We could take them along with the cakes and put up a sign. Everyone needs a good mouser, and if these little fellows are half as good as their mother, they should be champions."

Mary agreed readily because while cats were wonderful mousers, no one wanted a barn full of cats any more than they wanted a barn full of mice. So when the day of the sale arrived, Bernadine set off with a large basket full of cakes on one arm, a large basket full of kittens on the other, and a wooden sign marked "FREE TO GOOD HOME" clutched in her hands.

On the way, she ran into Nancy Weber, a friend from school. Nancy's parents had come from the Rhineland, but Nancy had been born in Wisconsin and only knew a few phrases of her parents' native tongue. This made her especially interesting to Bernadine, who couldn't understand how someone could hear German being spoken but not understand it. The two talked and giggled all the way to the church, where Nancy discovered another girlfriend and ran off to talk to her. Bernadine smiled, carefully made her way through the crowd, putting the sign that read, "FREE TO GOOD HOME" on the table.

"Bernadine," Nancy shouted across the din, "come meet Annabelle Murphy. She's from Ireland."

"I'm coming." She looked into the room to see which way Nancy had gone and dropped the basket on the table. Nodding with satisfaction, she went in. This was a good thing, people would see the kittens before they even got inside and even the toughest, most grizzled farmers would have a hard time resisting a six-week-old kitten.

"Good as gone," she murmured. Inside, an even bigger crowd blocked her way to the section marked "CAKES."

"Bernadine, are you coming or not? Annabelle wants to hear you speak German."

"Coming," she set the basket down next to the biggest chocolate cake she'd ever seen. She goggled at the coconut frosting for a moment. Whoever bought that monstrosity would have a stomachache for sure.

"Bernadine," Nancy called again, and Bernadine ran off to join her.

Henry Seimer had seen her drop off the basket. She was pretty, he thought, wondering if she baked as nicely as she looked. He went to the basket and lifted the cover—and a kitten jumped onto his chest, its tiny claws sticking in the coarse weave of his woolen shirt.

Henry had not expected to be attacked by the contents of the basket, and he yelped in surprise then he burst into a sneezing fit as the rest of the kittens made their way out of the basket and onto the high table. Four headed for the huge chocolate cake. The last one jumped on the head of Mrs. Montgomery, the church organist, who was wearing a straw hat with a big fake bird on the side. She screeched and began frantically batting at the sides of her hat. Just then, Joseph Rahm walked into the church—with his dog.

Pandemonium ensued.

"How was I to know Henry is allergic to cats?" Bernadine whimpered, tears running down her face as Mary took her home. "Or that someone would bring a dog in?"

"I don't understand what the cats were doing in the church," Mary questioned. "I thought you were going to put them by the door."

"I thought I did," Bernadine stood still, thinking. "Oh, but Nancy was calling me. Oh, no. Mary, I think … I think I mixed up the baskets."

Mary smirked. "That much I already knew. Well, look at it this way. You wanted everyone to know who you are. Now they do."

"But this is not how I wanted it to happen. I wanted them to love my cakes and adopt the kittens. Instead, the kittens trampled the cakes and anything they didn't destroy, the dog did. And someone took my cakes home without paying for them."

"Well, of course you put your cakes under a sign that said, 'Free to a good home.' What did you expect them to do?" Mary began laughing, and only the look on Bernadine's face kept her from going into a full-fledged paroxysm.

"Ach, there," Mary put her arms around the girl. "I'm not laughing at you. I'm laughing at the thought of all those kittens covered in coconut frosting."

Bernadine huffed, "And the one trying to eat the fake bird."

"And the one who nearly killed Henry."

"And the one who left the church riding on the back of that big shepherd dog," a grudging smile appeared, and then Bernadine began to laugh herself.

"Look on the bright side," Mary said when they had stopped. "It's Sunday afternoon. By next Sunday, it will be a thing of the past, everyone will forget."

But they didn't, and even years after all the cats had grown old with their adopted families and departed for cat-heaven, Bernadine was still known as "Kitten-Cakes."

"Mary," Bernadine asked one day, "what is the 'basket social' everyone is talking about?"

Mary set aside the pudding she was cooking. "Young girls and ladies prepare a lunch, put it in a box or basket, and decorate it. The box is put up for sale or bid, meaning the young men or boys let the auctioneer know they want to buy a certain basket. Of course, someone else may want the same one, so whoever agrees to the highest price gets the basket. The new owner pays for it and eats with the young lady who prepared the lunch and decorated the basket."

"That sounds like fun."

"It is."

Bernadine noticed the twinkle in Mary's eye as she wiped her hands on her apron and continued. "According to the rules and regulations, no one is supposed to know who brought which basket. Sometimes, though, if a certain young man wants to buy a certain young lady's basket and have lunch with her, little secrets are revealed to one another.

"Sometimes two young men want the same basket and there's a bidding war, and that means more money. All the money goes to the church or group sponsoring the function," Mary reported. "Mostly it gets funneled back into the school funds, so that's a good thing."

"There's one coming up soon. I'd like to go."

"We'll go, together, Bernadine, and I'll help you with your box."

Mary found the basket she had decorated for her first box social—the one her husband had bid on and won not only her lunch but eventually, Mary's hand in marriage.

"This basket means a lot to me, Bernadine, but I'll be happy to help you decorate it for some lucky young man."

Katherine contributed some lace and ribbon leftover from a sewing project, and Bernadine picked some flowers from the garden to decorate Mary's basket. The box socials had become increasingly popular as more immigrants settled in the area. Bernadine surprised herself at how much she enjoyed meeting different young men and sharing her lunches with them.

At one social, Henry Seimer bought her box. Bernadine—who had longed to attract him before—now found herself terrified.

"I heard they were your cats," he said with a little smile as they ambled across the church grounds to the park.

Bernadine's face grew so hot she thought her head might explode. "I ... I am so very sorry."

He laughed. "Don't be. Once I stopped sneezing and the swelling in my eyes went down enough that I could see again, I thought it was pretty funny."

"And how long did that take, for the sneezing and swelling to stop?"

"Two days." Henry chuckled.

She learned that he had been born in Bavaria, immigrating with his family when he was twelve years old. They had first settled in Wisconsin and then come to St. Benedict. He worked at various jobs to earn a living, primarily helping other farmers. Eventually, he purchased his own land and now managed several hundred acres.

"A lot of people don't understand," he explained, his eyes animated and his hands waving as he spoke. "But Iowa is God's perfect farmland. People claim their forty acres, and they set about growing oats, corn, and hay, all of it for animal consumption. They don't realize that corn is the REAL producer. People eat corn, too. They don't like to admit it. They say it's fitting only for pigs and horses. But people love corn—and why not? It's delicious, sweet, juicy, filling. You can make anything from bread to starch to syrup out of it. You can pop it, can it, chop it and cook it, or gnaw it right off the cob. Iowa is now the nation's foremost corn-producing state. I can see the day coming when everyone in Iowa will be growing nothing but corn."

"You are so passionate," Bernadine exclaimed, impressed as the young man continued to rattle on about the glories of corn.

However, Henry's passion for corn did not seem to translate well to humans. Once he had finished his soliloquy, he finished the slice of pie still remaining in the basket, stretched out on the picnic blanket, and went to sleep. When he woke from his nap, Bernadine had thrown away the trash and taken her empty box home.

At the next basket social, Bernadine did not contribute. The box Henry bid on had been made by Nancy Weber.

But Nancy Weber understood Henry's passion for corn in a way no one had ever understood before. By the end of the summer, they were engaged.

Elizabeth did not write with the regularity she had promised. The railroad strike of 1894 was a thing of long ago, and even Judith wrote every couple of months. But Elizabeth had married Hans in May of 1894. Now it was 1897 and she had sent only sixteen letters in three years. She had yet to visit Iowa again, nor had she invited Bernadine to visit them. Bernadine knew she was doing well, because the letters that came were written on creamy vellum rather than the more common foolscap, and there were occasional references made to a trip to Virginia, or Pennsylvania, or Ohio. Once, she and Hans visited the US capital in Washington, DC. That letter was long, carrying pages of description of this or that senator or congressman, and a great many word pictures of the buildings and monuments of "our nation's capital," as Elizabeth proclaimed. She even sent a picture-postcard with that letter, mentioning that she wished Bernadine had been there to see all these things, too.

Bernadine had given up on the notion of seeing her sister again when Elizabeth wrote to say she would be coming that summer for a month while Hans traveled to Pittsburgh for a conference. Bernadine felt more surprised than anything else. But the Leonards were delighted, and they repainted the room that had been Elizabeth's in her honor.

When the train pulled into Wesley station that July, Bernadine, along with Mr. and Mrs. Leonard, were there waiting. Elizabeth, traveling with more luggage for a month-long stay than she had used for her whole trip to America, rushed to greet them all with hugs and smiles.

"Bernadine, I can't believe it—you're taller than I am now," she cried. "And Mrs. Leonard, you don't look older at all. Mr. Leonard—oh, it's so good to see you all."

She dominated the conversation on the way to the Leonard's house, talking about everything from West Virginia cooking to the price of sheep in Montana.

In fact, Bernadine noticed that she talked about everything ... except Hans.

Upstairs in her old room, she begged a chance to talk to her sister alone for a while. With the door shut safely behind them, she sat on her old bed, tucking one leg under herself, and smiled coyly. "Who's this Henry you wrote about? Is he a prospect?"

Bernadine smiled. "Not anymore. His passion was for corn, not for me. I think he's paying court to Nancy Weber now."

"His loss," Elizabeth tossed her head. "Is there anyone else?"

"No."

At that, Elizabeth looked sad. "Well, I'm sure there will be soon."

"I don't know." Bernadine looked at the lovely suit Elizabeth was wearing, pale blue, with little white flowers at the bottom of the skirt. "I've been giving some thought to returning to Germany."

"What?"

"I have enough money saved that I could pay my passage now, but I want to travel first-class. I read there's a lot of disease for those who travel in steerage. For first-class, I need another eighty dollars. I figure about three more years should give me time to save up enough."

"Don't be silly. You can't go back to Germany. I won't allow it."

"You won't have to. I'll be eighteen next month. In the three years it will take to save money for passage, I'll be twenty-one and an adult."

For a moment, Elizabeth just sat, looking stunned and staring at Bernadine. Finally, she spoke. "We've discussed this before, you know. Why would you want to go back to Germany?"

"Because I still don't feel that Iowa is my home, I have no ties here—in fact, the only tie I have to the United States at all is you. And, let's face it, you are not a very strong tie."

"What's that supposed to mean?"

Bernadine opened her reticule, pulling out a beribboned bundle. "I mean that counting the note announcing that you were coming here, I've received a total of seventeen letters from you in three years. This is your first trip here. And in spite of all the promises of bringing me to visit you, my feet have yet to leave Iowan soil. Mary and Katherine are more family to me than you are, and I have no blood connection to them at all."

Elizabeth sighed. "Must you always make me feel guilty, Bernadine?"

"I'm not trying to make you feel anything. You asked me why I wanted to return to Germany, and I told you the truth. Any feelings you have are coming from your own conscience."

"I wasn't able to write very often. I was busy. I'm sorry."

Bernadine looked at the ceiling. "In that same period Judith sent me twenty-nine letters, despite her having three children and a dairy farm to manage, even though it takes six weeks for a letter to get from Bergen to St. Benedict."

"I wanted to see you, Dena. I love—"

"I have come to believe all life is a matter of priority, Elizabeth. After you left, there was a great tornado that destroyed much of Iowa. Many people were killed; many farms were destroyed. I was in great danger too. While I sat in that dark cellar, waiting to see if the tornado would whirl us away, I realized the things I valued. And I resolved that I would put my life toward the things I valued. I valued you, so I wrote to you. I valued Katherine and Mary, so I helped them as best I could. I value the thought of having a home someday, too. But I won't get married just so I can have a home. Nor will I come to live with you and Hans so I can have a home. I will only marry for love, and I will only live in a place I love. I still love Germany, and as yet, Iowa has not captured my affection. Maybe someday it will and if that happens I will stay. Otherwise, I'll go back to Germany. It doesn't mean I don't love you. But you have Hans, after all, and I know you love him more than anything. I will always be a poor second to him, and I'd rather not compete."

"Do you really think so little of me, Dena? You know I love you."

"Yes, I know. But you love Hans more. This is no sin, I don't claim it is. You should love your husband more than anyone, I guess, except perhaps your child. No, probably more than your child, too, although that doesn't seem a problem with you and Hans. So, you are doing right. But knowing that your priorities have changed, should I not adjust my own?"

Elizabeth looked stricken. Just then, Mrs. Leonard called up, "Girls, I have cake for you."

Elizabeth spent three weeks in St. Benedict. She visited Bernadine twice a week—once at Katherine's, and once at Mary's. Bernadine took her weekly afternoon off to go over to the Leonard's home and see Elizabeth. They also went to church together on Sundays and to a couple of dances and card games on Saturdays. But the balance of power had shifted, and Elizabeth knew it. Bernadine had gone from being a frightened girl to a self-confident woman. In fact, her confidence was stronger than Elizabeth's. Caring for six children, cooking, baking, working in the garden each day, dealing with winter blizzards and summer tornados, she was used to responsibility and making important decisions in the blink of an eye. Elizabeth, who taught school and managed a few servants at home, had comparatively few responsibilities. She and Hans had no children and spent their time together in leisurely pursuits.

"Don't worry," Mary told her once. "I'm sure you'll have a house full of your own children before long."

Elizabeth shook her head, deep in thought. "That hasn't worked out too well so far. I conceived three times in three years, but I lost each one. Sometimes I think I'm being punished."

"Oh, you poor child, but you mustn't think that. God doesn't work that way."

"Then why did they all die?"

"I don't know, but surely they are all with the Lord right now, and they are happy. You must be happy too. Someday you'll have a child."

At that, Elizabeth looked as if she would cry, and Bernadine, bringing in plates to set the table, looked at her sister and shook her head.

"Hans is attending a mining convention," Elizabeth said when asked about her husband. "The miners formed a union at around the time we got married, and they're threatening to strike. It is a silly thing because Hans treats his men much better than most miners have it. But they're unhappy all the same."

And while Bernadine knew these things were true, she also knew it was not the real reason Elizabeth was there. But she did not ask what was going on between them until one day she found Elizabeth sitting out in the Leonard's barn with Bovine Dena and sobbing on her shoulder.

"I couldn't tell you," Elizabeth confided.

Bernadine put her arms around her. "You don't have to. We're not all blind here. Something is wrong with you and Hans."

At that, Elizabeth only cried more.

"Hans didn't need to go to the conference," she finally admitted. "He gave me an ultimatum. He said when he comes home, I need to quit my teaching job. He wants a wife who stays home, chairing committees of charitable organizations and playing music for him and his friends when they come over."

"How foolish, doesn't he know most rich wives end up straying from their husbands and going with other men? It's in all the magazines."

In spite of herself, Elizabeth giggled. "I don't think he reads the same magazines you read. Anyway, it was the first argument we ever had."

"But what will you do? You won't give up teaching, will you? It's who you are."

"That's what I said. I told him I gave up my surname for him, but not my whole identity. Then I gave him an ultimatum of my own, that I was going back to Iowa for a visit, and if he does not withdraw his demand before my visit is up, I will stay in St. Benedict for good."

"Good for you." Bernadine nodded. "Stupid man, I really thought he was smarter than that."

"He said he'd given me three years 'to play with children,' but now I needed to stay home and have some of my own. He said I probably lost the babies because of the stress of teaching. 'Women are not designed to be intellectuals,' he told me. 'Too much brain work will ruin their bodies.'"

"Elizabeth, I think that man used up all God's blessings on his body instead of his brain. Truly, he's handsome, but he's an idiot."

Elizabeth laughed out loud at that and hugged Bernadine.

The tender moment was interrupted by Isaac Laube, the telegraph boy. "Halloo the barn; I have a telegram for Mrs. Hans Hartmann."

The two gaped at each other.

"Do you think—" Bernadine began.

At the same time, Elizabeth said, "Do you suppose—"

Elizabeth tore open the envelope. The telegram was from Hans.

LIEBCHEN STOP

I PINE FOR YOU STOP

PLEASE COME HOME AND TEACH ANYONE YOU WANT STOP

MY HEART IS YOURS ALWAYS STOP

HANS

The next day, Elizabeth departed for home.

# ᴄ᷾ᴅᴡᴏChapter Seven᷾ᴅ

B y the time of the next box social, Bernadine was ready to try again. She still had not met a boy she liked well enough to have two lunches with, let alone marry, but there were at least ten young men in town she had not yet tried. Joseph Rahm, Jr., the boy she had long ago hoped to entice with her chocolate cakes, had been walking out with Greta Frei. That left nine unmarried young men within her age range. "I'm almost eighteen," she told the mirror one day. "If I don't marry soon, I'll lose my looks and be an old maid. That might not be so bad. I wouldn't have to live in fear of disappointing some man, as Elizabeth does. But if I want children, and I do, I must at least try."

She heard from Nancy that a lot of the young men, unlike their forebears, had no interest in pickled or deviled foods, so she left the pickles and deviled eggs alone and concentrated on what Mary and Katherine called, "hungry-man classics."

For the next box social, she made a two-part sandwich, the right half was brisket, and the left was chicken breast. Both meats were on roggenmischbrot, rye-wheat bread most Germans loved, and for sides, the lucky boy could have both spätzle and potato salad as well as apple slices and cheese cubes. A chocolate cake rounded out the meal.

"That," Mary pronounced, "is a banquet. All the men will want it."

"I don't want them all to want it, just one, one special man."

Katherine was a talented seamstress who had taught Bernadine to sew, and together the two of them made a green dress with small white flowers on the skirt. They decided that should be the dress Bernadine wore and not only that, she would also cover the box with leftover green-flowered fabric, with dried flowers glued on the top.

"It's a piece of art," Bernadine announced. "But will a good man notice it?"

To Bernadine's surprise, young Joseph Rahm was at the box social, and he was carefully examining the boxes.

"I heard he and Greta are a thing of the past," Mary observed when Katherine commented on it. "They quit walking out at least two weeks ago."

"Does Bernadine know?"

"She will when we tell her."

"Don't tell her yet," Katherine advised. "Let me talk to the young man first and see if he has any interest. He knows me; I've made a lot of clothes for his family."

Katherine made her way through the crowd to Joseph, who was looking at a white box containing a bowl of goulash and a slice of apple pie.

"It looks rather plain," he observed.

"So does its owner," Katherine said with a smirk. "Take a recommendation from me. That green box over there, with flowers—I saw its ingredients cooked and put together. The fellow who wins that box will have a satisfying meal."

"Who's the cook?"

"Bernadine Vornhold."

"Ah, the kitten-cake girl, may I trust the meat is not made of cats?"

"Bite your tongue, child."

Joseph smiled and made his way over to the green box.

Katherine nudged him. "Well?"

"The flowers were unnecessary. Everything inside the box is beautiful."

"So is the owner." Katherine looked at him. "Am I, or am I not, the one who always knew what you wanted when you were younger and no one listened to you?"

"You are. You did."

"I still know what you want. Trust me."

She walked away, and Joseph, smiling, watched her.

Old Dieter Randolph was the auctioneer. His voice was as gravelly as the quarry pits. Everyone watched as he climbed up on a chair and hollered above the chattering, "Let's begin." Instantly he had their attention. Holding up a pink box with hearts drawn all over it, he shouted, "What am I bid on this lovely box?"

"'Lovely' is a little over-complimentary," Mary offered. "It's pork and dumplings."

Bernadine wasn't listening. She was staring at her own box, the fifth in line, and crossing her fingers.

In little time the first four boxes had been sold to eager buyers, and the girls and boys had gathered on the other side of the room to eat and talk.

Someone shouted, "One dollar," as Randolph held up the green box.

"I haven't even said anything yet," Randolph protested.

"It's for sale, ain't it?" The would-be buyer was Patrick Murphy, one of the town's few non-Germans.

"What do you think?" Mary whispered to Bernadine.

She looked distressed. "He's a nice young man, but … freckles?"

"I'll raise it fifty cents," another voice piped up, and Bernadine strained to see who the bidder was.

She gasped. "It's Joseph Rahm."

"Two dollars," said Murphy.

Joseph Rahm smiled, "Two-fifty."

Bernadine's heart began to flutter as Patrick shook his head, "Three dollars."

Joseph Rahm stared at Patrick Murphy, "Five dollars."

The hall went silent. All eyes were on Patrick Murphy, who gave a harmless little shrug and walked away. Joseph Rahm stepped forward and handed over the money.

"Son, you just bought a very expensive meal," said Dieter Randolph.

"I think it will be worth it," Joseph Rahm replied, and the audience began to giggle. "Where's the maker?"

Bernadine had frozen in place and could not move. Her heart was beating so hard and fast she was sure the entire population of the town would hear and begin a war dance.

Mary and Katherine nudged her forward. She resisted, and together, the two women gave her a mighty shove that sent her stumbling into his path.

"Hello, Kitten-Cakes," Joseph said with a grin. "I'm Joseph Rahm. I've wanted to meet you for some time."

The brisket was seasoned to perfection and the chicken had a touch of spice. Everything was wonderful, from the meaty sandwiches to the heavy potatoes and rich cake, to the light, almost delicate apple slices that concluded the meal.

"I'm glad your friend Katherine let me know which box was yours," he boasted as he washed everything down with a swallow of ginger beer. "I knew you had a heart for little strays like me."

"Are you a little stray?" Bernadine repeated, feeling foolish.

"Think of me as a lost kitten, desiring only cake and companionship."

The teasing tone made her want to giggle, but she restrained herself. "Well, in that case I'm glad Katherine interfered. I've wanted to meet you for a long time, Joseph."

"Since before your war-cats attacked my dog?"

Bernadine blushed. "Oh, long before then."

"Well, in that case …" Joseph wiped his mouth with a napkin, stood up, and pulled her to her feet. "I think we need to dance."

131

If Bernadine could have asked for a perfect dance, she would have wished for a romantic waltz but the little orchestra immediately struck up the Radetzky March. Laughing, Joseph and Bernadine got into line.

Four steps forward, four steps back, two to the side and back again. Change partners; four together, back to your partner and repeat. Clapping and laughing, Bernadine and Joseph moved through the routine as the fast-paced music played. They giggled when Hedda Strommberger and Patrick Murphy, neither of whom knew the moves, got mixed up and created a mess in their line. Everyone hooted and clapped, reforming the lines and trying again. When the dance ended, the whole room was full of laughter.

"Where did you learn to dance so well?" Joseph asked, not letting go of her hand.

"Oddly enough, from my friend and employer, Katherine, she watches over me in great and mysterious ways. How about you?"

"I have older sisters. I'm glad for their teaching, but you are definitely more fun to dance with."

The orchestra moved on, this time to a waltz. Bernadine smiled at Joseph. It was perfect. They floated around the room to the *Voices of Spring.*

At some point, the whole day took on a dreamlike quality for Bernadine. She lost track of the waltzes, polkas, and mazurkas. She only remembered Joseph, and how he never relinquished her to another partner, how his long legs effortlessly swept her across the floor, how they never made a misstep.

"I'd like to see you again, Bernadine," he said when the day was over and it was time to go home.

"I'd like that, Joseph."

He gave her hand an old-fashioned kiss. "Look for me next Saturday at one. I'll take you for a buggy ride."

HORSE AND BUGGY SIMILAR TO WHAT JOSEPH AND BERNADINE RODE IN WHEN HE SHOWED HER HIS PLOT OF GROUND FOR THEIR HOUSE.

She went out to the wagon with Mary and Katherine. "Do you believe it? He wants to see me again."

"Of course he does," Katherine replied. "The boy's no fool. By the time he comes to call, he will have asked about you all over town. He'll get nothing but good reports from us all. Watch out, Bernadine. You could be halfway to the altar."

"Don't listen to her, Bernadine," Mary cautioned. "Nobody is pushing you to marry. If you like the young man, all is well and good, but if you don't, you mustn't feel obligated. You take your time and listen to your heart. And of course, you can always ask us for advice."

Katherine rolled her eyes. "Listen to you. You're the one pushing her."

"I am not."

Bernadine giggled, "Girls, girls, settle down. It's late. We must go home."

As the big bay mare clopped along, Bernadine looked at the young man next to her and wondered if he was glad to be with her. He had said little since she had stepped nervously into the buggy, and now he hummed tunelessly to the horse.

More nervous by the minute, Bernadine was determined to get him to talk to her.

"Joseph, I know your parents are German. Were you born there too?"

"No."

"Oh. Where were you born?"

"Here."

"Have you traveled much?"

A shrug, "Been to St. Louis, I guess."

"You know I was born in Germany."

"Yup."

This was going nowhere. And speaking of nowhere, just where had he taken her? They were some twenty minutes from town now, and there were no houses in sight. A wooded area was alongside the road. It was as if they were alone in the world, with just the red and gold trees around them.

He stopped the buggy near another dirt road and jumped out, then turned and reached up for her. She did not move. "C'mon," he asked.

"Where are we?"

He grinned. "You don't trust me."

"Joseph Rahm, I am a good girl. I don't accept buggy rides out to the middle of some forest like Hansel and Gretel."

"If I didn't think you were a good girl, I wouldn't have brought you out here in the first place. C'mon." Without asking permission, he took her by the waist and lifted her down.

"But why are we here?" she asked, looking around.

He took her hand and led her down the curving dirt road to a grassy area marked off with twigs and twine. "I want to show you something. Nobody else has ever been out here with me. I've never shown it to another soul."

"What?"

"My house," he pointed. "Bernadine, my Pa's a good man. He's made his mistakes and taught me to avoid them. I'm following in his footsteps as a farmer.

"My father owned five hundred acres of land. Two years ago I turned eighteen, and he gave me some money. I invested it in the railroad, and this spring it paid off. I took the proceeds and bought this land from my father, one hundred acres. It's small, I think, but it's more than twice what most settlers start out with, and I think it'll do for a start for me and my family.

"This twine marks off my house. Look, kitchen, dining room, living room, two bedrooms. I'm working with an architect so the house can be modified if necessary, to add more rooms."

"Oh."

"Do you like it?"

"Um … well, it is a little hard to see right now."

He chuckled. "True." He took her by the hand and they walked around the marked area as he described to her what he envisioned.

"I can see it in my mind," she said when he was finished. "It sounds beautiful."

"It will be."

"But … you hardly know me. Why are you showing me this?"

"I remember you from school, you know. We didn't talk to each other, but I watched you. You paid attention, studied. Didn't gossip or act like a peahen with some of the other girls. I've spoken to the Leonards about you. They told me how you kept your head and delivered a calf way back when you were just a kid. Mary and Katherine both praise you to the skies for your taking care of children, cooking, baking. They say hard work doesn't scare you, that you are downright religious about keeping their houses clean. Everybody who knows you thinks you'll be a good wife."

"This is probably true," Bernadine conceded. "But if this is a proposal, I can't accept it."

"No?" He grinned.

"No."

"That's interesting, why not?" Now he looked serious as a funeral director.

"I remember you from school, too. Everyone said you were the best at math. You're very handsome, too." Feeling the blood creeping into her face, she looked at the ground. "But call me naïve, or romantic, or silly, I don't care. I don't want to marry a man who thinks marriage is an equation and if you just drop the right girl in as the unknown variable, the problem will be solved. A while back I had an experience that made me think about things, and I decided that if I couldn't marry for love, I wouldn't marry at all. I'm not afraid to be an old maid."

"You know," he said, the beginnings of a slow smile stretching across his face, "it's been a long time since that box social, a whole week. I missed your conversation. And I missed you. Bernadine, the day your cat jumped my dog I told my mother about it. I told her about you. She said I was plumb smitten. It was true, but I didn't want to believe it. After all, you were just a youngster."

"I was almost sixteen."

"Yes, but I was eighteen. I'm nearly twenty now." He gestured to the woods behind them. "I'm as old as some of these trees."

"Don't be silly." She began to smile too.

"But Bernadine, I'm a romantic, just like you. I want to marry a woman I love. The difference between us is simple. I know my own mind. I love you already. And I think if you get to know me better, you might just love me too.

"Here's my plan. It's autumn in the year of our Lord 1897. What do you say we walk out together for a bit? Your opinion of me may improve a little, and I can build my house and a few fences and maybe put some crops in. And then we'll look at that mathematical equation again. Say, winter of next year."

She found herself wearing a silly grin, uncertain what to do with her hands, not even sure whether to stand or sit. She said the only thing that came to mind. "Are you sure you never brought Greta Frei out here?"

"Never even thought about it. I called on Greta a couple of times because her mother is a friend of my mother. I never had any interest in her, though. Remember, I was pining for you."

Feeling a courage she'd never known before, she reached out and took his hand.

"Autumn is a beautiful time of year, all red and gold. Next week, we'll come out here again. And I'll bring a picnic. Would you like that?"

For a moment he didn't reply; he only looked at her, and she noticed the green flecks in his hazel eyes. Then he smiled. "I'm hungry already."

When they returned to Joseph's land the following week, it looked vastly different. A white clapboard fence encircled a large paddock, and a barn had been staked out. A distance from the "house," she could see the formerly green grassland as long black furrows.

"Me and two horses," he held up his arms and flexed his muscles. "Six days, ten hours a day. I plan to have eighty acres plowed before winter sets in, so we can get started with planting as soon as it's spring."

"We?"

He laughed. "Well, maybe it's the royal we."

She had brought along a large basket filled with sandwiches, fried potatoes, sauerkraut, and a large jar of tea.

"Say, that looks good and I'm thirsty," he said.

"I got the recipe from the 1890 Missouri State Reunion of Ex-Confederate Veterans," she explained, pulling out two plates and two glasses. "Careful, I stored it in the cellar last night, so it's pretty cold."

While they ate and drank, he talked about the work he was doing on the land. "It'll take me at least a month to get the whole eighty acres done. I just hope it's finished before the ground freezes. They say spring planting is easier if you plow up everything in fall and let the stuff you plow under nourish the soil."

"What will you do with the other twenty acres?"

"I'll save the other twenty and we'll pasture a couple of milk cows and horses on it."

"We again, you must be very kingly." Bernadine smiled.

"Well now, Kitty-Cake, I do believe that's the first time you've given me a genuine, warm smile. You should do it more often, it brings out your eyes, and your eyes are awfully nice to look at."

"You think so?"

"I do." He swallowed. "Your lips are nice, too."

"Oh." Color suffused her face again. She hated it, but she had no idea how to handle these compliments. He seemed serious. Did he really think she was pretty? Katherine and Mary said so; even Elizabeth did, now. But didn't they have to? They were all related to her or almost related.

By the time of the church hayride, Bernadine and Joseph had walked out four times. She knew all about his farming, his future plans and a good bit about his family. She knew she spoke more, and better, German than he did which she found funny. She knew his two older sisters had taught him not only how to dance, but how to talk to and treat women with respect. He adored his sisters, and while he had remembered their teachings with every girl he'd ever walked out with. "How many would that be?" Bernadine asked, and got a shrug in reply. "Um, a few," he finally admitted. He was putting his lessons into best practice with her.

She had also told him as much as she could about her own family. How she had been born in Coesfeld, how her parents were buried there, and how desperate for a good future for them both, Elizabeth had sold everything they had for a chance to come to America.

"But why did she leave you here?" he asked. "That seems wrong, somehow. I can't imagine one of my sisters leaving the other alone, especially if they were like the two of you, with no one else in the world."

Bernadine cocked her head, feeling an obligation to defend Elizabeth. "I'm pretty sure she loves Hans more than anything in this life. I'm sure he feels the same way about her. But I don't think either of them felt it necessary to include me in the dowry. Besides, she made sure I was happy with Katherine and Mary before she left."

"Hmm, I suppose." His serious look was back. "Well, it's not as if she was a mother abandoning her child, anyway. But I want you to be happy, Bernadine, and I think I must love you a great deal more than Elizabeth does. I can never imagine myself leaving you, not for any reason."

She admired his looks and intelligence, his great strength, and his honesty. She loved his kindness to children and animals. His sense of humor was broad and occasionally mischievous. He told stories of his Bavarian forebears that brought tears to her eyes. And he wanted her to meet his family. But, and he said this with his funeral director expression, so she knew he meant it, not until she was sure she loved him and wanted to marry him. "Because if you don't want me," he said matter-of-factly, "there's no point in getting my mother's hopes up."

"What do you mean? Is your mother worried about you?"

At this, he grinned. "She's already in despair of me ever finding a girl, seeing as how you ruined me for other women all those years ago."

"It was only two years."

"Two years is a long time to a woman wanting her children to marry."

The annual church hayride was held on a cold late afternoon in late October. Everyone was bundled in sweaters under their thick coats, and all wore gloves and hats. More than two dozen couples showed up, and three large wagons full of hay and pulled by four-horse draft teams were standing ready. Eight or nine couples climbed up and squashed themselves into each wagon, and waving goodbye to their less-fortunate friends and relations, everyone started out, laughing and joking, all smiles and games. Before long they were singing. They started with a couple of German songs most of the riders knew, but after a while, everyone was singing contemporary sparking songs. Bernadine was hesitant to join in, but Joseph was singing along lustily:

She's my sweetheart, I'm her beau.

141

She's my Annie, I'm her Joe.

Soon we'll marry, never to part.

Little Annie Rooney is my sweetheart.

His voice was just the slightest bit flat. It made her laugh helplessly, and so to keep from laughing at him, she had to join in as they moved to another:

Daisy, Daisy, give me your answer, do.

I'm half crazy, all for the love of you.

It won't be a stylish marriage. I can't afford a carriage

But you'll look sweet upon the seat

Of a bicycle built for two.

"I've never even seen a bicycle, except in pictures," she murmured to Joseph.

"I'll buy you one," he declared and kissed her hand. Maybe it was the cold, or maybe it was the warmth he radiated, but she found herself sliding closer to be enveloped in his arms.

It was a long, cold winter, and elsewhere in the United States there was tension. President McKinley had discovered evidence of Spanish atrocities in Cuba after an aborted rebellion. He demanded the Spanish withdraw from Cuba. Shortly after this, an American battleship called the Maine had exploded and sunk. America was poised for war.

But in Iowa, Bernadine was busy. The rest of the world could hang itself. She was in St. Benedict and so was Joseph Rahm. She had had a wonderful man holding her heart in his two hands, and he kept it warm day in and day out.

"When do you think you'll want to marry me?" he asked one day in late April as they walked to the dry-goods store.

"You're awfully sure of yourself." Somehow it didn't sound as tart as she had meant it to.

"I have to be," he told her, "Because I'm desperate for your love. If I don't have it, I will have to go to the war in Cuba and die on some forsaken hill."

"Oh, Joseph, don't even joke that way."

"You can't help but love me." He smirked. "Remember, I'm your own lost kitten." With that, he dropped to all fours like an overgrown cat and rubbed his side against her skirt. "Purrrrrrrrr."

"Get up, you silly boy. I can handle your foolishness when we're alone, but did you have to do this in town?"

"Purrrrrrrrr."

A lady stepped out of the dry-goods store and stared as Joseph circled Bernadine on his hands and knees.

"Oh Joseph, people are gawking at us. Please get up."

"Not until you say you'll marry me. Purrrrrrrrr."

"All right, all right, I'll marry you."

"Purrrrrrrrr." Joseph jumped up and kissed her full on the lips then. He had never kissed her before. Not on the lips, a few polite kisses to her hand and a few chaste pecks on the cheeks. But now his soft, warm lips were right on hers, and she didn't want him to ever leave. A little whimper escaped and her arms went around him and then she heard applause and opened her eyes to see twenty people gathered around them, clapping and hooting.

"Oh!" She hid her face in his coat front.

And Joseph bent his head down and said into her ear, "Purrrrrrrrr."

Bernadine crumpled up the sheet of foolscap and began again. Sticking her tongue out as she wrote and frowning so hard her eyebrows nearly touched, she was sure her hands were shaking, too. But finally, the words were coming out in what she hoped was a sensible fashion.

She looked over the letter and decided to read it aloud. If it made sense to her, maybe it would make sense to Elizabeth.

*"Dear Elizabeth,*

*"You must remember Joseph Rahm from your teaching days. I know you called him 'that giddy Rahm boy,' but he is anything but giddy now."*

She found herself blushing. *Except for the way he makes me feel—giddy, indeed.*

*"We've been courting for more than six months. I've lost count of how many times he has asked me to marry him, and I finally broke down and said yes. Now I'm wondering what made me hesitate. Truly, Elizabeth, he is the best man in the world. He's handsome and strong and gentle and sweet and ..."*

She sighed. *Well, Elizabeth will surely fuss at me for using so many adjectives, but I can't help it. He's all those and more.*

*" ...more wonderful than you can imagine. He's building a farmhouse now on his own land, and it's all plowed under and ready for spring."*

She remembered earlier that same day going out to look at the land and the house again. The foundation had been laid, and the frame was complete. For now, the house was single-story, but there was an option for a second floor to add bedrooms if necessary. This made her wonder how many children they might have. After four years of marriage, Elizabeth and Hans still had none.

*"Do you know, Elizabeth, when you and Hans married, I didn't believe it possible for any other two people to feel the kind of love you had. But now I know it can happen."*

And now she'll lecture me for starting a sentence with "but." I don't care, though, this is important.

*"Because I think Joseph and I share that same deep, committed sort of love that you and Hans have. I can see the years stretching out ahead, a long and happy future with this lovely, wonderful man."*

For a moment she just sat and smiled. Then she looked back at the page again.

*"We're planning to be married next year. Please be there. I'll let you know the date as soon as it's set. I'm meeting his parents tomorrow. I so hope you will come."* She nodded and added a hasty, *"Love, your Dena."*

As she sealed the envelope, she remembered the secret Elizabeth had made her promise to keep, and a dark cloud seemed to envelop her, but only for a moment. She would not let it ruin her life too.

# ⌘Chapter Eight☜

**B**ernadine wriggled in her chair. The Rahm's formal dining table was enormous, easily seating Mr. and Mrs. Rahm, Joseph's brother and his wife, both Joseph's sisters and their husbands, and herself and Joseph. And there was still room for more.

JOSEPH SR. FAMILY, LEFT TO RIGHT, JOSEPH, JR., ED, MRS. JOE RAHM, SR., JOE RAHM, SR., LAURA, AND FRANCES

Papa Rahm, known around town as "Old Joe," fixed her with a stare from under his bushy-eyebrows. "How long have you lived in Iowa?"

"Seven years now, Papa Rahm." She kicked Joseph under the table as she said it, and he jumped and began to snicker. "May I just say that Fair View Farm is lovely?"

"Yes, it is." The response was a simple acknowledgment, with no indication of pleasure or displeasure at the compliment she had paid. "From where is your family, Miss Vornhold?"

"My family is originally from Füssen, near Austria," Bernadine began, with a tremor in her voice. "However, we moved to Coesfeld when I was young."

"And you have no other family?"

"Just Elizabeth. She married back in '95."

"Elizabeth is Bernadine's sister," Joseph Jr. put in.

His father glared briefly at him before turning back to Bernadine. "Where is she now?"

"Bramwell, West Virginia, sir."

"And why is she there?"

Bernadine cleared her throat and looked back at the heavy-set man. "I guess she wanted to be near her husband, sir."

With that, everyone at the table burst out laughing, and Bernadine gained entry into the Rahm family's hearts.

Despite Bernadine's worry that her wedding would never happen, the year sped by. Mary's two sons were now old enough to help in the fields, and Mary was teaching her daughter to cook and do laundry, so Bernadine's child-care and laundry responsibilities went entirely to Katherine now. Katherine had already taught Bernadine to sew, and Bernadine picked fabric for a couple of new day dresses while Katherine worked on Bernadine's wedding gown.

Katherine sat at her sewing machine, feet rocking the treadle back and forth as she put in darts, gathers, tucks and pleats. She kept the machine humming as she straightened the bunched-up fabric and pushed it under the needle.

"Katherine, may I ask you something?"

"Of course," Katherine smiled but did not look up. Her eyes were fixed on the creamy satin in front of her.

"You know that you and Mary have been like mothers to me. And Elizabeth too, but not as much and not in a long time." She blushed. "Mrs. Leonard once told me that it's customary for a bride's mother to speak to her before the wedding. About what would happen ... after the wedding."

"This is true." Katherine reddened a little, and then looked Bernadine in the eye. "What would you like to know?"

"Well, I think I know what happens, actually. Elizabeth once told me that people are created exactly the way calves and colts and kittens are created, and I've seen animals breed. It's just—well, it looks terribly uncomfortable for the female. Male cats always bite the female's neck to hold them in place, and bulls are so heavy, it must be terribly hard on one's back."

Katherine had turned bright red and was holding her breath, but little snorts kept escaping. Finally, when she could contain herself no longer, she erupted into an explosion of laughter punctuated with little howls and hoots of mirth. Tears escaped from her eyes, despite her best efforts, and Bernadine backed away, flushed with embarrassment and shame. Katherine reached out, still laughing, and grasped Bernadine's hand.

"I'm sorry, my dear," Katherine finally gasped. "I don't mean to laugh at you. Those are some real concerns you've expressed. Sit down, please."

Bernadine had her doubts, but she pulled up a chair.

Katherine wiped her eyes. "All right, fortunately, our dear Savior loved us and didn't make us the same as he made horses and cows and whatnot. Joseph will not bite your neck, but he may kiss it. And he won't break your back either. The good God made people different from animals, and when we make babies, it's usually not uncomfortable. It can even feel downright good. Like being kissed makes your lips all warm and glowing but it feels that way all over. All right? Now, Joseph is a man, and he loves you. Anyone can see he does. The main thing to know is that when you love someone, you're gentle. You'll both learn together, and you may be a bit shy at first, but that's all right. If you're both patient and gentle with each other, you'll have no problems at all. It may hurt a little the first time, not much, just like the other day when you accidentally touched that skillet that hadn't finished cooling down. An occasion for 'ouch,' but not screaming, all right?"

Bernadine nodded.

"Other than that, just remember that he's showing his love for you in a physical way, and you're showing your love for him in a physical way. Our God gave us lots of ways to love each other. Friendships are good, and loving relatives like your sister are wonderful, but the love between a man and woman is just about the most special thing on earth."

"Oh, you really came," Bernadine was standing on tiptoe, her shoes squeaking in protest, and yelling above the crowd, as Hans put his arm around Elizabeth and pushed their way through.

"Did you think I would miss this?" Elizabeth replied, smiling.

Actually, Bernadine had doubts. But she said nothing, just threw her arms around Elizabeth.

"I remember young Joe Rahm," Elizabeth said as they walked off the platform to the waiting carriage below, "Rather a handsome boy, although he acted as if he knew it."

"He's even better-looking now," Bernadine told her. "And if he knows it, he doesn't let on. He's ever so humble."

"And I'll believe that when I see it," Elizabeth chuckled. "Where will you live?"

"Joseph finished building his house. It's lovely. We'll take you out to see it if you like. His fields are all planted, too."

Their luggage loaded, Hans and Elizabeth joined Bernadine and the driver in the carriage. "Fritz, would you mind taking the long way to Mr. Leonard's house? I'd like Hans and Elizabeth to see where I'll live."

When they got to Joseph's farmstead, she walked them through the house, not yet furnished, although everything would be in before the wedding. And she walked them through the barn. "Joseph has a two-horse hitch. He says his plow makes a twelve-inch furrow, and that to plow one acre of field he has to walk about eight miles behind the horses. He works ten hours a day, Elizabeth, imagine how strong his limbs must be."

Trying not to smile too broadly, Elizabeth agreed, nodding with enthusiasm.

"Have you had your dress made yet?" she asked.

Disappointed, Bernadine nodded. "Yes, and it's a lovely dress, to be sure. Katherine and Mary have worked hard at it. But I only plan on wearing it once, whereas I'll be living the rest of my life on this farm, so I'm more interested in this place."

Elizabeth laughed. "Indulge me, Dena. I won't be here for the rest of my life, and I'll only get to see the dress for a little while."

The finishing touches had been done on Bernadine's gown, headpiece, and veil. Her gown had a fitted bodice that accentuated her tiny waistline, long sleeves that narrowed at the wrists, and a toe-length skirt. The light cream satin dress came alive with darker ivory embroidered flowers at the hemline, on the bodice, and sleeves. Her shoulder-length veil was attached to the headpiece which sat high on her head, like a hat, with beads and teardrop pearls covering it.

"Ohhhhhhhh," said Elizabeth. "What a shame you can't wear that every day."

"Why would I want to? I'm already afraid of staining or tearing it."

"It makes your waist look so small."

"My waist is small," Bernadine replied, "although Mary says when I have some babies, it won't be small anymore."

Elizabeth sighed. "I do envy you, Dena. I'd love to be a mother. But so far, that hasn't worked out."

Bernadine put the dress away. "I guess I'd better get you and Hans over to the Leonards now."

The enormous dining room at Fair View Farm was getting a workout. In addition to the three married Rahm children and their spouses, Mr. and Mrs. Rahm, and Joseph and Bernadine they had added Elizabeth and Hans, Mr. and Mrs. Leonard, Katherine and Ralph Schmidt, and Mary and Herbert Wagner. Bernadine was sure they could've squeezed in another couple if she had had anyone else in her "family," but currently every important person in her life was sitting around the same table.

"I remember it like yesterday." Old Joseph Rahm's bushy eyebrows had drawn down over his nose. "It was 1874, five years after we came here from Wisconsin."

"That's even before we came," said Mr. Leonard. "You've been here a long time, Herr Rahm."

"Almost thirty-one years," came the gravelly reply. "Hasn't it been, Mutter?"

"Yes, dear, we got here just before poor Silas Stevens got caught on the tumbling rod of his own threshing machine. Poor man left a wife and four children."

Rahm grunted. "It was my fifth crop year, and the little buggers had already ruined half of my crop the year before. I was out with the oxen, didn't have the money for horses in those days. Took me a month to plow all forty acres back then. With a good team of horses, I can do it in two weeks now. But there we were in the field—Mrs. Rahm was with me—and I recall hearing her shriek and slap herself. Then I heard it, the roar almost as loud as a tornado. That's what I thought it was, at first, that dark cloud hanging above us. And then they were upon us, and I knew how Pharaoh felt when Moses called the plague of grasshoppers down on him."

"I believe those were locusts, dear," reminded Mrs. Rahm.

As if she had not spoken, he went on, "They were everywhere. In half an hour they had stripped the field we were in, we had already run. We set the oxen free and bolted. Not that we were afraid of being bitten, of course. Grasshoppers usually bite plants, not people, it didn't mean I wanted them in my clothes, though."

"But they were," Mrs. Rahm said, looking around the table. "In his clothes, I mean. Mine, too. It was awful. They stripped the corn down to the stalks. They were in the house, all over the furniture—they even ate my roses by the front porch."

"Bugger the roses," Mr. Rahm declared. "But the blasted—excuse me, ladies—pests ate my oats, sucked dry the entire crop. That year we went hungry. Before your time, Junior, and your brother's, you were too young to notice. Your sisters remember though."

The two women nodded soberly.

"If we men figure a way to free this world from grasshoppers and the like," Rahm declared, "then our time on earth won't have been wasted after all."

"What brought all that on?" Hans chuckled as he helped Mr. Leonard hitch the horses for the drive back.

Joseph had overheard him, and Hans ducked his head in embarrassment, but Joseph was laughing too. "Don't blush, Hans. My father loves dragging out those old stories. Most of them are directed to me. I am a disappointment, you see. I should have gone to college and been an engineer. But I am too much like he is. I feel the black soil in my fingers and must make it grow."

"You could never be a disappointment," Bernadine protested, her eyes flashing.

Joseph shook his head, smiling. "And my fiancée is a Valkyrie who will rain down in fury on anyone who thinks so. Goodnight, beloved. See you tomorrow."

As Bernadine rode with Ralph and Katherine back to the Schmidt's house, Katherine commented, "I hear your parents-in-law are giving you and Joseph some furniture."

Bernadine grinned. "Oh yes, they had some almost new living room furniture, and a table with chairs, even a bed. None of it was new, but it was all in good shape sturdy, tasteful stuff. I thought anything that helps us save money is a good thing."

Katherine clapped her hands together. "Mary and I have been working on a patchwork quilt. If your new parents are giving you furniture, there's no reason Mary and I can't give you a few furniture coverings. Would you like that quilt?"

"The beautiful star pattern with so much blue, oh, would I."

"That settles it, then."

Unknown to Bernadine, however, Katherine put the word out that Bernadine had never had a hope chest. Within the next two days, friends from church and town had brought over an entire wagon full of gifts—china, silver, linens, and a couple of framed prints from picture magazines. There was even a little spinet piano.

Seeing the wagon and hearing that the gifts were all for her and Joseph, Bernadine began to cry. Perhaps she had a tie to this country after all.

"I suppose you're not thinking of going back to Germany now," Elizabeth teased, "Or marrying some relative of Judith."

"Not now, no. Why, were you giving me ship tickets as a wedding gift?"

"The cheek on you, sister," Elizabeth chuckled. "No. I just remember the last time I came to visit, you were talking about having no ties to this country."

Bernadine gazed steadily at Elizabeth. "I have you and Joseph. I have friends here, it's true, but they wouldn't hold me if I wanted to leave. If something were to happen to you and Joseph, I would have a decision to make. And yes, home still has a powerful call."

"You can still call it 'home' when you've spent almost half your life here, in this country?" Elizabeth blew out an angry exhalation and mumbled something under her breath. "Well, do as you like, but I intend to draw my last breath in America. I've applied for citizenship."

"Have you?"

"Yes."

"Well, congratulations to you, but I neither need nor want citizenship. Joseph was born here, so marrying him makes me practically American. But if anything were to happen to him, I might still go back."

"Do you remember so little of home?" Elizabeth demanded. "Don't you recall all the name calling—and worse—that happened to us all?"

"I've been called a few names here, too. But really, does it matter? I'm marrying Joseph and staying here. Can't we just drop it and move on?"

Elizabeth gave her a weak smile. No more was said on the matter.

On May 30, 1899, a woman named Pearl Hart robbed an Arizona stagecoach and gained nationwide fame.

A week earlier, Bernadine Vornhold had married Joseph Rahm, but outside of St. Benedict, nobody cared. Then again, Joseph, with his typical sense of humor, read the headlines about Pearl Hart the week after their wedding and commented that both Pearl and Bernadine had gotten life sentences. Bernadine laughed and admitted it was true, but somehow, she didn't mind.

The night before their wedding, Bernadine had slept one last night at Katherine's. Wedding jitters had kept her awake long past her usual sleep time. She rolled and tossed until she finally fell into a restless, dream-filled sleep.

She took Joseph's arm. "Joseph, there's something you need to know about Elizabeth. You don't know, but I should tell you."

"Why do you need to tell me about Elizabeth? I'm marrying you, not her."

"But, Joseph, you need to know."

"All right, then tell me."

She woke with a start, screaming, chilled but sweating, her heart pounding, as Katherine rushed into the room. "Bernadine, are you all right? I heard you cry out."

"I just … had a strange dream. I'm all right now."

Katherine pulled the covers up and snuggled them around Bernadine. "Wedding nerves, I'm sure. Go back to sleep."

But she had gotten precious little sleep that night. The next morning, she thanked God for the veil she'd be wearing, as her eyes bore all the signs of sleep deprivation. Well, maybe the church lighting wouldn't be very good. Maybe her eyes would recover by the time the veil came off.

The church bells announced Joseph and Bernadine's wedding day from one end of town to another. Guests arrived in their buggies, coaches, and wagons, tied their horses to the hitching posts, and eagerly filled the church.

Bernadine arrived with Mary and Katherine. After a few adjustments to her gown, headpiece, and veil, they stepped back for an approving look.

"You look elegant, Bernadine," Mary declared.

Katherine agreed. "Joseph will not be able to take his eyes off you."

Joseph, dressed in a black suit and top hat, waited for Bernadine outside Father Henry's office. Mary opened the door of the dressing room, made sure no one else was around, and motioned to Katherine. Bernadine lifted her skirt and stepped across the threshold. She heard Joseph gasp and saw his hands go to his face.

"Kitty-Cake," he whispered. "I'm marrying the most beautiful lady in the whole world."

"Is she prettier than I am?" Bernadine replied with a giggle.

But for once, Joseph had no comic rejoinder. "My beautiful, beautiful bride," He took both her hands in his, kissed them, and then kissed both cheeks.

"You're quite handsome, yourself," Bernadine announced. "I love you, Joseph."

"There's the organ," Mary whispered, "Time for you two to make your entrance."

Bernadine took Joseph's arm, and they began their slow walk down the church aisle. Bernadine beamed as every head in the church turned to the bridal couple. Every face smiled back at the handsome couple. Many she did not recognize because they were friends of Joseph's parents. And there—there were Elizabeth and Hans. Her heart jumped and skipped a beat. Her dream of last night came back to her, and her heart raced. No. Not here, not now, not ever. She has her destiny. I have mine. Elizabeth's life and mine are parallel tracks from this day forth. There is only Joseph. He is my "forever."

They knelt at the altar and repeated their wedding vows. Joseph helped Bernadine to her feet as Father Henry said, "I now pronounce you husband and wife." Before the last word was out of the priest's mouth, Joseph was kissing his bride. The congregation laughed and cheered as Mr. and Mrs. Joseph Rahm, Jr., turned to face their guests. Joseph hurried Bernadine back down the aisle to the rear of the church where they held a long embrace and deep kiss before taking congratulations and well-wishes from every guest.

BERNADINE AND JOSEPH'S WEDDING PICTURE

BERNADINE AND JOSEPH'S WEDDING PICTURE WITH
ATTENDANTS

Joseph's parents hosted the reception at their large farm home. A meal of roast beef, mashed potatoes, vegetables, salads, cake, and pie was served. After eating, a couple of Joseph's friends helped clear the party room for the dance. Local musicians arrived, and Bernadine and Joseph danced their first dance as husband and wife. The guests joined in as the band played polkas, waltzes, and even responded to individual requests.

At four o'clock, the music and dancing stopped. Ladies put sandwiches, relishes, and cake on a table for guests to eat before leaving. Joseph and Bernadine took well-wishes again from every guest.

"Lovely wedding."

"Great celebration."

"You're a lucky man, Joseph."

"You're a lucky woman, Bernadine."

Then only family members were left. Her arms open wide, and her eyes full of tears, Elizabeth approached the newlyweds and embraced her sister.

"Little Dena, what can I say? I can see how happy you are, may it always be so. I can see that you love and are loved. What is any gift I could give you, compared to that?"

Bernadine swallowed and forced a grin. "I hope that doesn't mean you're not giving me a present."

Elizabeth laughed. "Your present from me is at your house, silly girl. We love you."

Hans was shaking Joseph's hand. "Congratulations, young man. If you and Bernadine are half as happy as Elizabeth and I, you'll be happy indeed." Then he put a long white envelope into Joseph's hand. "Please buy something special as a remembrance from us."

Stunned, Joseph nodded. "Thank you."

Elizabeth and Bernadine hugged each other one last time. The tears they shed were not the sad tears they had cried after Hans and Elizabeth's wedding. Though they did not know when they would see each other again, these were tears of joy.

"Come back to see us soon," Joseph said as Hans and Elizabeth made their way to Mr. Leonard's carriage.

"Here." Joseph handed the envelope to Bernadine. "Open it."

Bernadine slipped a finger under the tab and slid it across the envelope. She pulled out a check made out to Mr.

and Mrs. Joseph Rahm Jr. and involuntarily squealed. Wide-eyed, she handed the check to Joseph.

"A thousand dollars," he whistled long and low. "Talk about a pretty penny."

Bernadine's wits returned and along with them, an unwelcome thought. "Yes. A generous and thoughtful gift," she said softly, the price of a conscience.

Only a few family members were left at the Rahm's home when Joseph and Bernadine changed into their travel clothes. "Good night," Joseph called, and the couple took their leave without waiting for a response.

Arriving at their new home, Joseph held Bernadine's hand as he led her to the porch. There he lit a lantern. Inside, he set the lamp on the table, held one candle to the flame, and handed another to Bernadine.

"Let's light a few candles so we can relax a bit together. Are you as tired as I am?" he asked.

"Yes," Bernadine answered. She put her arms around Joseph's neck. "But it's a happy tired," she said and kissed him.

Before they could settle into the sofa, they heard clattering and clanging outside the windows.

"What is that racket?" Bernadine clutched Joseph's arm.

Joseph loosened her fingers and smiled. "I think it's some friends having a little fun with us. It's a chivaree. We'll let them carry on for a bit. Then we'll step outside and give them some money, and then we'll have the evening to ourselves."

The friends kept up the merrymaking for thirty minutes, singing bawdy songs along with their noisemaking. When the pauses between the shouting and banging grew longer, Joseph and Bernadine opened the front door and thanked the group. Joseph slipped some money to Klaus, who seemed to be the leader, and the crowd bid the newlyweds good night. At last, Joseph and Bernadine were alone.

# ᴄ⨪Chapter Nine᰾

A s the weeks passed, Bernadine found she loved being married to Joseph. She already knew he was a good man and a hard worker. She had seen his sense of humor throughout his courtship of her, but it had never occurred to her that it was a part of him. That even during a hard day weeding, he would find things to joke about. It was one more thing to love about him. Bernadine thought her own sense of humor had always been limited, and it was fun to discover things to laugh about, under Joseph's tutelage.

Fair View, Joseph Sr.'s farm, owned four hundred acres of fertile farmland, most of which was now planted to corn. They also had a large herd of dairy cattle and sold milk and cream to the local creamery. The land was productive enough that the Rahms, like many other Iowa farmers, fed part of their crop to their livestock and sold the rest for cash. Successful farmers were able to acquire more land and livestock with the accumulating cash equity. Joseph had worked alongside his father and brothers and had begun investing in his own land and livestock as a young man. And St. Benedict was booming.

ST. BENEDICT MAIN STREET, 1899

Bernadine had little recent experience with farm life as her duties as a domestic helper had been limited mostly to housekeeping and childcare, with some minor seasonal weeding work in Katherine's little garden. Now she took advantage of every chance to be with Joseph even coming alongside to help with chores. Despite the cold, Bernadine relished the time outdoors. But cold quickly became warmth in May and heat in June.

Joseph awoke before dawn each day, ready to feed the stock and milk the cow before going out to attack the land. Bernadine was usually already up and fixing his breakfast, but today she was still burrowed under their beautiful quilt.

"Bern," Joseph whispered.

No response.

"Bernadine." He gently shook her shoulder, "Time to wakey-uppy."

"Uhhhhhhhhhh," Bernadine sat up—and her face went white. "I think I'm going to—" She grabbed the chamber pot and heaved.

"Bern…?" Joseph took a handkerchief and handed it to her. "Are you all right?"

"I don't think I am."

"Should I call for Dr. Richter?"

"No, just …please, Joseph …let me sleep a little longer. I don't feel well at all."

When this scenario played out twice more in two successive days, Bernadine put it all together. "Joseph, I think I'm with child."

"Oh …" He stared at her. "Are you sure?"

"I think so." He didn't need to know the details of her reasoning, so he didn't ask. He just nodded slowly, the news settling on him like a calf he had once carried three miles on his shoulders.

"Are you …happy? Joseph?"

"Yes, yes, I just need a minute to get used to the idea." A slow grin spread across his face. "You'll be a mother. Ohhhh …Great Gott im Himmel, Bern, I'll be a father." He pulled her into a bone-crushing hug that lasted a long time. Then, shaking his head in wonderment, he left her for his chores.

Bernadine reviewed what she had been told about pregnancy. The tired, sick part shouldn't last that long. I'll get back to helping him soon enough. Today I think I'll write Elizabeth. She watched through the window as he headed to the barn, whistling. Then the remembrance hit her and she felt nauseous all over again. The wistful sigh that was unique to Elizabeth …"I do envy you, Dena. I'd love to be a mother. But so far, that hasn't worked out."

166

Bernadine's fists clenched. "Maybe I'll write Judith today."

Joseph and his father used a wire-checked corn planter like most of their neighbors. They stretched a long cable with knots at regular intervals across the field. The check-head at the planter moved each time a wire knot came through the pronged lever and the valves opened, dropping corn through the shoe into the furrow. This planting method also helped with weed control as it ensured straight rows through which the farmer could pass with a cultivator in any direction.

"Joseph, do you suppose you could plow up a patch of ground so we could have a garden?" Bernadine asked one spring morning. "I know a lot about gardening from Mary and Katherine. And you know how we enjoyed all the canned food this winter that we got as wedding gifts."

"Sure, I'll do that and help you plant it when I have time."

Eventually, Joseph purchased a single riding plow and used four horses to turn a fourteen-inch furrow, making his work easier.

With the seeds planted, Joseph faced another task, removing rocks that worked their way to the top of the ground. If not removed, they damaged farm machinery. Since it didn't require driving a team of horses or plowing a straight row, Bernadine volunteered to help.

"I can help you pick up small rocks today. My housework is done and I have time to spare. And the exercise and fresh air will be healthy for me and the baby."

"I can use all the help I can get, Joseph added. " There are lots of rocks out there."

They walked beside the wagon drawn by the team of horses and tossed the rocks into it. Bernadine worked as hard as Joseph. "Looks like you've done this for years, Bernadine. Keep up the good work."

Farming had always been physically demanding work. A day seldom ended with Joseph not sore all over. Bernadine had bought a bottle of liniment and rubbed it into his shoulders, back, and legs. The more she worked with him, the more she found herself sore too and then Joseph would return the favor, rubbing the liniment into her exhausted muscles. "You have to take care of yourself," he exhorted her one night. "I don't want my son to have a mama who's too tired to take care of him."

"Your son, how do you know it's not a girl?"

Joseph laughed out loud. "I am Joseph II, King of Jo-Bern Farm, and I hereby decree that even my girls will be called sons."

Farmers often worked together on tasks that required many hands, like haying and harvesting. Most farmers planted part of their land to alfalfa to provide food for their livestock. They mowed the hay, loaded it on racks, and pulled it up into the haymow of the barn.

Curious about how the hay got from the rack to the mow, Bernadine made sure she had her housework done on the day the farmers were helping Joseph. She stationed herself on the front porch where she had a full view of the barn and a shady place to tip and snip green beans.

A large door opened to the haymow under one gable where a track and pulley ran under the peak of the roof. The person working in the barn lowered a rope sling to the hay rack. The men below placed it securely under the hay. A horse pulled the long rope attached to the carrier down to the sling full of hay and got it to the crest of the barn. The men in the haymow moved the load along the track inside the barn. When they had the load where they wanted it, they shouted to the men below. A quick pull of the trip rope released the load in the haymow where it was stored until the farmer needed it later to feed his livestock.

"What a project," Bernadine remarked as Joseph sat down on the porch steps at the end of a long day. "I'm glad you had plenty of help."

Joseph wiped chaff and sweat from his neck. "It's the only way to do a job like that. Papa says they'll be ready to put up his hay tomorrow. I'll be over there all day."

By July, patches of golden yellow could be spotted among the fields of oats and alfalfa.

"It looks like the oats are almost ready for harvest," Joseph announced.

"Will you have someone to help you?" Bernadine asked.

"Sure," Joseph answered. "This is another time when farmers help each other."

Oats harvest, threshing, was another physically demanding job. A horse-drawn reaper cut the oats into windrows. One farmer walked along the windrows, picked up enough to make a bundle, and bound it with a band of straw. On some machines, someone rode on the reaper and tied the bundles by hand.

Often a group of five to eight farmers owned a threshing machine and agreed to work together. They made the rounds to each farm until every farmer's oats were harvested. The Rahms belonged to one such threshing ring.

"We'll begin soon, and I want you prepared for what happens," Joseph told her.

When the threshing machine arrived at a farm, men loaded bundles onto the rack, hauled them to the machine, pitched the sheaves into the feeder, stacked the straw, and took care of the grain. The grain was collected in spouts that measured the amount of grain into one-bushel sacks. When one bag was full the door closed, and another sack was filled from the other spout. A counter on the machine tallied the number of bushels threshed, and in this way, the owner of the thresher knew how much to charge the farmer. The bags were tied and hauled to the granary or barn where they were stored.

Some straw from the oats harvest also went into the barn to be used as bedding for horses and livestock. The rest was blown out from the thresher into a straw stack in the barnyard or a field for easy access by the herd. The straw had to be stacked and packed to withstand heavy winds, rain and snow and positioned to provide shelter for cattle from winter's strong northern winds. This job required knowledge and skill and the person assigned to it usually received above the average daily wage.

"It's a hard, dirty, itchy job," Joseph added. "We're covered with straw, chaff, and dust at the end of the day, and we're tired."

"I don't think anyone would want this kind of work," Bernadine commented. "It must be hard to find a person to do it."

"It is, but so far we've been lucky to hire someone."

Joseph laid a hand on Bernadine's. "I must tell you, Bernadine, the wives of the men in the threshing run work almost as hard as their husbands. They prepare meals to feed all those hungry men. The women all help each other just the way the men do."

"It sounds like fun," Bernadine laughed, and at Joseph's look of surprise, she smiled. "I know it will be hard work. That's all right. But it will be fun working with other women." She gave him a wink. "I haven't had a chance to be a 'silly, gossiping peahen' in a long time."

As he chuckled over that remark, she went on, "I also hope to get a lot of advice for when the baby comes." She rubbed her growing belly.

"I thought you were used to taking care of children."

"Children, yes, but newborns, no. I'm told there are differences."

The harvest began on Fair View. Bernadine rode in the wagon with Joseph to help her mother-in-law and the other wives prepare the meals. She tapped on the screen door and hollered hello before letting herself in as Mother Rahm slid a pan of homemade rolls into the oven.

"Schön Morgen. Are you ready to learn how we feed an army?" Mrs. Rahm teased.

"I'm here to learn and help," Bernadine replied. "What's first?"

Soon laughter and chatter filled the air. Pots clattered. The reservoir lid clanged as the women fed more cobs and wood to keep the oven hot. Aromas of freshly baked bread and roasting meats wafted through the open windows.

As noon approached Mother Rahm filled a basin with warm water. "Bernadine, would you get some washcloths and towels from the bathroom? Set them out on the table under the maple tree where the men can wash for dinner."

"Can I ring the bell?" Katherine's oldest daughter, Izzy, asked.

"I think we're ready to bring the food out," Mother Rahm said. "Yes, ring the bell."

The younger boys assigned the task of bringing jugs of well water to the crew arrived first, followed by a few older boys who pitched bundles onto a wagon to haul to the thresher. Then the men, hot and sweaty, found their spots at the long table. Father Rahm led the group in singing table grace, and the hungry workers piled their plates high with mashed potatoes, chicken, green beans, and rolls.

When the table looked like a horde of grasshoppers had passed over and eaten everything in sight, the men pushed back from the table, patting their stomachs and praising the women for "the best meal I've ever had."

"But don't ever tell anyone else they said that," Mother Rahm insisted with a mischievous smile. "Their wives would be angry."

The corn crop and Bernadine's pregnancy continued to progress. Joseph kept a watchful eye on both.

"If it doesn't freeze too early or we get a late hailstorm, we'll have a bumper crop. And then," he kissed Bernadine, "a baby. I can't wait to see him ..."

"If it weren't getting so difficult to get around, I'd help you with the harvest," she stated. "But Mother Rahm says I should take it a bit easier."

Corn harvest began in early October. Every morning Joseph hitched his team of horses to a wagon to which he had added a two or three-foot bang board on one side. He wore gloves and slipped a husking peg over one. With one hand he grabbed the stalk of corn. With the hook on the husking peg, he ripped the ear from the stalk and tossed it into the cart. The bang board kept the corn from falling to the other side of the wagon, thunk, thunk, and thunk. Joseph walked up one row and down the next husking, throwing, husking, throwing. On a good day, he picked sixty to seventy bushels, and then shoveled the corn into a slatted crib where it continued to dry.

Bernadine continued to marvel at her husband's capacity for physical labor. Though he rarely admitted to weariness, he welcomed the back rubs and shoulder massages she offered. He winced when she found a knotted muscle and massaged it with her thumb.

"Does that hurt?" she asked.

"Yes, but don't quit. I sleep much better after you've rubbed all the aches away."

Harvest and fall plowing kept Joseph busy in the fields into December. After the harvest, it was customary to plow again before the ground froze. As Joseph had said before, "spring planting is easier if you plow up everything in fall and let the stuff you plow under nourish the soil." There was a symmetry to it all that Joseph, with his liking for mathematics, and Bernadine, with her love of beauty, could appreciate.

Still, as Joseph worked morning to night, Bernadine hoped he would remember his indoor responsibilities. She had a "nest" to build.

"Joseph, when will you slow down?" she asked one morning shortly before Christmas. "I need you myself. Do you have time to help me get a room ready before the baby comes?"

"Of course, Liebchen, What do we need?"

"Mary and Katherine have given me some of their used baby things, but we need a cradle or a crib. The baby can sleep in our room for a few weeks, but eventually, we'll put him in the other bedroom."

"There's a cradle at my parents' house that my father made for us. I'm sure we can borrow that. Do you feel up to making a trip over there tomorrow?"

"Yes, I'm getting a little bored here all alone every day."

"You should enjoy the quiet now because soon you'll be a busy, tired mother." Joseph placed his hand on Bernadine's belly. The baby kicked. Wide-eyed, Joseph looked at Bernadine.

"Was—was that the baby?"

Bernadine laughed. "Yes, just letting you know he's going to need larger quarters soon."

Joseph hugged her. "Oh Bernadine, I can't wait to meet this little one."

Joseph stayed nearby throughout the rest of December and into January. In St. Benedict, the newly opened railroad spur posted its schedule. The growing town expanded to welcome new buildings and businesses. A new blacksmith came to town and the shingle that listed his name also promised, "No one has a bigger bellows."

And as St. Benedict planned for expansion, the young Rahms planned for expansion as well. They made room for the Rahm family cradle in a corner of their bedroom and cleared out one of their dresser drawers for the baby's things.

"We're ready whenever you are, little one," Joseph said to Bernadine's belly.

That night Joseph woke to Bernadine gently shaking him. "I think I'm having labor pains."

"Let me know when you're positive," he mumbled.

"Joseph, wake up. I'm not sure it's labor, because I've never been through this before but I'll tell you this. It hurts."

Joseph sat upright. "What should we do, Bernadine?"

"You can go for the doctor in the morning. The pains are not intense or regular yet like Mary and Katherine told me they would be. I'll try to rest. You should too."

"You woke me up to tell me I should rest? Humph," Joseph flopped back on the bed. Soon his breathing was deep and even again, but Bernadine was wide-awake. Trying to relax didn't work. She could only think, "This is going to happen. Oh, God, be with me you promised to comfort the orphans, and you know I have no father or mother. Stay with me, please. I'm so afraid."

Joseph set out for St. Benedict at the first light of day to get Dr. Richter. On his way, he stopped at Mary and Katherine's and asked them to stay with Bernadine while he was gone. They kept Bernadine calm, directing her to take deep breaths and relax between contractions to save her strength for the delivery.

On the return trip, Dr. Richter tried to prepare Joseph for the next few hours. "I know you're anxious for your wife and the baby," he instructed. "It may be a few more hours of hard labor before you meet your young one. Bernadine needs to focus, so I need you to stay calm and out of the way. The little one will let you know when he gets here."

Joseph swallowed hard and nodded.

As Dr. Richter had warned, the delivery took some time. Joseph paced the kitchen and living room and then stepped outside in the cold January air to take a break from listening to Bernadine's labor cries. He didn't dare venture as far as the barn to check the livestock or he might miss the baby's first squall. He stopped. Was that a creaky board on the porch? Or was it a tiny cry? Joseph rushed back into the kitchen. Dr. Richter met him at the door.

"It's a baby girl, Joseph. Congratulations, Papa. I've checked her over, and she is healthy. Bernadine is doing well too. You can go in and see them now if you want."

Joseph pushed past the smiling doctor and rushed into the bedroom. Bernadine was sitting up in bed, holding a tiny bundle on her chest. He glanced at the bundle, but he focused on his wife. Her hair hung in limp strings, and the dark circles under her eyes made them look huge. But she was smiling, and to Joseph, she had never looked better.

"She's beautiful, Bernadine. And so are you." Joseph kissed Bernadine's forehead. "Doctor Richter says you're both healthy." He sat on the edge of the bed and gazed at his wife and infant daughter. "I'm so glad it's all over."

"You're glad?" Bernadine laughed, "Me too."

"You did great, Bernadine. Now, what should we name her?"

"Let's think about it for a couple of days," Bernadine advised. "But remember we mentioned Sylvia if it was a girl. I think I need to spend a little time with her to see if Sylvia fits her."

"Of course," Joseph said, "just rest. Mother is coming to help. Do you know, Bernadine, now we're a real family."

After a few weeks of regaining her strength and learning Sylvia's likes and dislikes, Bernadine told Joseph they were ready to host a family gathering to celebrate their daughter's baptism.

The following year, John Bruns opened a restaurant and meat market in St. Benedict. Next door, Mr. Gerleman, the shoe repairman, was a favorite with the children. He gave them candy while their parents waited for him to repair their shoes.

These were additions to the town that both the railroad and the construction employees appreciated. And while Bruns was hosting his grand opening, the young Rahm family expanded again to welcome daughter Eleanor, who was soon after dubbed "Ella."

In 1903, while Joseph waited outside reading in the newspaper about a man named Henry Ford who had just organized the Ford Motor Company, Verena arrived. By that time, three-year-old Sylvia was banging joyfully on the spinet, hinting at a lifelong love of music, and two-year-old Ella proudly told Papa that if she had three blocks and he took two of them, she would only have one left.

When Verena was two—in 1905—telephone service came to St. Benedict. Located in Joseph's General Store, "Telephone Headquarters" offered a quick means of communication, but little privacy. The young man who wanted to ask a young woman out had to go through the operator (assuming, of course, that the young lady had access to a telephone). The operator would place the call, and then hand the receiver to the caller, who stammered his invitation to the unseen girl while curious onlookers listened in. The following year—the same year Laurie joined the family—rural areas were connected, with four or five households sharing a party line. Calls went through a switchboard, often housed in a private home, with the lady of the house serving as the operator. She used a general ring, five long rings, to announce a community event or alert the people that help was needed somewhere. All parties listened in and acted accordingly.

The direct line was convenient but no more private than making a call at the general store. Sometimes others on the party line listened in on personal conversations. The two parties might hear laughter when they discussed a funny subject or the telltale clicks of a receiver being taken off the hook or put back on.

That same year, the local stock buyer started shipping cattle to Chicago by rail. As many as two or three carloads of hogs were shipped out at one time. Farmers drove their livestock up the road to the stockyards, and neighbors along the way joined in with their animals. Though no one knew what price they would be paid, the stock buyer offered, "If you ship a carload of livestock, you can ride free to Chicago. Then you know the price firsthand." Presumably, sellers could negotiate with buyers and secure a better price in person. The farmer who had two carloads to sell was also assured a free ride back home.

"Son," Joseph Sr. suggested, "do you think we could come up with enough hogs together to take up Huber's Livestock on their offer?"

"For a round-trip ticket to Chicago, I'll have 100 head ready in about a month."

"Good, I should have enough to fill another car."

"I'm surprised you want to make such a trip."

"I'd like to see those big stockyards and talk face-to-face with the buyer. And I thought it might be interesting to see where our other products are bought and sold at the Commodity Exchange. And how else would we get a free trip to the Windy City?"

Any time a neighbor or friend joked to Joseph about his production of nothing but daughters, Joseph declared, "I am planning to have an all-girl baseball team, any objections?"

But the kidding stopped in 1908 when Magnus was born. Joseph Sr. offered Father Henry ten dollars to ring the church bell and let St. Benedict know that Joseph had finally fathered a son, but Father Henry said he would announce it at Mass instead. When Bernadine gave birth to another boy in 1910, Joseph named him Clarence.

"Six children," Joseph kept saying. "Can you believe it, Bern? Six."

"Let's say half a dozen, it sounds like even more," Bernadine said with a laugh. Her heart was full. She had gone from having no one in the world to having a wonderful husband and six healthy, beautiful children. What could possibly go wrong?

# ᴄᴀ♥Chapter Ten♥ᴀᴏ

C larence was eight months old when the grasshoppers came. He was sitting on the back porch watching his mother teach the girls and Magnus a little circle dance when the giant bug landed on his arm. He grabbed it with a pudgy hand and was about to put it into his mouth when it managed to squirm out of his grip and hop away. Just then, the insects swarmed down on his mother and siblings, sending them shrieking and running back to the house, Bernadine herded them all inside and closed the door and windows. Then the massacre began. She pulled the bugs off each child and threw them down to the floor, where Sylvia would bat the insect with a broom.

Out in the field, Joseph was fighting a losing battle. And he knew it. He remembered his father's rant right before he and Bernadine had married. "They were everywhere. In half an hour they had stripped the field we were in" and as he cursed and swatted, he knew now what his father had meant. "Go for the ropes," he shouted, and his hired men looked as if they thought he was mad, but they went for the ropes.

Unlike the smallish, dusky insects he had seen occasionally and identified as grasshoppers, these were big, plump, and bright green. They flew as well as they hopped, and although their bites were not terribly painful, he knew they were tearing his corn apart. Their mouths seemed to work in four directions, sideways in both directions as well as up and down. The critters seemed to have no fear of people and would land on them as well as the plants.

Joseph had read about ways to fight them, and while there were many suggestions, finding one that worked was difficult. He and his father had decided to go with long ropes that had rags tied on at intervals. A man held the end of each rope and stretched the line taut, then waved it rapidly back and forth. This made the rags flutter. The idea was to frighten the grasshoppers away from landing on the plants. But with four men, they could only do two rows at a time. And nothing would stop the braver bugs from returning to the plants once the men had moved to the next row.

"It won't work," Klaus cried, but he and Heinz took one rope while Joseph and Dietrich grabbed another. They stretched the ropes out and began yanking them from side to side, up and down, and were rewarded by seeing a small cloud of insects rise into the air. However, it was not long before they settled on another plant.

"Don't stop," Joseph yelled, "With me. Keep going, no matter what, row to row and back again, as fast as you can."

When this failed, they tried one last trick Joseph had read about. They brought out two horses and an array of long sticks. Two men would ride the horses on either side of a row, carrying a long stick between them. The stick would drag over each stalk, bending it down. Then when the stick had passed over it, the stalk would leap upright again, jouncing the insects off. Two more men following with burlap sacks bagged up as many insects as they could. But within an hour they had filled all the sacks they had brought. And still, the grasshoppers kept coming.

For the rest of the day and half the night they fought to keep the grasshoppers from landing. Bernadine came out at sunset, dressed in winter wear to keep her skin covered, and carrying sandwiches and a jar of hot coffee, but she saw defeat in Joseph's eyes. They might fight the critters until they dropped, but the battle was over and the bugs had won. The crop was lost.

The main lesson learned from the 1911 infestation was to get more dairy cows. Grasshoppers had no interest in cattle, and a farmer who could sell milk, cream, butter and cheese could still make a profit. Until then, Joseph had only had two cows. One, named Bovine Alberta, was the granddaughter of Bovine Dena and a wedding gift from Mrs. Leonard (whose Christian name was Alberta). After the grasshoppers, Joseph bought six more dairy cows and three shorthorns, which could be used for dairy or beef.

Pregnant again, Bernadine watched all the developments, wondering how this or that would affect her children. She had never had much interest in community growth or new technology, but that was before she realized that she no longer had only herself to consider. The grasshoppers of 1911 could have made her family go hungry. Had it not been for Papa and Ed Rahm, they would have gone hungry. It was time to be forward-thinking.

But then Bernadine began passing spots of blood, and for the first time in her life, she was terrified. Not for herself, but for the unborn life within her.

At almost the same time, St. Benedict, a growing community in which nearly all the buildings were constructed of wood, fire was a constant threat. The August 9, 1912, Algona Courier carried a story common to the era:

*The entire business section of our little city was
threatened by fire last Thursday afternoon. The fire originated
in the building just north of the bank and was quite well under
way when help arrived. Immerfall and Raskopf's threshing
outfit was luckily near at hand and their water wagon quickly
brought to the scene. The bucket brigade in the meantime was
busy carrying the available water. After much hard work, the
blaze was extinguished. A strong wind blew from the north at
the time and had the fire gained headway, the wind would
have swept it down the entire business section.*

Bernadine read the article and thanked the Lord for the
crisis averted. Then she redoubled her prayers on behalf of the
baby developing inside her. "You can avert any crisis, Father.
I'm so afraid I'll lose this baby. Please avert this crisis too."

Emma was born just before Christmas of 1912. She
was an easy birth and a happy little girl.

But the winter that ushered in 1913 was a harsh one.
Colds and flu passed from one child to the next throughout
January and February, finally settling on two-year-old
Clarence.

His cough persisted, and his fever rose. As Joseph
watched in concern, Bernadine applied damp cloths to his
forehead and liniment to his chest. She rocked as she sang to
him, but he grew listless and struggled to breathe. Bernadine
felt panic clawing at her throat, but she would not give in.
"Joseph, he's not getting better. We need to call Dr. Richter."

Dr. Richter took Clarence's temperature and listened to
his chest. He shook his head. "Bernadine, I'm sorry. Clarence
has pneumonia. There's not much to be done but pray his

lungs clear and the fever breaks. In the meantime, keep him as comfortable as possible."

"We'll all take shifts with him," Joseph insisted. "Bernadine, you've rocked him for hours. Let me help."

Feeling numb, she handed the baby to his father.

Joseph gave her a ghost of a smile. "Get some rest, Liebchen. I'll call you if anything changes."

Only an hour later she was back. "Is he better?"

Joseph bit his lip. "No change."

"Let me have him." Bernadine clutched him to her. Clarence wheezed a little and waved a tiny hand.

"He wants his mutti," Joseph said, trying again and failing to smile.

When Bernadine made no reply, he stood, shifting his weight from one foot to another. I'm a farmer. I know the seasons, I know when to sow and reap. I am strong, I can work all day and half the night if need be. I would give the boy all my strength if I could. But even the best farmer can't control life and death. They just are.

He turned and walked out of the room.

Soon Bernadine heard him chopping wood outside. He needs to do something, she thought. But there's nothing we can do. "Clarence, listen to me, we need you to get better. We can't do it for you, little one, you must do it. Please?" She clasped him to her chest, willing her own life force to strengthen his.

The next morning Joseph came in to find Bernadine still holding Clarence to her chest. She was peering into his little face, now white and still. Joseph looked too, and suddenly he realized he had never known any pain like this

Dear God, why this? You could have ripped my arm off and it would not have hurt this much.

"He died an hour ago," Bernadine said softly.

"Give him to me."

"Not yet, Joseph please, not just yet. I'll have the rest of my life not to hold him. Please let me hold him just a little longer."

Mary and Katherine helped Bernadine wash the body and dress Clarence in his Sunday clothes. Joseph and Magnus retreated to the barn where Joseph built a tiny coffin, and five-year-old Magnus carefully applied a coat of white paint.

Winter's gloom seeped into the house that was usually so full of laughter and life. Numb with grief, Bernadine went through the motions of feeding and dressing the children and sending them off to school. Joseph dealt with the loss by spending more time tending to the livestock, alone in the house except for Emma, Bernadine wept. But Emma, less than a year old, had her own needs.

Mary and Katherine made their visits more frequent. Father O'Neill spoke gently to Bernadine every Sunday. "Think of Clarence as your angel watching over you," he suggested.

That year, with five of his six children in school, Joseph Rahm, Jr., decided to take a seat on the Kossuth County School Board. "It's not that I know much about teaching," he told Bernadine, "But since our children need a good education, this seems the best way to make sure they get it."

Bernadine, however, saw through him. "We didn't protect Clarence well enough, and he died. So now, Joseph thinks he must work harder to protect the others. Father in heaven, is this really the way life works?"

Life never stopped. Still more changes were in store for St. Benedict. In 1913, many of its homes were fitted with acetylene lights. At about the same time, a system of gasoline lights was installed in the general store. "What a sight to behold," people shouted. Candles were slowly going the way of horses.

As Joseph's land holdings grew, he began welcoming the labor-saving devices that mechanization brought about. After years of shoveling corn into the crib by hand, he built a new corncrib for drying and storing corn. The new corncrib, with its central aisle, meant Joseph could drive a wagon through. He added a cupola and used an elevator to move the corn into the crib through the opening. Initially, horses supplied the power to operate the elevator, walking in a circle to turn a large wheel attached to gears and shafts that powered the lift. In a few years, portable engines or tractors powered conveyors and other farm machinery.

In 1914, Mr. Witte began selling gas-powered tractors in St. Benedict. Curious and eager to learn about more time- and labor-saving ways to farm, Joseph joined the crowd gathering for a demonstration. The massive tractor weighed 28,000 pounds and stood more than ten feet tall. Its drive wheels alone were seven feet high, and it was billed with "the power of sixty horses." The manufacturer, Minneapolis Steel and Machinery Company, called it the most powerful tractor of the day.

Mr. Witte hooked the Twin City 60 gasoline tractor to a twelve-bottom plow on a piece of land.

"Twelve," Joseph repeated. "Did I understand him right, he really said twelve?"

"Imagine how much ground you could cover in a day," his neighbor answered.

Another man shook his head. "Say goodbye to your horses." In awe, they watched the tractor make plowing look easy.

Joseph marveled and calculated. By the time he got home, he was almost beside himself with excitement. "Bernadine, you should have seen how easy that tractor pulled the plow and how fast it turned over the soil. You know, to pull a four-bottom plow would require a well-trained, four-horse team. Considering you need to harness each horse, feed, water, and rest the horses during a day of plowing, the tractor has many advantages. I think I'm ready to buy one, along with a new plow. What do you think?"

Bernadine had not seen the demonstration and had no idea what a tractor was except that it was a machine. However, Joseph wanted one, and he knew enough about farming to understand what he had seen. "If we have the money, and it makes your work easier and saves time, I'm all for it. It might give you a little more time to spend with your family."

The next day Joseph drove the tractor home by himself. Bernadine heard the roaring outside and thought another tornado was coming. She snatched up Emma and headed for the cellar, only to see Joseph riding in on a monstrous machine about half the size of their barn. It belched black smoke and stank to the skies. She shut her eyes and prayed. "Dear Lord, don't let that thing kill him."

It was a long time before Bernadine made her peace with the huge, noisy, smoking contraption. But Magnus called it "the dragon" and loved riding on it with his father.

187

Joseph used most of his corn crop to feed livestock. He sold the excess for cash. It was easier and more profitable to ship shelled corn. St. Benedict boasted two elevators, giving farmers some bargaining power when it came time to sell their corn. Joseph's Uncle Ed owned one elevator as well as the lumberyard where he sold coal, fencing, cement, and other items Joseph used on the farm. "We're blessed," Joseph observed one day. "We have so many relatives who are in this business; it helps us with the money angle. And since all our friends are farmers too, they know when we go through hardships. We all look out for each other."

"We live on home-raised beef, pork, eggs, chickens, milk, cream, butter, and garden produce," Bernadine agreed. "There's plenty of wood in the grove and corn cobs for fuel for heat and cooking, and St. Benedict has everything we need close by."

"Our children are healthy, and we even have an angel looking out for us," Joseph said with a small, sad smile.

Bernadine felt the tearing pain in her chest that so often accompanied her thoughts of Clarence. "Do you think we'll ever stop wondering what he would be doing now, what kind of boy he would be?"

"I don't think so, Bern. Maybe one day the pain will ease. But I think our hearts will always ache when we think of Clarence. Still ..." Joseph gave her a brave smile. "We have much to be thankful for."

"Much indeed."

At the end of June, 1914, the heir to the throne of Austria-Hungary was gunned down. It was an act that would change the world forever. But in Iowa, Bernadine realized she was pregnant again. She prayed fervently. "You took Clarence from me," she said to the crucifix in her bedroom. "He's with you now, I know. I can't blame you for wanting him. Do you find him as adorable as I did? I hope you're treating him well. But dear Father in heaven, I'm going to have another baby. You won't take this one from me, will you? Please?"

While the world watched, heads of state talked to and about each other, made threats and exhortations, and held meetings. Telegrams and letters flew across borders.

Bernadine, whose interest in the news these days seldom turned to the international stage, knew that the emperor of Austria had issued an ultimatum of some kind to the Serbian government. What it all meant she could not guess until the letter from Judith arrived in August.

*They say we are going to war. Kaiser Wilhelm and the Austrian Emperor, Franz-Josef, are friends, so the Kaiser has said the Austrians will have whatever they need from Prussia, including soldiers. But the Russian tsar says Serbia will have whatever they need from Russia, including soldiers. Most people are excited, there are parades and songs and people are polishing their guns. For myself, I'm not worried; Bergen is a small town of no military significance. But for my son Jacob, I'm terrified. He is like any other young man of 19, eager to make himself heard, wanting to be a hero. He will volunteer, and I'm so afraid of what will happen if he goes off to war.*

"But Germans are smart, practical people." Bernadine murmured. "The Kaiser wouldn't do anything foolish. There won't really be a war."

Joseph heard her. "Bernadine, didn't you know? Last week Germany declared war on France and Russia, and Austria declared war on Serbia and Russia. England hasn't declared war on anyone yet but they have an agreement with France, so they will have to. All of Europe will be at war."

"But Judith lives in Bergen. What will happen to her, and to David and Jacob, and all the other children?"

"I don't know. We'll have to pray for them. And for all Germans, everywhere. A lot of people are saying it's all the Kaiser's fault."

Matilda, known all her life as Tillie, was born in early 1915. By that time almost every army in Europe had mobilized. The war that would come to be known as "The Great War" was underway.

By 1916, the Germans and English who had been friends for years before, and who were ruled by first cousins who had played together as boys were using poisoned gases on each other in the battlefield. And in Iowa, St. Benedict's population was about seventy-five percent German. Suddenly, the non-Germans were looking at their German neighbors with suspicion and distrust. Signs started going up at the post office (run by a Scotsman) warning people to guard what they said, especially around people of German descent. "Spies are everywhere," the signs warned.

Gas lights gave way to more modernization—electric lights. Various homes in St. Benedict proper as well as the church, rectory, and schoolhouse were fitted with the Delco electric lighting system. The Britt Light and Power Company installed power lines between Wesley and St. Benedict and turned on the electric current. And some of the English-descended residents of St. Benedict talked about roasting "Frankfurters" on the wires. Berta Feingold, who had come to

Iowa from Frankfurt more than forty years earlier, sold her neighboring farm to Joseph and moved to Chicago.

Meanwhile, the Kaiser declared "unrestricted submarine warfare." Bernadine thought this was horrible of him, even before she knew what it meant. But learning that it meant German U-boats could fire on any ship in the ocean without warning was even worse. It was that unrestricted submarine warfare that led to the sinking of the American ship, the Lusitania, even though the United States was not involved in the war. Then a telegram was intercepted from German Foreign Secretary Arthur Zimmerman to Mexican President Venustiano Carranza. Proposing a military alliance between the two nations, the telegram offered Mexico the return of Texas, Arizona, and New Mexico in exchange for starting a war with the United States. Woodrow Wilson, the American president, asked Congress for a declaration of war on Germany. Bernadine, pregnant again, watched the international goings-on with a feeling of dread in her throat that worsened every time she or Joseph went into town. Across Iowa, many German immigrants were dragged out and beaten by their non-German neighbors. People who had been friends for years became enemies. Throughout Iowa, town councils began outlawing the speaking of German and the celebration of German holidays like Karneval.

"Ain't fair," Magnus observed. "In Louisiana, they get to have Mardi Gras. Why can't we have Karneval?"

Joseph and Bernadine did not know what to tell him. People now refused to play German records on their Victrolas. "As if Schubert and Beethoven were some kind of savages," Joseph Rahm, Sr., muttered. This was the least of the insults, as German books were burned and the names of foods were changed—sauerkraut became "Liberty Cabbage" and hamburgers became "Liberty sandwiches." Even Dachshunds became "Liberty Pups." The world had gone mad.

Rose, always known as Rosie, although her papa called her his little bunny, or Häschen was born in 1917 as the first American troops landed in France, and by that time Bernadine refused to allow her children to go to school. Even after the school board declared that German would no longer be spoken in school, Joseph argued with Bernadine. But when he learned that another German-descended child had been bruised and beaten, he changed his mind.

Patrick Murphy who had once tried to buy Bernadine's offering at a box social still counted the Germans in St. Benedict as his friends. However, he enlisted in the Army, although at thirty-six he was a bit long in the tooth. All told, seventeen men from St. Benedict served overseas. Fourteen were Germans. One was killed in action, and one died of influenza. Patrick Murphy returned legless and in a wheelchair. But he told side-splitting funny stories about his military service and always smiled at the people who came to see him. Everyone was surprised to hear of it when he committed suicide.

Bernadine often thought of Judith and especially her son, Jacob. But it always came back to one thing, thankfulness for her own situation. Even with the suspicion of the other people around them, her situation was better than Judith's. At thirty-eight, Joseph was too old for military service. And at eight, Magnus was too young. For those facts, Bernadine daily thanked God.

The war ended in 1918, and tensions throughout Iowa gradually diffused. Everyone celebrated the American victory.

Ultimately, the best thing about the war was that agricultural prices rose during that time and when it was over. Most of the European countries had been devastated. It would be a while before the farms of France, Belgium, Germany and Austria could produce food again. Joseph considered the situation and purchased more land, doubling, and then tripling his farm. He bought more farm equipment and reveled in the technological improvements.

Then an influenza breakout nearly destroyed the world. People called it "Spanish flu." Whatever it was, it hit hard and fast. Old people and children were hardest hit. Many of the families in St. Benedict lost babies and toddlers. Down in Des Moines, almost a thousand soldiers died at Camp Dodge. But now the Rahm family's isolation, which Joseph had fought so hard to prevent, became a good thing. No one in Joseph Rahm, Jr.'s family caught the dreaded disease, and by the time 1919 rolled around, it had burned itself out.

The elevators in the area saw more grain in those years than they ever had before or ever would again. The people of Iowa and especially St. Benedict had a reason to celebrate.

It seemed almost like part of the celebration when Rita was born in 1919, and Ardyth in 1921. Electricity came to the Rahm household. And in celebration, Joseph finally completed the second floor of their house. They now had a little breathing room.

JOSEPH AND BERNADINE'S HOUSE WITH ADDITION, THEIR AUTO, AND FAMILY, LEFT TO RIGHT, SYLVIA, ELLA, VERENA, LAURIE, MAGNUS, EMMA, JOSEPH, JR., AND BERNADINE

# ᢙ Chapter Eleven ᡣ

I n late 1923, Bernadine received a letter from Judith, for the first time in eight years.

*...My darling boy Jacob died in 1916 at the Somme. Two years later, influenza took my beautiful David. I still have my younger son Michael, and my two daughters and their husbands also survived. We are all living together on the remnants of our farm.*

*One of the greatest ironies is that living on a dairy farm, we never went hungry during the war, although I heard people in the cities were less fortunate. But now the French are here. They left us the land, but they confiscated our cows. I had a little cheese hidden. That's the only thing keeping us from starving now. We are the pariahs of the world. It's funny; I was almost used to being hated by other Germans for the crime of being a Jew. Now I'm hated by other nationalities for the crime of being a German. One has to laugh.*

"There must be something we can do for them," Bernadine told Joseph. "Do you think we could sponsor them to come here?"

Joseph's eyes showed the pain he felt, but his voice was hard and cold, "Absolutely not."

"But why, the war's over. Surely the Americans don't still hate us."

"I'm not so sure of that," Joseph said. "Maybe you didn't hear, but there are now immigration laws in place that put limits on the numbers of immigrants the United States will accept from each country. They started doing it in the war when everyone hated Germans, but now it's official, the Immigration Act of 1921 established a quota of people allowed to immigrate. Three percent of the number already here, and for Germans, I think the numbers are even smaller."

"I don't understand. Before the war, they ran an article about General Pershing, his real name was Pfoerschin, and he came from German immigrants. Now he's a hero. He commanded the whole American army in Europe. Why is he a hero but someone like Judith, who has probably never touched a gun in her life, is a threat? Do they really think the haus fraus started the war?"

Joseph took her hand. "I'm sorry, Bern, truly, but there's nothing we can do."

"Can we at least send her food?"

"What could we send that wouldn't spoil or be confiscated before she ever saw it?"

"How about money?"

"Do you think money sent through the mail is going to reach her? Someone would open the envelope before she ever saw it, and any money would be stolen."

"What about a bank draft?"

Joseph thought long and hard. "I can try, but no promises."

Joseph did try, but Germany was undergoing an economic depression worse than it had ever known. Inflation ran rampant. Soon the German mark was losing value every minute. A loaf of bread that cost 20,000 marks in the morning would cost 5,000,000 marks by night. When the economic collapse came, it took 4.2 trillion German marks to buy a single American dollar.

"I could send her five dollars and she'd be rich," Joseph said. "But since the French are occupying the Ruhr Valley, the whole country is sliding into hell. It would take her life savings just to buy a train ticket into town. If she tried to claim the money, chances are she'd be killed, and even if she could get it, she couldn't feed her family for a week."

The question became moot when a group called the National Socialists, or Nazis, tried to overthrow the government in Munich, calling for the whole country to take arms. Although the insurrection didn't last long, there was no hope of sending money to the desperate country.

Bernadine resorted to prayer. The Weimar government stabilized the following year. Slowly, the economy began to grow again, and civil unrest lessened. In 1924, Judith again wrote to Bernadine:

*Things here are a little better. But it does beg the question, is this what things are like in a republic? How has the United States survived for 150 years as a republic? I can't see it happening in Germany. We need a king again, a strong leader. But hopefully, one who won't be interested in starting wars.*

"Oh, God, please let it be," Bernadine murmured. "Germany is still my country, and I don't know what the Kaiser was thinking, but please, give Germany a strong leader—who won't start anymore wars."

Bernadine's life revolved around her little ones. Even with electricity and labor-saving devices, keeping the family fed, their clothes and the house clean took nearly all her time. The Rahm family now numbered twelve, Papa Joseph, Mama Bernadine, and ten children. Even with the upstairs bedrooms, the family frequently tripped all over each other. This was something of a marvel to Bernadine. Sylvia was twenty-three, Ella twenty-two, and neither showed signs of getting married nor did twenty-year-old Verena. By their age, Bernadine was already married and a mother, so there was more than a generational gap between them. There was a matrimonial and maternal gap as well. Almost overnight, so it seemed to Bernadine, her oldest daughters matured into beautiful young ladies. Their girlish giggles and bickering turned into concerns over how they looked. They were interested in the latest fashions and hairstyles and trying out some new makeup. Lacking experience with a sister closer to her age, Bernadine wondered how to handle all the changes they were going through.

At least the older girls helped with the chores. Magnus was daily helping his father in the fields. On days when the household grew hectic, Bernadine escaped to the barnyard to help Joseph. The livestock didn't bicker or yell at each other.

"What are they up to now?" Joseph asked when she walked into the barn.

"Don't ask," she replied. "How can they be so close sometimes and such bitter enemies at others?"

"You should know," Joseph offered. "You had a sister. Weren't you friends sometimes and sometimes enemies?"

Bernadine looked at the ground. "It was different with us, age gap and all that."

"There's an age gap between ours too. Sylvia's twenty-four, Emma is twelve. Isn't that about the same as between you and Elizabeth?"

"It was different, that's all."

Joseph looked thoughtful. "Do you know, we've been married twenty-five years, but every now and then I realize how little I know of you. What your life was like when you were young and what your parents were like. What life was like in Coesfeld or even why your family left Füssen?"

Bernadine grabbed a bucket and shoved it into the grain bin. "I have to feed the chickens."

Before she got to the barn door he intercepted her. "What did I say, Bern? I can't fix it if I don't know what I did."

"Nothing, you didn't do anything. I have to feed the chickens." She pulled away, but he wrapped his arms around her in a fierce hug.

"You don't have to tell me anything if you don't want to," he murmured. "When the angels come for me I'll still love you as much as I do now. I don't know what it is about your past that upsets you to think about it, but Liebchen, don't be angry at me. You're the reason I get up in the mornings. Don't you know that?"

At that she dropped the bucket, burst into tears, and held onto him.

Magnus came in a minute later to find them together. Bernadine was still crying.

"What's wrong with Mama?"

Joseph held his sobbing wife and gave Magnus a warning look. "She dropped the chickens' breakfast and it upset her, son. Would you mind picking it up and feeding the birds for her?"

When the boy was gone Joseph cradled her protectively close. "It'll be all right, Bern."

After her crying binge was over, Bernadine cringed, wondering how on earth she had lost her composure to such an extent. Maybe it was being surrounded by so many girls with whom she had so little in common. Maybe Mary and Katherine had some advice. They'd been through this stage with their girls. One morning she went to see them and ask.

"It's a phase, Bernadine." Mary refilled their coffee cups and offered Katherine another slice of banana bread.

Katherine smiled in agreement," Just keep loving them, love and prayers."

"Patience, too," Mary added. "Someday they'll make you a grandma, and you'll forget all the annoying things they put you through."

"A grandma, well I hope that's a few years off, but I like the idea of cuddling a newborn again."

Rosie, in third grade, hit her thumb against her chest with pride. "I'm learning to write cursing." She pointed to her composition book. "See my loops?"

Tillie looked at the ceiling as if praying for patience. "It's cursive, dummy, not cursing."

"We don't call each other names," Bernadine admonished. "Rosie is just learning. We help each other, not make fun of each other."

"Colm Murphy makes fun of people," Magnus snapped.

"Colm Murphy is unfortunate. If his father was alive, I'm sure he wouldn't be so surly. He's lonely without his father, so he does things that sometimes hurt people. In this family, we help each other. Understood?"

Everyone nodded. The younger children took their places around the kitchen table to work on their lessons.

"Rosie, maybe you can practice your cursive by writing a letter to Aunt Elizabeth," Bernadine suggested.

From the kitchen, Verena snorted, and Ella, just home from her job at the bank, shushed her. Sylvia said something unintelligible to both of them, and Bernadine resolved to get in the kitchen quickly to find out what the older girls were up to.

"Mama, we have a special program for our mothers next month," Rita said. Will you come? We're practicing hard."

Tillie jabbed Rita. "Shhh. Don't give it all away."

Bernadine raised a hand, "All right, you two. Yes, I'll come to your program."

Rita gave her sister a "so there" look and Bernadine hid a smile behind her hand.

Leaving the younger children to their homework, she went into the kitchen. Sylvia was putting a large pork shoulder roast into the oven and Verena and Ella were both giggling.

"What's got everyone in an uproar?" Bernadine asked.

"We just wondered if Aunt Elizabeth and Uncle Hans would come this Christmas." Sylvia's voice was about an octave too high and determinedly innocent, and she glared at her sisters as she spoke.

"Well, they've come every Christmas since you were born, always with more gifts than you can carry, and playing with you more in a week than I do in a year," Bernadine smiled. "I don't know why this year should be different from any other. Now girls, you know I don't interfere between you much."

"True, Mama," Ella said. "And now would be a good time to keep it that way."

Verena giggled again.

"All right, what's going on?" Bernadine demanded.

"Nothing, Mama, it's just that Sylvia and Louis were making eyes at each other at Mass Sunday. We wanted to ask her about it, but she won't say anything."

"What?" Bernadine felt as if the air had been knocked out of her lungs.

"Tattletale," Sylvia snapped.

Bernadine made her way back to the kitchen table. "Magnus, do you know a young man named Louis?"

"Yes," Magnus replied. "His family farms to the west of us, and they go to our church. He used to have a brother my age, but he died back when everybody had the flu."

"Mama," Sylvia called from the kitchen. "Can I talk to you?"

Bernadine stepped back into the kitchen. Ella and Verena were gone. Sylvia sighed. "I was not sneaking around, Mama. I just didn't want to say anything until I was sure. Louis and I have been walking out together, and I like him. I think I love him. How do you know for certain if you love somebody, Mama?"

Caught off guard, she managed a smile. "Can you imagine the rest of your life without him?"

Sylvia thought for a while. "Maybe, but it would be awfully empty and bitter. I think I must love him."

"Then you'd best marry him."

"He asked me, but I panicked. I said I'd have to think about it."

"Oh, that's all right," Bernadine assured her. "Only a very silly girl wouldn't want to think about it. Marriage is a commitment and not something you do lightly. Does your father know the family?"

"Sure."

"Does he think well of them?"

"I think so." A mischievous look crossed Sylvia's face. "By the way, Mama, now that the cat's out of the bag with me, you might ask Verena about a young man named Cliff, and Laurie about Ben."

By the time Elizabeth and Hans visited at Christmas that year, Sylvia, Verena, and Laurie were all married. Not that this made any difference in the number of presents they received. Elizabeth and Hans doted on their nieces and nephew, and Bernadine's claim that they arrived with more gifts than they could carry was accurate. With the arrival of the motorcar Hans had purchased a new touring car every year, and they arrived each Christmas week with the entire back of the car stuffed to bursting with gifts. This year was no different. Their 1923 Duesenberg Model A was literally overflowing with presents. They even had to put some in the front. Elizabeth's face shone when she told them, "But we didn't mind. Having so much in the front seat gave me an excuse to sit right next to Hans. When he wasn't busy shifting gears he kept his arm around me."

Joseph, who finally bought a car, a used Model T Ford, raised an eyebrow. "Nice automobile," he commented.

"It's a Duesenberg," Hans told him excitedly, "A German car. You probably haven't heard of it before."

Joseph and Bernadine exchanged smiles but neither said anything. They had been in Des Moines before the war when the Duesenberg brothers, a couple of German immigrants who settled in Iowa, opened their company.

"When we get the gifts under the tree and change our clothes I challenge everybody to a snowball fight," Hans announced.

Bernadine shook her head. "Hans, wouldn't you like to meet the new family members first?"

"Bernadine, gross Gott, are you in a family way again? There should be a law."

"Not me, silly, but three of my daughters have married. Don't you want to meet the husbands?"

"Married?" Elizabeth's voice broke, "Really?"

"Didn't you get the latest letters?"

"We just got back from overseas. Most of these gifts are from England and France."

"All right," Hans said. "We'll meet the husbands, put the gifts away, and get our clothes changed. Then comes the snowball fight.

Louis, like Joseph, owned a Model T, but since cars were regarded as barely a step up from horse-drawn carriages, they had no heaters. Joseph and Louis were lucky enough to afford completely enclosed cars. Many automobile owners did not have that. They relied on blanket-wrapped hot bricks on the floorboard and long bearskin wraps and lap robes to keep the occupants warm. When the families bundled into the three cars for Christmas Mass, they could have complained about the tight fit. They were grateful instead for the additional body heat provided by all the occupants.

Mary and Katherine were there when they walked into the church. After rounds of hugs, the two dragged Bernadine off to one side.

"How are you feeling these days? Sylvia looks pretty good." Katherine remarked.

"She does. So do Laurie and Verena. What of it?"

The two exchanged glances. "Has Sylvia had any problems so far?"

"Not that I know of and Louis treats her well. She already knew farming work since she grew up with us, but why are you asking?"

"Really, Bernadine, have you not noticed?" Mary demanded. "Sylvia's expecting."

"She's expecting?" Suddenly, almost every eye in the church was on Bernadine. "What are you talking about?"

"Well, if you don't know after having eleven children of your own," Mary shrugged.

Sylvia, already seated with Louis, was laughing at something he said. Flushed and happy her blue eyes radiated joy.

"Lieber Gott," Bernadine murmured. "I'll be a grandmother."

She looked over at Elizabeth, whose eyes were full of tears.

Ella was upstairs putting the younger children to bed. Joseph tottered off to bed himself. Hans kissed Elizabeth good night and headed upstairs to the small guest room, and Bernadine removed the kettle from the stove and poured its contents into the china teapot. Elizabeth smiled. "So, you have Mr. Sullivan's silk teabags in Iowa, too."

"All the latest conveniences, although I doubt we are as sophisticated as you are in Bramwell."

"Did I tell you?" Elizabeth asked, smiling. "I was sworn in as a citizen last year. I'm an American at last."

"I thought you were going to do that twenty or so years ago, when Joseph and I were getting married."

Elizabeth shrugged. "I lead a busy life, and not everything I want to do gets done when I want it to. That's one thing I finally did."

They watched the teapot in silence as if they could make the tea steep faster.

"I need to tell you something," Elizabeth said at length. "Hans and I, well, you know this year we celebrated thirty years together."

"Congratulations," Bernadine said softly. "It's gratifying to know that some married couples do stay together, in spite of divorce becoming so fashionable."

"Hans is retiring this year. We were overseas looking at mining methods in coal mines in France and Wales."

"Not Germany?"

"There's no point in going there. The French have occupied the whole Ruhr mining district, and the Germans retaliated by refusing to work in the mines. Nobody knows if the plan Senator Dawes submitted will work. Germany is dead, and everyone who lives there might as well be. It's a good thing I got us out of there. Since the war, it's not a place for decent people to live."

Bernadine got two cups and saucers out of the cabinet and busied herself pouring the tea.

"Bernadine, I didn't finish what I wanted to tell you."

She looked back at Elizabeth. "I'm not stopping you."

"As I said, Hans is modernizing our mines, and we traveled abroad to get some new ideas. But he's sick. You know, he was never the sort of boss who sat at a desk. He went down below a lot with his men, and I guess it happened often enough that he got a disease in his lungs. He's not coughing much, but when it happens, it's bad."

Bernadine's eyes filled in spite of herself. "I'm so sorry ..."

Elizabeth shook her head. "He has a few years yet the doctors say, and so do I. There's something growing in me, you see, and they say it's too deep-rooted for surgery."

At that, Bernadine's mouth fell open, but she could not speak.

"Once the sale of the mine is finished," Elizabeth went on, "Hans is going to retire, and we're going to travel around the United States. We want to see places we haven't seen before and have different kinds of experiences."

"That will be fun," Bernadine said, determined to sound cheerful. "Do you know how long you'll be gone?"

"No, we're not making plans. We'll just stay in one place and have fun until we decide to move on. Hans says we might as well spend all our money now, and whatever's left after we die can go to charity. I wanted to make sure that you're all right. Can't leave my little sister with nothing, can I?"

She smiled and Bernadine's spine stiffened as if someone had thrown a bucket of ice water at her back. "I'm sorry your health is failing," she finally managed, "But you can die in peace, Elizabeth. I don't need to be rich. I have everything I want. I have children, and now I'll have grandchildren."

"I'm happy about that. You must believe it."

"It's not just you and Hans who are happy, you know." Bernadine was speaking fast, as if under a time limit. "Joseph and I are happy together. We have each other. Joseph has purchased more land and equipment, and in a short few seasons we'll have everything all paid off." She took a deep breath. "There's nothing we need or want from you and Hans."

# ᝡᝈChapter Twelveᝈᝈ

esidents of Kossuth County, like most other Iowans, had taken Prohibition in stride, albeit with a lot of grumbling. Many German settlers brought their knack for brewing beer and wine with them to their new country. They recognized that liquor could be intoxicating but chafed at the prohibition to drink or brew their own beer. While beer brewing was banned, winemaking—for home consumption—was not. Many families joined the growing home brewing trend, including the Rahms.

Earlier in the year, in fact, one June Sunday, pushing back from the dinner table Joseph asked, "Who wants to go along on an elderberry pick this afternoon? I've been checking the roadside bushes. They are loaded and at the peak of ripeness."

"I'll go. I'll go." Magnus, Emma, and Tillie were off their chairs and clearing the table before Bernadine could object.

"Then we'll make a pie, right, Dad?"

Joseph laughed. "Not this time." He winked at Bernadine. "I've got something else in mind."

"What?"

"We're going to make elderberry wine. Bernadine, can you find the recipe my dad gave us a few years ago?"

In a short time, Bernadine, Joseph, and the children harvested a couple of bushel baskets of elderberries. Joseph crushed the berries and added sugar and yeast. He poured the mixture into a large stone crock and let it ferment for three or four weeks, then bottled it. After it aged another six weeks, he told Bernadine, "It's time to try the wine."

Bernadine removed glasses from the cupboard, and Joseph opened one of the smaller bottles. Both opened their eyes wide and exclaimed in unison, "This is some of the best wine I have ever tasted." We'll have some when Elizabeth and Hans visit at Christmas.

The wine added special enjoyment to the going-away party for Elizabeth and Hans. The celebration featured three grilled hogs and enough homemade under-the-kitchen-sink elderberry wine to make a Volstead Act enforcer do a St. Vitus dance.

Most of St. Benedict was in attendance, many of Elizabeth's former students, now in their thirties and forties came along with their children. Mrs. Leonard was there alone because Mr. Leonard passed on the year before. She openly wept, calling Elizabeth the daughter she always wanted.

Bernadine scuttled about serving drinks and filling plates. It was easier than standing still and allowing her mind to drift. She had a terrified-little-girl feeling down deep inside that told her she would never see Elizabeth again. Despite the things she said a few nights ago, the thought of losing Elizabeth for good was like a clawed hand squeezing her gut, refusing to let her eat or even breathe. Not only that, but everyone, herself included, knew that crop prices dropped this past spring. Freight charges had risen, and every forecaster out there predicted more of the same over the next few years.

Their farm, which Joseph still called Jo-Bern, was mortgaged during the war to add more land. As long as the federal government guaranteed commodity prices for farmers, they prospered. Once the war in Europe was over, however, price supports were discontinued, and within a couple more years prices dropped everywhere. Joseph shook his head more than once over the recent days, worrying that the commodity prices would continue to fall. It all added up to a lot of surplus crops and no money. Both knew that if the crops didn't make a profit over the next five years, they could lose everything.

Not that Bernadine would have shared this information with Elizabeth. She had too much pride for that, and maybe too much faith in God. He supplied their needs before, and maybe He would do so again.

She heard Elizabeth talking to Mary and Katherine. "I can't thank you both for being such good friends to Bernadine over the years. I know she looks on you both as substitute mothers."

If she only knew. Bernadine picked up a glass of elderberry wine from the table and drained it before she realized it wasn't her glass.

"I'm sorry, Herr Rolfe," she muttered and went back to the kitchen. Ella and Tillie were laughing over something they'd heard outside, but they sobered immediately at the look on their mother's face.

"Mama, can we do anything?" Ella asked.

"Will you clean up when everyone leaves?" Bernadine asked. "I don't feel very well."

Elizabeth and Hans left the next morning. After Elizabeth and Hans were gone two or three weeks Joseph announced to Bernadine, "We have several bottles of that good wine left. Why don't we invite a few family members for a meal and we'll see how they like our wine." The next Sunday Joseph's parents and sisters joined Joseph and Bernadine for dinner. As Joseph finished the last of his chicken dinner, he pushed his plate aside and stood. With a twinkle in his eye, he asked, "Bernadine, don't we have something else to share with our guests?"

Bernadine returned Joseph's wink. "Why, yes, we do, Joseph. Emma, Tillie, will you go to the cellar and get our surprise."

Giggling, the girls ran from the dining room. The screen door slammed behind them as they raced around the house to the cellar.

"What are you keeping from us, Joseph?" Father Rahm gave his son a questioning look.

A sly smile spread across Joseph's face. "You'll see."

"Here they are, Papa." Each daughter carefully carried a dark bottle to Joseph.

Joseph held up one, "Elderberry wine from the family recipe with berries we picked from the roadside ditches last June."

"If I'd known you were serving wine today, I would have brought our goblets," Mother Rahm suggested.

"I don't think it will taste any different whether we drink it from a goblet or a tumbler," Joseph commented. He opened the first bottle and poured a small amount for his father to sample.

Mr. Rahm lifted the glass to his nose, sniffed, took a sip and rolled the purple liquid slowly over his tongue before swallowing. He raised his glass and announced, "This is some of the best wine I've ever tasted, Joseph."

Joseph beamed. "The berries were perfect when we picked them. I was hoping it would be one of my best batches."

"It's better than good," Mr. Rahm continued his praise. "You got the fermentation and aging just right."

The compliments continued as Joseph poured and passed the wine around the table.

"How 'bout trying dandelion wine next?" a sister suggested.

"Or try wild grape."

"Just don't try bootlegging. Stick to fermenting fruit and berries, and you'll be all right."

Mrs. Rahm smiled, "I supposed you've heard the jingle, 'Mother's in the kitchen washing out the jugs, sister's in the pantry bottling the suds, father's in the cellar mixing up the hops, Johnny's on the porch watching for the cops.' We don't need that kind of trouble."

During the war, wheat sold for $2.30 to $3.60 and corn from $2.00 to $3.00 per bushel. At the close of the war President Wilson ordered an immediate return to the free enterprise system, although price supports and foreign loans continued through 1919. Despite warnings of possible disaster, farmers were surprised when both were discontinued. The week after Elizabeth left, Joseph heard the news on the wireless radio. Corn dropped to ten cents per bushel. The following week, it plunged to eight cents. "I might as well stand on a street corner and give it away," Joseph said.

Even the one outlet that had always been open to farmers was closed. The Eighteenth Amendment banned the manufacture, transportation, and sale of intoxicating liquors. This meant no corn for whiskey, and that capped it. The Roaring Twenties were anything but for farmers. While industry and manufacturing prospered, flappers bobbed their hair, wore short skirts, and danced the Charleston, farmers across the country struggled to make ends meet. Many farmers had no choice but to sell their land at depressed prices. For the first time in the history of the United States, more people were living in cities, and less than twenty percent of the population was engaged in agriculture.

The stress of mortgage payments and low prices began to take its toll on Joseph, too.

Bernadine tried to cheer him. "It's not that bad, Joseph. We're better off than the city folks in some ways. We produce most of our own food while they cannot. We have garden produce and fruit from our orchards, milk and cream from our dairy cattle, and our own poultry, beef, and pork. I buy flour and sugar in fifty-pound sacks and bake our own bread."

"Many other things, too," Joseph smiled and patted his belly. "Then you take the used flour sacks and use them again, making pajamas and shirts and dresses from them. Remember all those years ago when I asked around and everyone thought you'd be a good wife?"

"I was a bargain," Bernadine chuckled, putting her arms around him.

"Well, I got more than I bargained for." He kissed the top of her head. "You're so resourceful."

"We do what we have to."

"I know what you do. I just wanted you to know. Sometimes I suppose you feel no one notices all the economies you make, but I do, and I'm grateful."

The agriculture economy continued to deteriorate as the decade progressed. Their worsening financial situation occupied much of Joseph and Bernadine's thoughts and conversations. Joseph turned from his ledger one day and looked at her gravely. "I should not have bought that wireless radio receiver."

"Joseph, don't reproach yourself. That was nearly five years ago when things were still going well. We couldn't see how much things would change."

"Do you think I could sell it?"

"Not for anywhere near what we paid. How bad off are we?"

He looked down. "Let's put it this way. I don't want to go into town because there are too many people I owe. I'm afraid to see my father or Uncle Martin because they're bank officers. I don't want to see other relatives who work at the bank. I don't even want to see Ella because now she works at the bank."

At times like those, Bernadine almost regretted not telling Elizabeth the truth about their finances. Elizabeth's last call came from California. She said that she saw the Pacific Ocean and the burgeoning town called Hollywood, where people made motion pictures. Let them enjoy the time they have left, and let them spend their money. Elizabeth owes me nothing. Joseph and I will get through this somehow.

By 1928, four of Bernadine's daughters were married and Ella, always independent, was living in town in an apartment she rented and paid for herself. Only Magnus and the four youngest daughters lived at home, and even they noticed the change in their father.

"I don't like seeing Dad so worried," Tillie mentioned.

"He used to be so happy-go-lucky," Rita admitted. "Now he always seems sad."

"When he's not sad," little Ardyth added, "he's just plain crabby."

"We all want to help him," Rosie said, "but he just doesn't want it from anyone. We wish we could do something to keep his mind off all the sadness, but we don't know what to do."

"I know how you all feel," Bernadine agreed. "I am concerned about your father too. He's depressed, but maybe things will change." What she didn't say aloud was what she finally accepted. It was time to swallow her pride and ask Elizabeth for help. Next time Elizabeth calls, that's what I'll do. She was in Oregon last week. Is that east of California? I should have learned more American geography. Wherever they are, I hope they're heading back this way.

January, and 1929 hit with a blizzard. Magnus had gone into town to see his girl Rosalia and found himself stranded when nine inches of snow fell on St. Benedict that night. It was three days more before the road cleared up enough for him to get home.

In the months that followed, the cold and bleak winter changed to a hot and dry summer. Joseph went about his chores with an air of defeat, moody and disconsolate.

Elizabeth called one weekend, excited. "Bernadine, you won't believe some of the wonderful things I've seen. I've been taking photographs to show you when we get there."

"Are you coming here, then?"

"Yes, and from there we'll probably go to New York. I'm having such fun."

Bernadine thought about asking for a loan then, but if she was coming to Iowa, it would be better to do it face to face. "When will you be in St. Benedict?"

"Day after tomorrow, I think. We're in Nebraska."

"Wonderful. I'll look forward to seeing you."

The following day two deputies from Dickinson County tramped up the steps to her front door and banged on the wood until she answered. "Are you Bernadine Rahm?"

Hand at her throat, she managed to say, "I am. May I, um, help you?"

"Ma'am, do you have a sister named Mrs. Elizabeth Hartmann?"

Joseph was suddenly standing beside her, his arm around her shoulders. "She does. Officers, what is this about, please?"

"There was a wreck." The older deputy looked at Joseph as if relieved to be talking to another man. "Mr. and Mrs. Hartmann were driving through our county when, according to his wife, he had a coughing fit and swerved off the road. He hit a telephone pole."

"Oh," Bernadine's mind went blank, but Joseph stepped forward.

"How bad are their injuries?"

"Mr. Hartmann is dead, sir. Mrs. Hartmann is critically injured. She's not expected to survive."

Joseph got the car out and they followed the deputies back to Spirit Lake. It was a silent drive of three hours over an odd collection of paved, partially paved, and muddy dirt roads.

By the time they arrived, it was dark, and a light rain was falling. The doctor who met them shook his head. "Her injuries were too bad for her to be moved, or I would've advised taking her to the Mayo Brothers' facility in Minnesota. There's nothing we can do. Her life span can be measured in hours."

Bernadine nodded in silence and pushed open the heavy door. Elizabeth was the only one in the room. She lay on a bed twice her size under blankets that seemed to swallow her. An intravenous line was delivering blood into her body, but transfusions were then in their infancy. According to the doctor, she was losing it faster than they could replace it anyway. Her face had a deathly pallor, but she was conscious. Seeing Bernadine, she smiled. "I waited … for you."

Bernadine took her hand. "How do you feel?"

Elizabeth moved one shoulder. It might have been a shrug. "Not too bad, they gave me something for pain. It hurts, but not too much."

Bernadine managed a nod.

"My Hans … he's gone," Elizabeth cried. "The last thing he said was, 'Are you all right?' Even at the end … he thought of me."

"Hans loved you more than anything."

"As I loved him …" Elizabeth whispered. "I loved him more than you, Dena. That was wrong, wasn't it? I'm sorry."

"Don't be. A woman should love her husband more than anything."

"Not more than …" She took a deep breath. "I'm sorry." She put a white hand out and tried to touch Bernadine's face, but her weakness betrayed her, and her hand fell away.

Bernadine picked up the hand and held it to her cheek. "Don't worry about me."

"You'll bury us together, won't you?"

"Of course, but it's too soon to think about that. You've got years yet."

"Don't. Last words … shouldn't be lies."

But we've lived all our lives as a lie, Bernadine thought. Aloud, though, she said, "I don't want you to leave me. Please, Elizabeth …please, don't leave me."

"Hush, baby, you'll be fine. You always have been. Remember … so long ago … I said, 'you don't have to … live in fear'?"

"I remember."

"I'm glad you took my advice. You don't need me … really, you don't. You never did."

Bernadine bit her lip and somehow brought herself under control. She sat down by the bed. "Well … I will stay with you."

Elizabeth moved her head. It might have been a nod. Then she sighed, too weak to say more. Bernadine kept a solid grip on her hand as if she could hold onto her and not let her go. Within the hour, Elizabeth stopped breathing.

The police gave the Hartmann's personal property to Joseph and Bernadine. The bodies were put in coffins and shipped to St. Benedict. They found about five hundred dollars in Hans's wallet, and that was enough to cover the hospital bill, coffins, and burial plots. There was even enough left over to buy headstones, but there was nothing for the farm. When Bernadine called Father Emmanuel in Bramwell, the elderly priest confirmed that the couple's will left all their funds to charity.

A few weeks later, the stock market crashed.

The post-war depression did not start with the stock market crash of 1929. For the farmers of the Midwest, it began in 1921, and those who depended on the land were hit hard. For eight years things went from bad to worse and nothing they or the politicians did could improve their lot.

"Stock Exchange to Close Two Days," can you believe it, Bern?" Joseph walked into the kitchen with the previous day's newspaper tucked under his arm, his furrowed eyebrows at war with his mischievous smile. "Isn't there a word, in German? I know my father used to use it, but I can't remember what it is. It's a word to describe happiness at the misfortunes of others?"

Bernadine looked up in consternation from turning bacon in the big iron skillet. "You mean schadenfreude."

"That's it. Bankers in New York are jumping out of windows, and investment brokers are selling their fancy automobiles for a hundred dollars. It's not that I'm happy for what's happening to them, but it's been happening to us now for years and nobody cared. I keep thinking, 'Now they know how I feel.' Do you think I'm selfish?"

He had another sleepless night, and Bernadine knew this because his tossing and turning awakened her several times. "Don't be silly. You know what your father says—sometimes things have to get worse before they can get better. Maybe this thing in the stock market is a prelude to things getting better."

"Maybe," he didn't sound convinced. He sat down, muttering when his suspender caught on the chair stile.

As she brought him his breakfast, she took a hard look at him. Streaks of gray wove through his once-thick dark hair. Deep creases lined his forehead.

"What's wrong?" he asked, looking at her.

She scoffed a little. "I was just thinking … we're not young anymore, Joseph."

"Speak for yourself, old woman. I can still plow a furrow with the best of 'em. When we work together Magnus has to beg me to slow down."

Magnus just walked into the kitchen, and he hooted with derision. "That's because usually you're going the wrong direction." He fastened his overalls as he dropped into a chair. "I can't make you too mad today, Dad. I need a favor."

"Ah yes. You're not even half my age, but I bet you want me to lift those feed sacks onto the truck."

Magnus chuckled. "I think I can manage that all right. But listen, Mom, Dad, I asked Rosalia to marry me. She said yes. I know this isn't the best timing, but you promised me fifty acres and help building a house."

"Oh," Bernadine cried. "When is the happy day?"

"We were thinking next January. By that time the harvesting will be finished and the busy rush of the holiday season over."

"Good work, son," Joseph said. "Sure, you already know which parcel it is. Mark out your house and we'll get to work on it."

"Thanks, Dad." He grabbed for the egg bowl, but his grinning father beat him to it.

MAGNUS AND ROSALIA'S WEDDING PICTURE

MAGNUS AND ROSALIA'S WEDDING PICTURE WITH
ATTENDANTS, MAGNUS'S FRIEND ED, AND ROSALIA'S SISTER,
ESTHER.

The two men left a little later, and Bernadine smiled, watching them through the kitchen window. They walked out to the barn together in the weak pre-dawn light. Bernadine thought she saw a bit of her old Joseph.

By evening, though, Joseph was tired and exhausted from the stress and strain of the situation. He suggested to Bernadine, "I don't sleep well these nights. I don't want to keep you from getting a good night's sleep, so I'm going to doze on the couch in the dining room close to the wood-burning heater. I will keep you awake if I am with you."

Bernadine started to protest but then decided to do what Joseph suggested. *I don't sleep well when he tosses and turns. Poor Joseph, he really is sick. I want to tell him my secret, and I will in the morning – promise or no promise. He is my husband, and he has a right to know I vow I will tell him. I will.* She finally fell asleep.

Bernadine woke at morning light. Joseph was right. I did sleep better than I have in months, she thought as she stepped into her slippers and put on her robe. She padded into the dining room. A log burned in the wood stove. She looked lovingly at Joseph. He was breathing deeply but still asleep.

Bernadine went to the kitchen and fixed a light breakfast then called to Magnus to come eat with her. He rushed to put on his overalls and hurried downstairs. "The breakfast was tasty, Mom. Before I go out to do chores, I'll check on Dad."

Before Bernadine finished clearing the table, Magnus was back, his face white and his blue eyes frightened. "Mom, you need to call Doc Richter. Something's wrong with Dad."

All the blood drained from Bernadine's face. "You call him, Magnus, and hurry." She dashed into the dining room. Joseph was sitting up, slumped over, and clutching his chest.

He looked at her through bleary, pain-filled eyes. "Can't ...breathe ..."

"Magnus is calling the doctor, Liebling. Lie back down on the couch. What can I do to make you more comfortable?"

Without waiting for a response, she grabbed one of the blankets at the end of the couch and tucked it around him. A light sheen of sweat was on his face, and when she touched his skin it was clammy. "Try to relax, Joseph."

He shook his head, reaching for her hand. "Kitty ...Cakes. Love you ..." His grasp on her wrist was convulsive and painfully intense, but she managed not to cry out. Then his grip loosened and his hand fell away. His head dropped back against the pillow on the couch.

"Joseph? Joseph, please talk to me. Joseph don't leave me," she whispered, but she knew her plea was too late. His eyes were open and his gaze still on her, but the pupils were huge and fixed in spite of the sunlight now pouring in.

"Oh, Joseph ...my Joseph ..." she said softly. She combed his hair back and kissed his forehead. She closed his eyes. "Say hello to Clarence and Elizabeth for me, my beloved."

She began to shake. A scream rose from her throat. "Joseph! Help me, dear God, help me."

"He's dead. He wanted to sleep on the couch last night, so he wouldn't keep me awake. Magnus, what will we do without your father?"

Magnus felt Joseph's forehead. It was cold. Then he took his pulse and found no beat. Fighting back the tears he gently lifted the blanket and covered Joseph's face. "I will go upstairs and tell the girls."

Tiptoeing upstairs and into the girls' bedroom, he tapped Tillie on her shoulder. He put a finger to his lips as she woke. "Shhh, come downstairs. Dad passed away early this morning."

Tillie watched in disbelief as Magnus repeated the news that their father was dead to Ardyth, Rosie, and then Rita. Together the sisters made their way downstairs where they found their mother rocking and weeping. As they sat and knelt around Bernadine, they heard Magnus on the phone.

"Father Murphy? It's Magnus Rahm. We need you to come to the farm." His voice wavered. "It's Dad. He died a short time ago. Can you come and give us some assistance?"

Within an hour Dr. Richter arrived with Father Murphy, the new parish priest. Father administered the last rites, Dr. Richter provided a death certificate, and Joseph's body was taken to the funeral parlor. "Based on the fact that you found a fresh log on the fire, Bernadine, it looks like Joseph got up early this morning to add wood to the stove and then likely died of a massive heart attack soon after that," Dr. Richter said.

News spread fast in a little town like St. Benedict. Before nightfall, Bernadine was inundated with visitors and had enough meals to sponsor her own box social. She purchased a two-grave plot near the spot where she laid Hans and Elizabeth to rest and planned the funeral for Saturday. When people commented on how well she was doing and how organized she was, she only shrugged and said, "I'm German. One thing I can do is organize." In truth, she was in shock. She could only focus on the chores of the moment. It was easy to brew tea or pour milk. It was easy to put a casserole in the oven, but thinking of the future without Joseph overwhelmed her and made her throat close and her ears pound. The glimpses she allowed herself of the future were long and lonely. She felt like running away, maybe even returning to Germany, but she knew the loneliness would go wherever she went. That only scared her more. Alone at night, she let her tears flow, but no one else heard or saw.

St. Benedict's Catholic Church filled for Joseph's funeral. The son of an influential family and a leader in his own right, Joseph was well-known and loved. Many in the community could empathize with his financial hardships. They were in similar straits, but to lose the family breadwinner at the age of fifty-four was a cruel turn of events.

Bernadine spent the intervening days in prayer and reflection. She knew her faith and family had sustained her in the past. They would again. The day after the funeral she called a family meeting. Her four married daughters brought their husbands and Magnus brought Rosalia.

She turned to her married daughters and their spouses. "Your father and I made all the important decisions about the farm together," she said. "Now I'm on my own. I know Joseph would want us to do whatever we can to keep the farm going, and for that I need your help."

"What can we do, Mama?" Verena asked.

"Well, first, I'll be leaning on Magnus to help with the farm, but since he and your father were working it together before, I think he can use some help." She fixed her four sons-in-law with a hard stare. "I would like each of you to donate a day each week to Magnus."

"But Mother Rahm, we all have jobs in town besides working our own land," Louis protested.

"If I remember correctly, it was Papa Joe who helped you all to obtain those jobs," Bernadine said, and the young men squirmed a little. "If you can't help, then you can't help, but you can contribute enough money for us to hire a worker on the day that you can't come."

The men all looked at each other.

"All right," Ben thought. "Since the bank is closing its doors, I can come on Tuesdays and Wednesdays—but only until the bank reopens."

"If it reopens," Laurie muttered.

"I can't come at all," Cliff remarked. "I'll hire a teenaged boy I know. He can come out on Thursdays and Sundays."

"I'll take Fridays," Frank added.

"I'll do Saturdays and Mondays," Louis apologized.

Magnus was moving a saltshaker around. He looked up. "Mom, you and I will need to meet with Uncle Martin at the bank and see if we can get them to help us."

"We're already in arrears," Bernadine cautioned. "The bank's no better off than we are, or they wouldn't be closing."

Ella cleared her throat. "I don't make much, but I can contribute a little."

"Me too," Tillie chimed in. "I have babysitting money."

"I'm cleaning houses in town," Emma said. "I can help."

"I wanna help," Ardyth shouted.

"You can help." Bernadine managed a smile at her youngest daughter. "For now, the best way to help is by being happy with what you have and not asking for new dresses."

Rosie looked around at all of them and sniffed. "It's not my fault Daddy died. Why do I have to do anything?"

"It's nobody's fault," Bernadine snapped, "But if we want to stay together, we all have to pitch in."

"Well," Rosie mumbled, looking at the floor, "I can gather eggs, I guess."

"That would be helpful."

Magnus and Bernadine went to the bank. Uncle Martin gave them a six-month moratorium on the mortgage, but nothing comes from nothing, and later that year, the bank closed. The Northwestern Mutual Insurance Company assumed ownership of the Rahm farm. Magnus rented the land from the insurance company. The farming operation changed little, but the pressure of meeting mortgage payments was gone, and the rent was less than half of what the mortgage had been.

One night Bernadine came back from the evening milking, pails in hand to find Magnus leaning against a fence post. He was looking out across the land.

"Son, you look like you lost your smile and can't find it. What happened?"

Jerked back to reality, Magnus shuffled a little, his eyes downcast. "It feels funny, Mom. From the time I was little, I could look out across this land and know it was ours. Now I'm looking at it, and it looks the same as ever. It's just not ours anymore. I'm farming the same land and nothing's changed, but everything's changed."

She put her arms around his trim waist. "I know. Your father would be disappointed, too, that we couldn't find a way to keep the land. It was all he thought of toward the end. We can't see the future, and it hurts to remember the past. So, we think of now. We should have enough from the crops to feed the livestock we're keeping. If we are frugal, we'll have enough to pay the rent to the insurance company. Someday things may change, and who knows? Maybe then you can buy back the land. For now, though, we hold on to what we can."

"It's good you can see hope in all this." Magnus sighed. "Me, I'm not so sure."

"Magnus, we must always have hope. If not, what else is there? I believe God is watching us. Eventually, things will be all right."

Soon all the economic growth of the previous quarter-century had been erased. Industrial production was especially hard hit, falling to almost half of earlier levels.

Despite good crop yields, commodity prices remained low, and Bernadine and her family struggled to make ends meet. Rita, Ardyth, Tillie, and Rosie all pitched in. They tended the chickens and gathered eggs. They washed and cased the surplus eggs to sell.

"Mom, could we use some of the egg money to buy real fabric?" Rita asked.

"Oh, yes, please," Ardyth echoed.

"I'm sick of wearing dresses made from feed sacks," Rosie said. "Mama, look at me. I'm pretty, but nobody will want me if I wear burlap."

"Calm down." Bernadine put aside her ledger. "For now, our choices are limited. The store-bought cloth is not among them." It hurt to say no. The older girls had not known such deprivation. "You're not the only ones wearing feed sack clothes. Everyone is sacrificing these days."

These were the times Bernadine missed Joseph the most. Joseph would have supported her in these difficult decisions. He would have said something funny or wise to the girls to sway the conversation. Now she had to deal with the girls' disappointment and resentment alone. In time, she became more comfortable seeking advice from Magnus and Rosalia, or from her married daughters and their spouses. The final decisions were hers though, and she always tried to think about how Joseph would have handled them.

There has to be a practical way of handling all this. What would Joseph do?

She could think of nothing.

# ᐸᔑChapter Thirteenᔑᐳ

I n the summer of 1932, a drought struck the land the likes of which had not been seen in decades. Crops failed. As she had in earlier losses, Bernadine turned to her priest for comfort and spiritual guidance. Father Colm Murphy joined the parish the previous year. At first, she felt uncomfortable with such a young priest. His late father had once tried to pay court to Bernadine, and at twenty-seven, he was only three years older than Magnus. He was a sensitive and soft-spoken man, and he had grown up in St. Benedict. He knew all the people, had many friends among them, and he knew what it was like to work the land.

Always a regular at Mass, Bernadine often spoke to him after services. "If things keep up at this rate, I don't think we can even afford to rent the farm," she told him. "Sylvia, Verena, Laurie, and Emma all think I should sell off the farming equipment. Naturally, their husbands agree. That would leave nothing for Magnus to work with, and all he's ever wanted is to farm. He couldn't work in town even if there was work to be had." She looked at the kindly young priest. "You must know what it's like for him, Father."

A gentle smile tugged at his lips. "Do you know, Miss Bernadine, I have an idea that might help. The way I see things, you have four married daughters in town, one single daughter on her own in town, a married son on the farm with a child of his own, and four younger daughters still at home with you. You're making decisions for the farm, although you don't know as much about it as Magnus and your late Joseph, and those decisions are going to impact a lot more than you. And you are …lonely. This also affects the decisions you make."

How had he known that? She tore her gaze from him, looking instead at a stained-glass window.

"Do you know," he went on, his voice quiet, "many years ago when my father took his life, my life was, well, it was awful. I didn't understand how he could do such a thing. I was miserable and I made everyone around me miserable too. Then one day Magnus, a boy I had never regarded as a friend, came to me and said, 'My mama says you're mean because you're lonely. Do you want to be my pal?'" He smiled at her. "Did Magnus ever tell you that?"

Bernadine began to blink. "He did not …"

"We didn't become terribly close, because not long after that, my mother moved us to Templeton. Just knowing that someone cared about me and didn't want me to be lonely meant the world to me. It taught me that God was watching, and He loved me and didn't want me to be lonely, either. As you see, it changed my life." He chuckled.

The urge to cry passed and she managed a smile. "I'm glad for you."

"Well, I wanted you to know that. Not that it helps your problem, but do remember that God cares."

"Oh, Father, if I didn't believe that, I couldn't go on."

"And it reminds me …" His eyes twinkled. "I was back in Templeton not long ago, and they told me about a gentleman in that area who lost his wife two or three years ago and wants to marry again."

Bernadine gasped and dropped her purse. Father Murphy retrieved it, and as he handed it back to her, he patted her hand. "Maybe the timing is not right, but think of all the good it would accomplish if you married again. Magnus and Rosalia could stay on the farm without worrying about the ability to build their own house. Magnus could be his own man and take over all the farming decisions. You'd have someone to keep you from being lonely and care for you and the younger children."

"But I loved Joseph, and I still love Joseph."

"Of course you do. I don't doubt he still loves you, but he's with the Lord now, and you are still on earth. Your life didn't end just because his did. Bernadine, there's no hurry. Just think it over."

Bernadine spent some time thinking, *marriage? Why? How could I ever love another man as I loved Joseph? Besides, I still have four daughters at home. What widower would want to bring four young girls into his house?*

She'd lost so much over the years, little Clarence, with his perpetually happy smile and his affinity for eating bugs. Hans and Elizabeth, and she had rejected Elizabeth's peace overtures so many times. Maybe they could have kept the farm if she had only forgiven Elizabeth for forcing her to keep that secret, that stupid, stupid secret. It wasn't even relevant now. Nobody alive could be hurt by it. Still, she'd kept it, even after Elizabeth was under the ground and returning to the dust from which she'd come. As a result, she held a part of herself back from Joseph, the man she loved more than life. *If I married again, I would still be holding back a part of myself, and I don't know if I can do it again.* She lost Joseph. Now she lost

Joseph's farm, and even much of the equipment would soon be sold.

Lightning never strikes twice in the same place. I don't want to marry because I have nowhere else to go.

Then again she made another discovery. Surrounded by four noisy, beautiful daughters, she felt more alone now than she ever had before.

Germany and Judith beckoned to her, faint as a forgotten whisper. Judith knew the cursed secret. Judith and her mother were even unwilling accomplices.

But no, she had ties here now, like it or not. She couldn't afford to go back to Germany with her daughters. They barely even spoke German. She wouldn't go anywhere without them. She had to do something to make things easier for her children, especially for Magnus and the younger girls. And she was lonely. She could at least meet this fellow. Maybe lighting could strike twice.

She told no one but Father Murphy about her decision. If she liked this fellow, she would think about introducing him to her children, but there was no point in talking about it this early.

Father Murphy said the man's name was John Bierl. "All his children are grown and away from home. He is not wealthy, but he has a little money from a government pension. He rents a house, and I understand he's a man of faith."

Well, those were good things. She didn't want a wealthy man, wealth could be lost. She didn't want to deal with that again, but a comfortable fellow who was careful with his money that was a good thing. She just about talked herself into meeting him when Father Murphy offered to drive her to Templeton. "I'm going to see my mother. I can visit her and my sister while you visit John. Then I'll bring you back."

The night before the meeting she didn't sleep at all. She even spent a large part of the night in the bathroom they put in ten years before. At least it was better to be sick in a bathroom than to be sick in an outhouse. Still, she groaned as another cramp racked her nervous stomach.

This is not life or death, she told herself. If you don't like him, all you have to do is say no. Marriages aren't forced on women anymore, are they? Besides, Father Murphy wouldn't recommend this man if he's a monster.

But this felt nothing like 1898 when she was getting ready for the box socials and hoping to catch Joseph's eye. Of course, she already knew him a little. She thought he was good-looking. He always made people laugh.

Don't go thinking about Joseph, and don't do John the grave disservice of comparing him to Joseph. Give him a chance, and be prepared to like him for his own qualities, not just the ones he shares with your first husband.

"You're very quiet, Miss Bernadine," Father Murphy said as they approached Templeton.

Bernadine looked out the window. "Oh, Father, I feel a little like a young girl going on her first date. That's what they call it now, isn't it? Dating? It's been so long since I walked out with Joseph. I'm not sure I know what to say or how to act."

Father Murphy smiled reassuringly. "Just be yourself, Miss Bernadine. I'm sure that's what Joseph loved about you." Father Murphy stopped his Model A Ford in front of a little house by a riverbank and walked Bernadine to the door.

A tall man of almost sixty was at the door before Father Murphy could knock.

"Looks like someone is eager for company," Father Murphy said. "John, meet Bernadine Rahm. I'll leave you two to get acquainted and will be back for Bernadine in about two hours."

Husky and strong, John had graying brown hair and a small bald spot on the back of his head. His eyes were large and stormy gray. When he shook hands with Bernadine his grip was warm and firm, and his smile made her think of the fresh smell after a rainstorm.

John brewed a pot of coffee and set out a plate of cookies. "Well, tell me about yourself," he began, "and your family. I want to know all about you."

She trembled, suddenly shy. "That's a tall order."

"Father Murphy told me you have a large family, including married daughters, a son, and grandchildren."

Bernadine laughed. "Yes, Joseph and I had eleven children together. It was a busy household for quite a few years." Better get it out of the way so if he doesn't want me, he can say so now. "My four youngest daughters still live with me."

"Ah," she could see his mind working. "How old are they? The ones still at home, I mean."

"Tillie is seventeen. Rosie is fifteen. Rita is thirteen. And Ardyth will be eleven next month."

John grunted. "I bet they eat a lot."

"I'm not sure what you mean. They're hardly fat."

"Hey, I don't mean any offense. Let's put our cards on the table, Bernadine. If we marry, I'll be taking on responsibility for your family, and I'll have to feed those girls. I need to know in advance if it's something I can afford."

Bernadine thought on it. "I suppose that's fair. Well, as I said, they're hardly fat. They all do their chores, both indoors and in the barnyard, and Tillie baby sits and contributes her own money to the household."

"Well, now I know a little about your girls. I'd like to know about you. Were you born here?"

"Oh, no, I came over from Germany. Um … didn't you?"

"No, my grandparents were some of the first Germans in the Midwest. Both my mother and father were born in Iowa right after it became a state. I was born about three miles down the road from here. Back then there wasn't a road or a town, and it didn't become 'Templeton' until 1882."

"Mmmm," Bernadine nodded, "That was the year after I was born."

"Really, you're younger than I thought."

"Oh," she wilted.

"Well hang on, I'm sorry. I keep saying the wrong thing, don't I? I didn't mean you look old. What I mean is, when Father Murphy described you, I thought you must be closer to my age. I'm ten years older than you. I'll be sixty in the fall."

"So, whereabouts in Germany are you from? My grandparents were from somewhere in Bavaria, although I'm blamed if I know where."

She smiled. "We came here from Coesfeld. Not in Bavaria."

"Hmm, I never heard of Coesfeld. Where is it?"

"In the Rhineland, but really, John, I was very young when we left. I'm afraid I've forgotten things, and I doubt it was an interesting story, anyway. Elizabeth, my sister, and I were orphans, and she brought us to Iowa in hopes of a better life."

He nodded. "That's why all our families came here isn't it?"

A dog barked outside, and he got up. "Just a minute, I gotta let Willy in."

"You have a dog?"

"Yep—does that bother you?"

"No, I like dogs and cats."

"Well, cats are all right if they catch mice, but I can't abide 'em in the house."

"Ours stay in the barn and are excellent mousers."

Willy was a brown, medium-sized dog with an oversized purple nose. He immediately shoved it into Bernadine's face, and then he snorted. Involuntarily, Bernadine broke out laughing, and the dog wagged his tail wildly and licked her ear.

"Well, he likes you. That's a good thing," John remarked. "He's always been a good judge of character."

Willy was also a great icebreaker. All the tension in the room vanished, and soon John and Bernadine were laughing and chatting, exchanging family histories and recipes. When Father Murphy returned he knocked on the door. Both of them were laughing over something John just said.

"Not certain, but promising," he murmured. "Lord, thy will be done. If thy will happens to include bringing a couple of lonely widowed people together as life partners, it would be all right with me."

The drought worsened all over Iowa, but Bernadine's second, third, and fourth visits to see John were successful. It was so good to talk things over with someone close to her own age that she could hardly wait to see him again. However, marrying John would mean leaving St. Benedict and moving to Templeton. That meant she needed her children to be in agreement. Making the decision to talk to them about John was difficult, but it had to be done. The days of Bernadine shrinking away from difficulty were long past.

It was the first time since Joseph's death that Bernadine called a family meeting. She looked around the long table. Tillie took charge of all the children, Bernadine's nine grandchildren and had them playing quietly nearby where she could hear.

"I called you all together because I'm considering a decision that could have a family impact," Bernadine said, and if there was a slight tremor in her voice, no one commented. "I'm being courted by a gentleman in Templeton."

Sylvia's eyes popped open, "What?"

Magnus looked at her. "Um…Mom…?"

"For how long," Verena demanded.

"How could you do this to Daddy?" Rosie began to sob.

Bernadine swallowed. For a moment she couldn't speak. Even with all of them talking at once, she could not have opened her mouth. Her stomach jumped into her throat, and for a moment, nausea overwhelmed her.

Then she took a deep breath and pounded both fists on the table. "Children, I can't answer anyone if you're all screaming at me."

A sudden silence followed. None of them could remember hearing her raise her voice before. Bernadine was always quiet and calm. Until now, her face was flushed and her fists clenched. She looked around the table. "I will answer polite and reasonable questions." She gave Rosie a pointed stare. "I shouldn't have to tell any of you this, but I loved Joseph with all my heart. I will always love him. Sometimes …sometimes I feel as if a part of me is in the grave with him. But the rest of me is right here on earth, above the ground, and I can't lie down and die. And perhaps it has not occurred to anyone, but since I didn't ask anyone's permission for my first marriage, when I was a lot younger and less experienced than I am now, I don't see why I have to ask permission for the possibility of a second marriage."

She looked around at all of them again, "And I said possibility. Nothing has been decided yet, but there is a possibility. I'm interested in everyone's thoughts, as long as they are reasonable thoughts and not just accusations. I hope you all understand."

Magnus cleared his throat, "Of course, Mom. It's just that we're surprised. I don't think any of us ever knew that you'd even consider getting married again."

She managed a smile. "Am I not allowed to be lonely?" She looked at Rosie. "Do you think I should stop living because Joseph did? Or should I say, 'I have ten children and nine grandchildren, and that's all anyone could ever want'? Maybe I do want more. Maybe I want a companion."

"You could get a dog," Rosie muttered.

Bernadine couldn't help but grin at that. "You'll be happy to know that if I marry John, I will get a dog. He has a lovely dog named Willy who likes me very much."

"Mom," Ella wondered, "please tell me you're not doing this just because you're afraid of inconveniencing the rest of us."

"Don't be silly," Bernadine answered, although that thought crossed her mind. "If John and I suit each other, it will be a good thing for both of us and the rest of my family as well. I'd like you all to meet him."

A fine cloud of dust blew in the open door. Bernadine shrieked and covered the chicken she was plucking. "Shut that door before we're all coated in dirt," she shouted.

"Right," Rosie shouted, and the door slammed so hard that if there had been glass in it, it would have shattered.

"Häschen," Bernadine called, keeping her temper and using Rosie's baby name, "Come in here."

Rosie walked in and slumped into a chair. Bernadine handed her the half-plucked chicken. "Make yourself useful instead of trying to break things, Little Bunny."

"Daddy called me that." Rosie grimaced and tore out a few feathers as Bernadine picked up another chicken from the pile on the counter. She planned to roast six chickens for this family feast to introduce John. In better days, they could have made do with a hog.

"Rosie," Bernadine began again. "It's not fair to decide you won't like the man before you even meet him."

"I don't dislike him. I just don't want him thinking he can replace Daddy."

"He could never replace your father, Häschen. Don't you think I know this? But he doesn't want to replace anyone. Do you think I can replace the beloved wife he lost? Of course not, but maybe we'll like each other, and maybe we'll do well together. Do you not understand that this could be a good arrangement for all of us?"

"No, I don't understand." Rosie tore out a few more feathers. "How can being taken away from all my friends to a place more than a hundred miles away be a good thing? How can living in a strange house with a strange man be good? How can going to a new school—in my very last year of school—be good? No, Mama, I don't understand it, and I don't think it is right."

"Well then," Bernadine said grimly, "I'm glad I'm the one making decisions. I know what's best for my family. Häschen, you are fifteen years old, and you think you know how the world works. You don't. Any hardships you think you have faced in your young life are small compared to what many people have seen in their lives. If you live long enough, you'll come to understand that there are always alternatives to one's situation. I'm looking at alternatives now, and I will decide on the best one, not you. You can come back to me in thirty years or so, when you actually do know a little about life, and you can tell me then how I should live."

Rosie didn't reply. She just tore out more feathers.

Bernadine sighed. "Give me the bird before you tear off its skin, too. Go, wash your hands and find something useful to do."

As Rosie left the room, Bernadine wished she felt as confident as she was before. The truth was she had no idea. John seemed nice, but anyone could be nice for a handful of social get-togethers.

Down at the end of the table, John faced the children and their spouses, wondering if this was what a condemned prisoner felt like when looking out at his firing squad. Bernadine's six older children and four spouses were drilling him with their eyes. The youngest girls and the grandchildren sat at a separate table and played under Rosie's supervision, but she never stopped looking at him, either.

"What do you young men do for a living?" John asked Louis and Ben.

"There's a question without an easy answer," said Ben with a nervous little chuckle. "I worked in town for a while, but you know how that goes. After some places closed I went back to my father, and he gave me some of his land. Now I farm to the west of this place."

"What kind of farming?"

Ben shrugged. "I keep a few milk cows, and I raise hogs. We also have a few chickens for eggs."

"Same for us," Louis said. "I farm a little farther to the west. During haying and threshing season we both work with our families to make things a little easier. What about you?" Ben asked.

"My wife died a few years ago, and I've been alone since then. It's lonely. I live on a pension, so I don't have much money."

Across the room, Rosie stage-whispered, "I bet it's an old-age pension." The little children laughed. Bernadine's face turned scarlet, but she resolutely ignored the girl. "Will you have some peas, John?" She passed a large bowl in his direction.

"Are you the oldest, Magnus?" John asked.

The young man laughed. "Not by a long shot, sir. I have four older sisters and five younger ones. There's a legend in St. Benedict that by the time I was born, my folks despaired of ever having a boy. They asked Father Henry, the parish priest back then, to ring the bell so the whole town would know the Rahms finally had a son."

Polite laughter followed.

Ella handed him the large bowl. "I have a job, Mr. Bierl. When the bank reopened, I went to work there. I make twelve dollars a week."

"Tell 'em what happened last year, El," Tillie said. "You know when the bank was robbed."

Ella shushed her sister. "You weren't s'posed to tell about that, stupid."

"The bank was robbed?" Bernadine gasped, "When?"

"Oh, Mother." Ella rolled her eyes. "No big deal. A couple of guys in a Ford Roadster pulled in. I was the only employee there at the time. They got away with three grand and locked me and my two customers in the vault."

"My God," Bernadine whispered. "You could've been killed."

"Yeah, and Tillie could get killed riding the horses all the time, but you let her do it."

"Horses are tame. People, I'm not so sure about."

"Mom, I was fine. As soon as the robbers left, I got a screwdriver and managed to open the vault. I called the cops and described the guys. Everything was okay."

"This is why I don't like my single daughters living away from me," Bernadine managed to say, looking at John.

He cleared his throat and spooned out some peas.

Later Bernadine walked him around the farm. "Too bad I can't move here," he remarked. "Nice place, except for all the women."

"I thought you liked a lot of women."

"Just one," he said, and smiled at her.

It was when Rosalia, Magnus's wife, was pregnant again with a due date around Christmas of 1932 that Bernadine made her decision. She had to be out by then. Magnus and his family needed the space.

John met the family and they all liked him well enough, except for Rosie, of course and it made sense. She hated leaving the farm, but more, she wanted Magnus to have his own family in his own house, just as she and Joseph had. She accepted John's proposal and began planning the move to Templeton.

On Bernadine's last visit with John before the marriage, John said, "How many of your daughters do you plan to bring with you?"

Her eyes popped wide at that. "What?"

"I told you before. Four girls, that's a lot to feed. I've been going through my books, and I can't afford to take all four. I can take two at most."

Still stunned at the thought of splitting up her family, she left early and walked to Mrs. Murphy's house four miles away in town.

On the way home that afternoon, she asked Father Murphy to stop at the Templeton market for flour, knowing it would be too late to shop when she got back to St. Benedict. Rosie was right. The two towns were almost four hours apart by car. In the market, two women were talking about John, and although a part of her was horrified at the thought, Bernadine couldn't help listening in.

"They say John Bierl is courting again," said the first woman, "Someone from out of town."

The second one snorted. "That's because none of the widows in town are silly enough to fall for him. What he put poor Elinor through …."

"Now, he wasn't that bad. Remember, I lived next door to them back then. Elinor was devoted to him."

"She didn't buy sugar for the last three years of her life because he was too stingy to allow it. Deny that if you can."

"They were poor."

"Poor, my eye, his pension would have kept his wife and daughters comfortable—all five girls. He was hoarding every cent. Why do you think his girls all joined the convent? At least there they could get sugar in their coffee. The man is a miser."

"He's not a miser."

"He is, and some of the men say he's a regular Mussolini. I heard he demanded his daughters go to the convent."

"I thought you said they went voluntarily, for the sugar. Which is it? It can't be both."

Bernadine left quickly only to discover later that she paid for her flour but left it behind.

# ᴄᴘChapter Fourteenᴏ

The marriage was a quiet one, with just her family and a cousin of John's present. Ardyth and Rita packed their bags. Looking at them reminded Bernadine of how she felt at the prospect of moving, and how much of her own property she was able to bring to this country forty years before. It almost made her want to cry.

BERNADINE WITH SECOND HUSBAND, JOHN

Magnus agreed to keep Tillie and Rosie, but at that, Rosie pitched a screaming fit at Bernadine. "You never loved me, or you wouldn't leave me behind." Talking to her did not help, reminding her that she didn't like John was no help, and she claimed to hate Rosalia even more. By this time Bernadine was ready to enter a convent herself, but Verena and Cliff, whom Rosie had always liked, stepped in and offered to take her. They moved to Minneapolis, and that was even farther away than Templeton. Rosie brightened immediately at the prospect.

"I didn't want this," Bernadine told Magnus with tears in her eyes. "My family is fragmenting. I'm going away and abandoning my children. I never wanted that. It's so wrong."

"Mama, you can't think that," Magnus reminded her. "Verena already lives in Minneapolis. If Rosie lives with her, it just means you have two daughters together in Minneapolis."

"But not here."

"True, but you're not going to be here either, Mama. That doesn't mean you're abandoning us. We'll all get together sometimes, but the days of everybody living together are ending everywhere. People are going all over the world to make their mark, just like you and Aunt Elizabeth did years ago. Now Verena's gone with Cliff because he had a wonderful job waiting for him, and Rosie's going to be with them. She won't be left alone. Neither will the rest of us. We'll be fine, and we'll all see each other when we can," he gave her one of Joseph's smirks that made her almost cry again, "And you're leaving Tillie with us. We'll have a built-in babysitter."

John lived on a small acreage near the Raccoon River (whether it was the North, Middle, or South Raccoon River was never established. He changed the answer every time he was asked). His house had only two bedrooms. He sold the larger house he and his wife lived in after she died. Bernadine realized he probably really could not afford having all four of her younger daughters here. Certainly, he had no space for them. Even his kitchen was small, narrow, and minimally clean. Bernadine's first big project was a floor-to-ceiling cleaning project, with both Ardyth and Rita helping.

Although his income was limited, John and Bernadine were able to supply almost all their own food, a self-sufficiency that would become more important to them later. The Bierls ate well with John's cow supplying milk, his chickens furnishing both eggs and roasting hens, and his hutches of rabbits that always seemed full to provide a nice dinner.

John, fishing pole in hand, often invited Bernadine to join him on the river. "It's a beautiful morning. The breeze is from the south, and you know the old saying, 'When the wind is in the south it blows the bait right in the fishes' mouth.' Maybe we'll catch a few."

"I'll pack a lunch, and we can eat it right at the river. It's so peaceful there. I think you'll probably enjoy that as much as the fishing."

John chuckled. "You're on to me."

John cleaned the fish, and Bernadine cooked them. She rolled the catfish in flour and cornmeal, added a little salt and pepper, and fried them in lard.

"I don't know what you do different, Bernadine, but these fish are delicious." John reached for another filet.

"It's the lard," Bernadine laughed. "It's one of the by-products of butchering your own meat. You trim the fat from the pork, heat it until it becomes liquid grease, and pour it into crocks to harden. Lard makes the best pie crusts, too, flaky and tasty."

251

"Well, you can make a pie anytime. We've got plenty of fruit trees."

Bernadine continued many practices from the Rahm family farm, planting a large garden, preserving vegetables and fruit, and sharing the surplus with neighbors and friends.

"We eat just as well here as we did on the farm," Bernadine said to John. "Although it's good we have the fish and all your rabbits, or we wouldn't have much meat. Meat's far too expensive at the grocery store."

While John appreciated Bernadine's thriftiness and culinary skills, there were things he did not appreciate and these, in turn, made her appreciate him less.

Joseph always had a marvelous sense of humor. Bernadine, who never laughed easily, always laughed with childlike abandon at Joseph's wild remarks, his silly jokes and impersonations. John had all the sense of humor of a deathly ill mortician. It was that more than his miserly qualities that worried her. On the rare occasions when John laughed, it was done stiffly, as if it hurt. Most of the time he was polite, but brusque as if he had something better to do than associate with his wife or her daughters. Occasionally he was not polite at all. When he wasn't being polite, he sometimes made bitingly sarcastic remarks. Those remarks frequently found their targets in her daughters.

One day Ardyth and Rita quietly approached their mother. They looked at each other, and then Rita spoke up, "Mama, it seems like John is awfully crabby."

"And stubborn," Ardyth said. "When he makes up his mind, there's no changing it."

Rita smacked her fist into her palm. "He's been fussing and fussing at us, and we don't even know what we did wrong. We came all the way here to live and all he does is yell."

"He is set in his ways," agreed Bernadine. "We have to remember he's been living alone for quite a while and now three women have taken over his home. I will talk to him."

"Thanks, Mom." Ardyth kissed Bernadine's cheek. "I know you'll set him straight."

That evening after the girls went to their bedroom John and Bernadine were relaxing, Bernadine began. "John, I know you've lived alone with no one bothering you since your wife died. Now you have a new wife and two young girls to figure out. We've upset your routine, haven't we?"

"You might say so," John said. "I'm not used to all the noise, and giggling, all the time giggling."

"Really, John, you had five daughters of your own. Did they never giggle?"

"Not all the time like yours. Their mother kept the house quiet."

Now for the first time, Bernadine wondered if she made a wise choice in marrying this man. She drew on all her determination and smiled. "Perhaps our family was a little noisier than yours. I can admit this. Our children do have discipline, and they are not bad children. I've uprooted my daughters from the home they knew all their lives. I want them to be comfortable and happy here. You want peace and quiet, but one of the first things you told me when we met was that it was too quiet, and you were lonely. I think we both must make adjustments now that we are married. We must get used to your ways, and you need to get used to us. We need to compromise and work together. Can we agree to that?"

John thought for a while before nodding. "I suppose."

Ardyth and Rita, listening through the opening to the stovepipe, grinned at each other.

"I knew we could count on Mom," Rita whispered.

There were parts of John's life that Bernadine knew nothing about. Most of them did not bother her so much, but at least once a week he left in the middle of the afternoon and did not return until late at night. On those nights, he smelled of whiskey, though he was not drunk. Ardyth, whose sharp eyes never missed a thing, decided John must be a bootlegger. The Volstead Act was still in effect, but people all over the United States were breaking the inconvenient law and making their own hooch. In most cases, it was not a serious problem. Even Joseph made his own wine with elderberries, right under the kitchen sink. But hard liquor, that was different.

When she asked him about the whiskey, his eyes widened. "Are you spying on me? How dare you!"

She trembled and gripped the kitchen counter before replying. "Spying is not required to smell whiskey, John. Since my sense of smell is one thing that makes me a good cook, it shouldn't surprise you that my sense of smell can detect alcohol on your clothing."

"I suppose you're one of those women from the Temperance Society then? Wasn't voting the country into this position enough for you?"

Bernadine laughed in pure shock. "I knew you didn't know me well, but even so, this is a surprise. John, Prohibition, the Volstead Act, was the 18th Amendment. The law allowing women to vote was the 19th Amendment. While women may have run the temperance societies, it was men who voted for Prohibition. Since you know me so little, you might want to know that I have never been, and likely never will be, an American citizen, so I can't vote anyway."

His voice was hard and cold when he replied. "Elinor had enough sense to stay out of my business."

Bernadine, leaning on the counter for support, now took a deep breath, let go of the counter, and stood as straight as she could. "I am not Elinor. Nor will I be spoken to as if I am a servant. I am your wife. If you are breaking the law, and possibly consorting with mobsters, you are endangering this house and the other people in it. If my daughters inconvenience you with giggles, you threaten our lives with alcohol."

John rolled his eyes looking up to the ceiling and finally managed a sigh, "You silly, silly woman. No, it isn't like that. Look, Iowa shut down the state's breweries back in 1916 before Prohibition even started. People need their booze, and that's a God's truth for you. Templeton has a... a... well, it's like a consortium, a partnership of a few men who make rye whiskey. We use only quality ingredients, and although we started locally, people all over the country buy Templeton Rye these days. It's not legal, exactly, but we're not mobsters. Politicians all over the country order from us. Even Al Capone loves it. He calls it 'The Good Stuff.' We sell it for upwards of five dollars a gallon, and it's that little extra money I make that keeps us eating."

"Now you're being silly, John. It's having our own garden and raising our own meat that keeps us eating. You praised my thriftiness only last week."

"We buy flour and sugar from the store. We buy bacon and sausage from the butcher. Last week I gave you money for dress material for your girls. Where do you think that came from?"

Bernadine's hand went to her throat, "Oh, dear God, John, this is wrong. If I had known the money was illegal, I wouldn't have touched it."

"Then don't touch it. Drinking is harmless enough unless you do it too much. I'm not gonna have the government that's s'posed to protect me takin' away my right to make liquor."

"Then vote for Mr. Roosevelt," Bernadine snapped. "He's promised to do away with Prohibition as soon as he's elected. If you're going to do things that endanger the lives of my children, I will take them and return to St. Benedict."

"What? You can't divorce me."

"No, and I won't. But I will assuredly leave you."

John swallowed.

A week later, he dropped out of the consortium.

By 1933, it was evident that Prohibition did not achieve the economic and social objectives predicted. Economically, the industries that were expected to thrive under Prohibition were losing revenue. Restaurants failed from lost revenue for liquor sales. The entertainment and amusement industry suffered, as well. Tens of thousands lost their jobs as breweries, distilleries, and saloons closed. Abruptly shutting down the alcoholic beverage manufacturing industry caused a ripple effect that resulted in job loss in related trades such as trucking, barreling and bottling, distributing and many more. Government revenues declined at every level with the absence of liquor taxes, and hundreds of millions of dollars were spent to enforce the laws associated with Prohibition. Overall, the economic effects of Prohibition were more negative than positive.

From a social perspective Prohibition also failed. The widespread illegal liquor trade made criminals of thousands of American citizens. Organized crime flourished, government agencies battled corruption, and users of bootlegged alcohol endangered their health.

One man said, "Prohibition didn't improve health but threatened it, didn't reduce crime but increased it, and didn't raise public morality but corrupted it. Based on laudable intentions, Prohibition failed in every way."

Franklin D. Roosevelt took office on March 4, 1933. On March 22, he signed the Cullen–Harrison Act, which effectively ended Prohibition. Even before Congress ratified the 21st Amendment in December of that year, Americans across the country went out to have a drink.

Most of the bootleggers went out of business, but the gentlemen of the Templeton "consortium" were not among them. They continued selling "The Good Stuff," as it became known, and people kept buying it. The company eventually went legitimate, and John blamed Bernadine for his not becoming rich.

Bernadine didn't care.

By the following year, the dust that covered most of Iowa was now blowing even farther west, covering the plains in sepia. John's only cow sickened and died, and the river that flowed near the house shrank to the size of a stream as the drought went on.

With the plants dying, there was nothing to hold the soil in place. The winds picked up still more soil and carried it in dark, swirling clouds. Sometimes there were so many yellow clouds hanging in the sky that the sun could not be seen. Cars drove down the street with their headlights on in broad daylight. Despite John's hatred for using the electricity, he was frequently forced to keep the electric lights on in the daytime.

In St. Benedict, Magnus scheduled the equipment sale. When he wrote and told Bernadine of the problems he was having, she took Rita and Ardyth and headed to her old home for a visit.

She arrived to find Sylvia and Laurie arguing with Magnus. Even her arrival did not stop the shouting, and she physically walked between them to get them to notice her presence.

"What's going on?" she demanded.

"This jackass won't sell the John Deere," Sylvia shouted, giving Magnus a shove that failed to move him even one inch.

"You're right, I won't," he replied, his voice quiet and far more dangerous than Sylvia's screeching. "I can plow more acreage in a day with that tractor than I can in a month with horses. The other tractors can go, but the Deere is the newest and best of the lot, and I'm keeping it."

Sylvia looked pleadingly at her. "Mother, we know you have almost nothing in Templeton, and we never hear from you. Only Ardyth and Rita write to us. They complain about John never allowing them to have oatmeal with breakfast or all the other things he makes them do without."

"What?" Bernadine looked at her two youngest daughters, who looked back in defiance.

"Well, it's true," Rita argued.

Bernadine crossed her arms and glared at both of them. "Ardyth, what did you have for breakfast before we left for the train this morning?"

"Hotcakes, eggs, bacon, and sausage," Ardyth replied in a small voice.

"Were you still hungry when we left home?"

"No, Mama."

"But I wanted oatmeal." Rita blurted out.

Bernadine looked to the sky for patience. "How dare the two of you tell your sisters such tales. I'll make you both go without breakfast for a week if there's any more of this."

She turned back to Sylvia and Laurie. "Nobody is going hungry in John's house, girls. I personally watched Rita stuff five hotcakes into her mouth this morning with at least three sausages. She had scrambled eggs and toast, too. Just because we didn't have oatmeal doesn't mean the girls are lacking."

"They said he wouldn't give them dresses, either," Laurie offered.

"Of course not, he gave me a bolt of cotton last month for the two of them. I made each a dress. Why would they need another?"

Ardyth gave an exaggerated sigh. "Nobody wears home-made dresses anymore, Mama. If you don't have a dress from Sears and Roebuck, you might as well not go to school at all. People will throw rocks at you."

"And that, to quote Father Murphy, is malarkey," Bernadine replied. "If I hear of anything like that happening, I'll tell the principal, and since he once bought my dinner at a box social I am sure he'll listen. Now you girls can stop telling these terrible stories to your sisters. The truth is, Sylvia, we probably eat better than you do here. We have three kinds of meat to choose from and fresh-caught fish. Nobody is going hungry in Templeton. Nobody is naked in Templeton. I may have done too good a job at sheltering these two, so they don't know what real hardship is like. The equipment sale will go forward, and you will divide the proceeds. If it isn't fair to everyone, I will say no to the whole thing. Does everyone understand?"

Ben, Laurie's husband, stepped forward. "You are right, Mother. Enough is enough." He looked from his wife to Sylvia and back. "You cannot sell everything out from under your brother and leave Magnus high and dry. I'm coming with my truck and will help Magnus take some livestock and machinery to my farm to keep for him until after the sale. I'll help him get enough other items, too, to give him at least a start in farming on his own."

"Thank you, Ben." Bernadine hugged him. "You are exactly right. Magnus helped me carry on the farm after Joseph's death. He is entitled to carry on farming on his own. We will leave some machinery and livestock and some tools for him. He can pick what he needs. We can sell the rest. Enough of this greed, and I don't want any bad feelings. We need to be a cooperative family and work together."

"It wasn't greed. I was worried about you. I thought you needed every penny you could get," Sylvia snapped.

"That's true," Bernadine said, "But isn't it true for all of us? I read in the newspaper that experts are saying the country is in a 'depression,' and everyone is affected, not just us. I will not profit at the expense of Magnus and his family. Remember, he's helped me since your father died. He is entitled to what he and his family need to get started in farming and furnish their own house, that's it."

The day of the sale dawned clear and cold. Curious neighbors and potential buyers arrived early to look over the items. Finally, the auctioneer called the crowd to attention and announced the terms of the sale. "We'll start with the small tools, move to the larger equipment, and end with the machinery. Now, who'll give me a dollar-fifty for this bushel basket?"

Bernadine and Magnus stood at the edge of the crowd. Every item the auctioneer held up for a bid brought back a memory for Bernadine: Joseph's husking glove, the crock he'd used to ferment the elderberry wine, the bridle for the team of horses that took them on all their Sunday afternoon rides.

"I'm so glad John didn't come with me. I don't think I could've stood it," Bernadine murmured, taking hold of Magnus's arm. "Son, it's too much. Will you help me into the house?"

"Sure, Mom," He put an arm around her shoulders and guided her behind the crowd, around the puddles of melting snow to the front porch.

"There are so many memories here. It's almost as hard as losing Joseph, seeing everything we worked so hard for gone."

"I'm sorry you had to see it," Magnus offered, "but it's for the best. And thank you … and Ben … for stepping in when it looked like everything was going to go on the auction block. Honestly, I didn't want to be difficult with the girls. We didn't want everything that was yours, but we felt entitled to some things to begin farming the place for all the work and time we gave to you after Dad's death."

"You certainly were entitled to everything you got. Don't you dare feel guilty, son."

Over the next few days, the farmstead was emptied of Joseph's possessions and the paperwork was finalized. The sale relieved Bernadine and her daughters of the pressure to maintain the farm and gave Bernadine a small amount. She put it in the bank in St. Benedict in her own account. It was the first savings account she ever had.

Returning to Templeton, Bernadine announced to her younger girls that she would now be reading their letters before allowing them to be sent.

"That's not fair," Rita argued. "This is America, and the Constitution says you can't search my stuff."

"I'm not an American," Bernadine replied. "While you're worrying about fairness, was it fair for you and your sister to embarrass me in front of my other children? I'm tempted to send you both to an Indian reservation, so you can learn what it's like to be deprived."

Judith wrote less often these days, but Bernadine always enjoyed her letters. This latest one, however, worried her.

*Germany has a new leader too. His name is Adolf Hitler and they say he is a great man. He wrote a book called*

262

*Mein Kampf. I read it. He says he's going to restore all the greatness Germany once had. Do you remember what I said to you, years ago? Well, we got half of it.*

Bernadine looked back through the shoebox full of letters, and finally, she found the letter she was looking for. It was written in 1924. *We need a king again—a strong leader, but hopefully one who won't be interested in starting wars.*

*Everyone seemed to think Adolf Hitler was a good leader. But war, surely not.*

Bernadine never would have imagined it, but it was Tillie, sensible, practical Tillie who changed so after Bernadine left St. Benedict.

Magnus and Rosalia looked forward to a more peaceful life after Bernadine, Rita, and Ardyth moved out. Tillie had other ideas. Without her mother's guidance and no longer needing to set an example for her younger sisters, Tillie spread her wings. She invited friends over. They stayed up late talking, giggling, and keeping the babies awake.

"Tillie," Magnus cautioned, "you and your friends have to quiet down. We want to sleep. The kids wake up easily, and they need their rest. Please, please, less noise."

Tillie also thought she should have a say in running the farm, or at least be free to express an opinion. Magnus listened patiently and then proceeded to operate as he learned from Joseph.

As pretty as all of Bernadine's girls, Tillie soon had a serious suitor Arthur, better known as Art. Within a year, she married this young man she'd been dating for several years and moved out of Magnus and Rosalia's home.

"Finally, for the first time since we've been married we are by ourselves and can move on with our lives, just us," Magnus smiled, "with this large house, farm buildings, and rented land. I'm looking forward to it."

FARM HOME WITH HITCHING POST IN FOREGROUND AND
BEFORE GRADING AND BLACKTOPPING OF ROAD

As the topsoil continued its swirling pattern across the country, America took notice. It wasn't normal, people said. Along with the dust, the grasshoppers that thrived in hot, dry conditions returned. Many plants not already destroyed by the dirt, the lack of rain, or overheating, were ravaged by insects. People abandoned their farms and headed westward, most aimed toward California. In those years, that came to be known as "the Dust Bowl." More people migrated to California than went in the great gold rush of 1849.

Not all moved because their farms were wiped out, though. Some were ordinary factory or mill workers and others were white-collar types like lawyers and teachers. All of them were let go in the economic downturn. More than five million people now were unemployed.

Watching the hobos and caravans of jalopies passing their house, Bernadine wondered how much longer this could go on. "Elizabeth, this was your land of opportunity. Do you believe what's happening here?"

The government got involved. Groups such as the Soil Conservation Service took photos of the land from the sky and used them to produce soil maps to identify areas that needed attention. Then groups such as the United States Forestry Service's Prairie States Forestry Project planted trees on private lands to create shelter belts or lines of trees or shrubbery to reduce soil erosion. The Farm Security Administration even encouraged small farm owners in drier areas to resettle on other lands.

As part of Roosevelt's New Deal programs, Congress passed the Soil Conservation and Domestic Allotment Act in 1936. It required landowners to share allocated government subsidies with the laborers who worked on their farms.

The government paid farmers and ordered more than six million pigs to be slaughtered. This helped to stabilize prices. Then the government paid to have the meat packed and distributed to the poor and hungry. The Federal Surplus Relief Corporation was established to regulate crop and other surpluses. They diverted agricultural commodities to relief organizations. Apples, beans, canned beef, flour and pork products were distributed through local relief channels. Cotton goods were later included to clothe the needy.

Reading about it, Bernadine wondered even more. She never remembered droughts in Germany and whether they happened or not, she did not know. She knew that the Kaiser would not have taken all these steps to help the people he ruled. "When he knew the Great War was lost, he ran away and left his own people to suffer and starve for the war he started," she said. "I wonder if this Hitler fellow would do the same. Judith is smart, and she's afraid of him."

When John began shouting that night about taxes and subsidies and how unfair it all was, Bernadine for a change did not listen and agree with everything he said. She thought about everything that happened in the afternoon instead. Of course, John was a real American. He had nothing to compare things to, except the way things used to be in Templeton. He couldn't remember what Germany was like because he was never there. Bernadine was, and suddenly she realized that the United States, the country she never acknowledged or felt a part of, tried to take better care of its people than the Kaiser ever did.

She couldn't help smiling. *And what would you think about that, Elizabeth?*

In fact, the U.S. government was so busy trying to take care of its own people that it preferred to ignore what Adolf Hitler was doing in Germany. In blatant rebellion against the Versailles treaty, he was rebuilding Germany's army and air force. He sent them to his friend, Fascist leader Francisco Franco, to be tested in battle in the Spanish civil war. In Nuremberg, a series of anti-Semitic laws were passed that outlawed marriage between Jews and Germans. Before long, even friendship between the two groups was illegal. As if she feared her letters now were being censored or read by others, Judith seldom spoke of anything other than the weather or the antics of her grandchildren. One letter contained a single, telling line, *I was always so thankful for your friendship and it's best for you that you left. I only wish I could have, too.*

Hitler again violated the Versailles treaty by marching his troops into the Rhineland, a territory that was stripped from Germany at the end of the Great War. No one was certain what he was up to. Since he was thousands of miles away America ignored his bullying, and the other European countries sat back and hoped his ambitions would stop there.

In Iowa, Bernadine found herself with another bully, John. It wasn't that John was physically abusive. In a way, he was worse. He abused people's spirits, like Ardyth, and Rita, and Bernadine. Soon his irritation at Rita's lipstick arrived at the point where he threatened her with the convent.

Bernadine was always easygoing, and with the exception of her threat to leave if he continued bootlegging, her response to John's bullying was always gentle reasoning and compromise. Threatening her daughters with anything, even a potentially good thing, like a life of Christian service was not something she would put up with.

She walked in on his tirade about women who looked like prostitutes, looked at him, and then said to Rita, "Go to your room, daughter."

"Just a minute," John began.

"Immediately, Rita," Bernadine insisted, crossing her arms and looking straight at John.

Half in relief and half in disbelief that John had allowed it, Rita fled to her room and dropped to her knees at the opening to the stovepipe to listen.

"Rita and Ardyth may have come with me, John, but they are not your property to abuse."

"Abuse, woman? I'm trying to teach them some morals, since you never did."

"My daughters are not perfect, but they are good girls. Your goading them isn't teaching them anything. It's just painful and embarrassing to all of us. There's nothing to guide or encourage them, you just scream. What kind of teaching is that?"

"It worked fine for my girls."

"Did it? They're all in a convent, and they never come to see you. No wonder you were lonely when I met you. You drove your own children away."

"How dare you say such a thing?"

"I dare a lot where my daughters are involved. They are mine and when they require discipline, I will be the one to hand it out, not you. You need to understand that right now."

His heavy eyebrows came down in battle-ready stance, "Or what?"

"Or we will go away," she blurted out. "Magnus told me that he'd welcome me back if I ever needed to come. I would hate to do that to him because he and his wife deserve their own life. I would hate to do it to you since I promised my life to you. I will not let my children be harmed. Not even by you."

"Fine," John said. "You've made that threat before. I backed down and look what it cost me. Go ahead and leave, and I'll let it be known about town that you found someone you liked better."

"You can do that," she insisted. "I don't care what people think of me. The people I love will know the truth. As for the people in Templeton, they may listen to what you say. Since they still believe you drove Elinor to the grave and your daughters to the convent, they'll think I had a merciful escape."

"What?" His roar made the rickety kitchen table quiver, but Bernadine did not move.

"There's been gossip about you in Templeton for years. I heard some of it even before we were married. I've never participated in it, but yes, I've heard it." She turned away. "If we're going to leave, I guess I'd better start the girls packing, then."

"Now wait a minute, Bernadine. I never said you had to go. Look, I don't mind your girls being here. They do run loose, don't they?"

"If my seventeen-year-old daughter wearing a dull red shade of lipstick is running loose, then yes, they do indeed run loose. That same daughter spent all yesterday right here, bluing and ironing every one of your shirts, not running around bars. Her younger sister helped me cook dinner last night and breakfast this morning. It seems to me that their version of 'running loose' is an awfully well-behaved lifestyle."

"Well, they just need to keep the noise down."

Bernadine stared at him and did not say a word.

"Fine," John said. "I knew you'd understand what I meant. Maybe I don't always say it right, Bernadine, but I mean what I say."

He returned to his chair by the fire and stretched out his long legs.

A minute later, Rita crept into the kitchen to meet Bernadine. "Are we leaving?"

"Not today."

"Mom, you really know all about how to handle men, don't you?"

"Don't be silly, Rita, and get out some onions and potatoes for dinner."

As the two peeled potatoes and chopped onions, Bernadine wondered about the fix she was in. All problems could not be solved by a threat to leave. First, she had to be prepared to carry it out, and second, John had countered the bluff with one of his own. She had to find a way to deal with him that he could understand and not involve threats of returning to St. Benedict.

# ᴄ🙑Chapter Fifteenᴄ🙑

In 1938, Time Magazine recognized Adolf Hitler as "Man of the Year." Austria, Britain, and France recognized Francisco Franco's fascist government in Spain. Hitler took advantage of the situation, demanding "self-determination" for the Germans living in "Sudetenland" (the German-speaking part of Czechoslovakia) and in Austria. Soon both were flying the Nazi flag, and not a shot was fired. Cardinal Innitzer of Vienna met with Hitler and then directed all Catholic clergy and laity to "unconditionally support the great German State and the Führer."

Bernadine heard once from Judith that year, saying she was saving money and hoping of immigrating either to America or Cuba in 1939.

When she thought about it, she wondered how it could be that she always wanted to return to Germany, and Judith always wanted out.

Rita got a job in Templeton and moved into a microscopic apartment near the office. When Bernadine looked dubiously around and said, "It's a little small," Rita only laughed. Finally, she said, "Maybe you haven't read Milton, Mom, but he said it was better to rule in Hell than serve in Heaven. I love you, but I've really had it with your husband. Tell Ardyth she's welcome to move in with me if she wants."

The year closed with a furious blizzard, and by January Templeton was under almost three feet of snow. John, who never allowed Bernadine to heat their bedroom even in the dead of winter, still saw no reason to do so.

"John, it's just too cold to sleep in this room." She was using her reasonable voice, the one she used when trying, gently, to get him to address a problem with logic.

"I'm not cold."

"You're not the only one who lives here. I don't know why I have to remind you."

"I'm the one who pays the money for us to live here, so I'm the one who's important."

"Are you saying I'm not important?"

"Not as important as I am."

"I see." Bernadine thought for a moment. "Well, John, I'm not particular to the notion of freezing. So, since I'm not important, I'm sure you won't miss me if I sleep in the kitchen from now on."

"Sitting on a chair all night? That's insane."

"Spoken by the man who would rather freeze," Bernadine replied sharply.

"I'm not freezing."

"Right," Bernadine nodded. "Well, then sleep alone for a while. Since you're the one who's important, you shouldn't miss me at all."

She could see right away that she had won. John was a man who wanted a woman with him, but he didn't want her to know.

"You go right ahead," he mumbled, and went off to bed, alone. She dragged the fifty-pound flour bag over by the stove and pulled the partly empty sack of cornmeal next to it, forming a lumpy but serviceable mattress. Then she got the blue, star-patterned quilt that was her first wedding gift, from Mary and Katherine all those years ago, and wrapped herself in it. Sleep followed quickly.

After three nights, John seemed to realize that any discomfort Bernadine suffered sleeping on the floor was more than soothed by the heat. That night while eating dinner, he asked how long she intended to sleep in the kitchen.

"I should think," she said, "until it warms up enough that sleeping with you and without heat is comfortable again or until you decide to buy us a little more coal.

"Well then, I'll join you here."

"I don't think so, John. I'm sleeping on these sacks, and there's not enough room for us both."

"I wouldn't need that much room."

"No."

He stared at her. "What? Are you really going to deny me my marital right?"

"I have marital rights too, John. One of them is to be loved and valued. You've already told me I'm not important to you, and you didn't marry me for love. I'm not entirely certain you love anyone, even your own children. So if you think it's fine to deny your children their rights, and to deny me my rights, I don't feel much guilt about denying you a night of carnal pleasure."

It took all her courage to say that. She never could have said it to Joseph that much was certain. With Joseph, she never would have to say it. She always felt loved and valued with him. Even when he was dying, Joseph showed her his love.

"I could kick you out of this house for what you're doing."

"Yes," she smiled, "but who would cook for you and do your laundry? You weren't much good at it before we married, and you haven't done it since. You've had no practice."

His face was so red she could almost see the steam coming from his ears, and he turned and walked away without another word.

The battle of the bedroom ended a few days later when the snow cleared and Ben and Louis drove over with a truck full of dried corncobs. "Oh, that's enough fuel for weeks," Bernadine exclaimed, clapping her hands. "How did you know we were in need?"

"I think an angel must've told us," Louis said with a shy smile. "We never had so many surplus cobs before, and it just came to Ben here that maybe you and John could use some."

John was wearing a frown that told Bernadine his exact thoughts, but she stepped up to both her sons-in-law. "You were so right, my darling sons. Please, while you unload them, I'll whip up something to eat. Thank you so much for driving such a long way just for us."

"Well, you and Papa Joseph sure went above and beyond the call for us many times," Ben said, kissing her cheek.

"We're family," Louis shrugged, and that explained everything.

While she cooked, the men unloaded the cobs. Then she heard chopping nearby. They were taking down trees in the forest. When they finished, there was a cord of wood stacked against John's little house.

The two men left after supper that evening, refusing to consider staying the night. "All the snow on the telephone lines," Ben said, "Our phone service hasn't been right lately. I don't want Laurie thinkin' I'm keeping company elsewhere." He winked at Bernadine.

"Yeah, our wives are just like you, Mama Dena" Louis said, "Terrifying."

They kissed her on the cheek, shook hands with John, and went back to their truck.

As the red taillights vanished into the night, John turned to Bernadine. "How dare you accept their charity?"

"All right," Bernadine said, putting her hands on her hips and stepping right up to him. "I knew your pride was beyond reason, but do you really not understand the difference between charity and family? I don't know how you raised your children, but Joseph and I raised ours to understand that family always helps family. When Louis and Sylvia were first married and when Ben married Laurie, Joseph went down to help them plant their gardens. When their first children were born I went down to help them with the babies. Not because we were doing charitable acts, but because Joseph and I believed family should help family. Now Ben and Louis— God bless their sweet souls—are doing the same thing. Here you are with your angry red face and hateful words, demanding to know how I could let them do such a thing to us. You talk as if they burned the house down rather than saved our lives."

John did the unthinkable. He took a step backward. "You are a mean little thing, aren't you?" he asked with a strange smile. "I had no idea you were so spirited."

"Huh. There's much you don't know about me, John, but next time you're busy thinking you are so much more important than I, think of this. We have about a month's worth of fuel right now that we wouldn't have if not for me. Do you think they would have brought those cobs, or chopped all that wood, for you? No, they did it for me. Whether I am important to you or not, I am important to them."

She spun about and headed to the full sink of dishes, but he grabbed her by the elbow. "You're right," he said, still with that strange smile. "You are important, very important. I'll bring in a load of cobs for the bedroom fireplace, and I'll help you with dishes." His eyes held a softness she hadn't seen before. "Then we'll go to bed."

She nodded, "Why not?"

In May of that year, an international event splashed the front pages of newspapers across America, but few paid attention to it. Bernadine, however, did pay attention. Judith wrote her in February when it was still freezing outside. She said in her letter that she, her daughters, and her grandchildren booked passage to Cuba on a German liner called the St. Louis. *"This will be my last cold winter,"* she crowed. *"No more snow. They say the sun shines every day in Cuba. It looks far from Iowa, my beloved friend, but once we get there we're all going to hire out and we'll save up. Who knows, maybe someday I will come to visit you in the United States."*

When the long overdue rains finally came that spring, the St. Louis set sail, and Bernadine cried with joy. She was happy partly because of the rain, partly because of Judith—not so much that she and her family were going to Cuba, more that they were getting out of Germany. While a tiny spark of homesickness remained in Bernadine, she read too many distressing headlines to deny the fact that for whatever reason Nazis hated Jews. Only the previous November, a pogrom that now carried the name "Kristallnacht" left dozens of synagogues torched, Jewish businesses looted and destroyed, and close to a hundred Jews dead in towns and cities all over Germany. Even President Roosevelt condemned the actions of the Nazis.

Elizabeth told Bernadine years ago that many people didn't like Jews, but Bernadine never understood why. John never seemed surprised to hear of anti-Semitic goings-on, and the Nazis seemed to have a positively pathological hatred for Jews.

So now Judith would be free of all that, and Bernadine smiled at her childhood friend's childish enthusiasm for the adventure of travel and new places.

It didn't work out that way. The St. Louis sailed into Havana on May 27th, and the Cuban government allowed twenty-eight of the 937 passengers to debark. The rest were denied entry into Cuba and lingered on the ship for five days while Cuba and the United States talked about the situation. The talks failed. Most of the passengers had ultimate destinations in the United States, so the ship headed for Miami. Miami also denied them entry. Several passengers used the ship's office to cable Roosevelt and ask for asylum, but the president never responded. Ultimately the ship was forced to turn around and head back to Europe. Four European countries: Great Britain, the Netherlands, Belgium, and France, agreed to take the refugees in.

The next letter Bernadine received from Judith was postmarked from Belgium.

*I'm so tired and discouraged, but I refuse to give up. Naturally, we have very little money now, but once again we're going to hire ourselves out. At least the Belgians aren't out to get us like the Nazis are. I can say that now, can't I? In Germany, I was so careful in my letters, because I never knew who might peek at my mail. At least we are safe now, even if we're still cold.*

Five weeks after Bernadine received the letter Hitler invaded Poland. The French and British, who gave in to every demand the dictator made before, put their collective foot down and said, "Stop and go back to Germany, or we are at war." Hitler did not reply. Once again, Europe was at war.

*Mom, thanks for sending me to Verena. I love Minneapolis. There's so much to see here, so much to do; things I never would've gotten to do back in St. B. Movies, plays, shopping galore. While my clerical job is boring, I do meet a lot of handsome young men. They all want to marry me, but I'm determined to remain free. I'm only 22, after all. I know you were long married and with children by that age, but I won't make that mistake. I want my freedom.*

Bernadine long ago stopped reading Rosie's letters in John's presence. He always wanted to know what she was chuckling about, or what she was clucking disapprovingly about. When she told him he just shook his head. "That girl is going to get herself into trouble."

Bernadine, however, saw youthful high spirits in every letter. At twenty-two, Rosie matured into a tall, slender beauty with blue eyes, blonde hair, and a great sense of fun. Elizabeth would have liked Rosie. She had that same desire for adventure, the same idea that life was a game to be played. She lived her whole life that way, and perhaps Rosie saw it in her.

Perhaps, with that personality, it was only natural what happened next. But Bernadine never could have imagined how it would turn out.

The first indicator was a young man whose name was mentioned more than once and in more than one letter. The next was the same young man's name being mentioned again in letters over a three-month span. For Rosie, this was serious stuff.

Bernadine couldn't help wondering if another wedding was on the way. Ella wasn't married yet, Rita was in her own place and self-supporting for a year, and Ardyth just turned eighteen. If there was going to be a bride in the spring of 1940, it would most likely be Rosie, despite all her protests of wanting freedom.

The thing that was lovely about the small bank account in St. Benedict was that one day each month Magnus sent her a small cash amount from it. John, of course, would not give her money for such frivolous things as telephone calls, but she wanted to keep in touch with her children, all of them.

One day in September of 1939, Bernadine walked into town, went to the corner drugstore, and nodded to the clerk that she'd be using the pay telephone. She always wrote to the children to schedule the phone calls since John did not have a phone. Bernadine did not want to have this conversation around him anyway. She placed the long-distance call to Verena and then purchased a Coca-Cola while she waited for the operator to connect her.

At last, the connection came through and Verena answered, sounding flustered. "Oh, Mama, I am so glad you called."

"Is something wrong?"

"Well—yes and no. Yes, it's Rosie."

"Shall I speak to her?"

"She won't come to the phone. I told her you were calling today, and she said no. She wouldn't talk to you."

"What is it? What's wrong?"

"Mama ..." Verena's voice dropped so low Bernadine could barely hear. "She's pregnant."

Bernadine remembered once slipping on the ice and falling flat on her back, knocking the wind out of her and leaving her unable to breathe for a good thirty seconds or more. That feeling hit her again.

At last, she found her voice. "Worse things have happened, Verena. We can make this right."

"Well, that's what I said. But Rosie was nearly hysterical. She was crying. She told Robert, her boyfriend."

"I know."

"And he said that was great. He wants to marry her, but she said no."

"What?"

"She said she wasn't going to be tied down, having a baby every year like you were. She said she's too young to marry. She said a lot of other stuff you wouldn't like, but anyway, she says she can't have it."

"Look, can you get her on the line? I need to talk to her."

"She doesn't even live here now, I might as well tell you. She has a little place uptown."

"Fine, I'll come to her. I'll take the train up tomorrow, all right?"

"Oh, thank God. Yes, please come."

Bernadine went straight to the station and purchased a ticket for the morning train, then rushed home to pack.

John walked in and watched for a minute. "What's going on?"

"Family emergency," Bernadine replied.

"Who's hurt? We are going to St. Benedict?"

"Nobody is injured, and no, I'm not going to St. Benedict. I'm going to Minneapolis."

"Oh," he said flatly. "What's Rosie up to now?"

"Why do you always think Rosie is up to something? Couldn't it be Verena, or Cliff, or one of their children?"

"Nope, Rosie's the type to cause problems, and I'd bet a dime to a doughnut that's just what she's done. I'll go with you."

"You will not." Bernadine snapped. "She is my child, not yours. This would never have happened if you only let her come here with me."

For a change, John did not reply. He looked thoughtfully at her. Then he shrugged. "Gone and got herself in a fix, I reckon. Huh, you can do that anywhere. She was the type to do it."

"You should be ashamed of yourself. How can you label her so easily when you never knew her? How can you?"

"Wer Feuer frißt, scheißt Funken," John said and walked away.

He knew only a little German, a few idioms and platitudes mostly, and the Rosary. But he'd picked a bone-driller that time: "If you eat fire, you'll crap sparks."

That night Bernadine got no sleep. She could think of only one thing, "That stupid, stupid secret has outlived its time. When I see Rosie, I'll tell her everything. Elizabeth didn't marry the father. She also didn't die. She had a happy life, not long enough, of course, but that wasn't related. Rosie can live with this, even if she doesn't marry the boy. It may even make her grow up a little. But surely, if I tell her about Elizabeth, that secret will finally serve a purpose."

She walked the four miles into town again the next morning and by eight o'clock she was on the train to Minneapolis. Trains ran faster now. She remembered so clearly thinking that thirty miles an hour was incredibly fast, but she was a child then on her way to America. So many things changed since then. This train went twice the speed of the one on which she went to Bremen. According to the newspapers, there were trains that traveled faster still. She saw the passing trees as a blur of red and gold. Autumn was settling in. It was spring when she and Elizabeth left Germany. Everything was vibrant and green, the end of life and the beginning of life.

I won't think about that right now.

She wondered again what to say to Rosie. It didn't matter if she wanted the baby. But Rosie could keep the baby and raise it. She might want to go to a different town, one where she could claim to be a young widow. Rosie could marry that young man, Robert. Why didn't she want to? He loved her, and she seemed to love him. Bernadine wanted a big family, but if Rosie didn't, she didn't have to have one. Not all women had a baby every year. Elizabeth was married to Hans for thirty years, and she never had a baby at all.

The point was she had a great many choices available to her. She didn't need to despair or think her life was over.

Cliff was at the Minneapolis station to pick her up and take her back to the house. Rosie wasn't at the house, he said. "She saved her money from the time she got that job, and she got a little apartment downtown just last month."

"She never told me that."

"I think she thought you'd say no and make her come back to us. We gave her a curfew, and she seldom met it," he sighed. "You can't really ground a woman who's over the legal age of consent and who insists on paying to board with you. Rosie thought she was all grown up and didn't want to be accountable to anybody."

At Verena's house, Bernadine went in just long enough to hug her daughter and grandchildren. Then she announced she needed to get to Rosie's place as quickly as possible.

"We figured that," Cliff said. "Verena will drive you over, and I'll stay with the kids. Thank God I have an understanding boss."

On the drive over, Verena shook her head again and again. "I don't see why she won't marry the boy. Robert's nice, and I'm convinced he truly loves her. He was talking about marriage before she even found out about the baby."

"She can marry the young man or not. I just want her to know that we'll stand by her and we still love her."

"Well, of course," Verena said. "I thought that was obvious."

"Did you say so?"

"Not in so many words, but I thought she knew— we're family. That's what we do."

The parking space reserved for Verena's apartment had a car parked there. "That's Robert's car. Good, maybe he's talking some sense into her."

They parked next to his car and went inside to find a young man standing in the hallway, knocking on the door. He looked at Verena. "She won't let me in."

"Robert, this is our mother. Mom, this is Robert Stone."

He blushed. "Mrs. Rahm, I'm sorry to meet you like this. I feel so stupid. Rosie and I talked last night on the phone. I told her I'd come over today, but she said not to bother. As you see, I didn't listen. I just want to make things right with her."

"We all do, Robert. Knock again, and I will call for her."

He knocked on the door, and Bernadine called, "Rosie, Hasi? Little Bunny, will you let me in? I want to talk to you."

There was no sound from within. Robert tried again, and Verena called out, "Häschen please let us come in."

"Maybe she isn't here," Robert offered.

"She's here." There was a grim note to Verena's voice. "Robert, can you break the door down?"

"Are you kidding? You can get in trouble for that."

"The building manager isn't here," Verena shouted. "We've got to get in. If she's really desperate, she may do something stupid."

Understanding dawned on his face, and with it, fear. He grabbed the doorknob with one hand and slammed into the door, leading with his right shoulder and putting his weight into it. When the door shuddered but stayed in place, he did it again.

On the fourth blow, they heard a splintering noise, and the knob turned in his hand. Panting, he pushed the door open. "Rosie? Rosie."

The small living room was sparsely furnished and tidy. Verena pushed past everything, heading for the back. Bernadine followed, and Robert, still breathing heavily, was on her heels. "If she's not in her bedroom, check the bathroom," he shouted.

Bernadine glanced back at him. He stopped dead and was bent over, panting. "Robert, are you all right?"

"Just catching my breath, Mrs. Rahm."

"Mrs. Bierl," she corrected him without thinking, just as Verena screamed.

Bernadine forgot all about Robert. She dashed forward to find Verena standing in the bathroom, her eyes and mouth open wide. She turned back to Bernadine with her hands outstretched, blocking the way. "Mom, no, don't come in."

Bernadine ignored her and strode in, pushing her aside.

Rosie was in the bathtub, her head hanging to one side, her eyes open and glassy. The lower half of her body was covered in caked crimson, and the ten-inch knitting needle was still gripped in her hand, bits of torn tissue stuck to the sharpened tip.

Robert took off his overcoat and covered her gently. He made not a sound, but his chin quivered, and his tears splashed down on the tub.

Bernadine was still trying to absorb what she saw, but her mind did not want to accept it. I came to you, Häschen. Why couldn't you wait for me?

# ◌ℐ◌Chapter Sixteen◌℞◌

John met her in St. Benedict for the funeral. To his credit, he did not say a word about this being destined to happen. He didn't even say, "I told you so," although when Ardyth began sobbing too loudly for his taste, he told her to be dignified or be elsewhere.

Bernadine looked around the little graveyard. She saw the graves and headstones of old Joseph Rahm, Mama Rahm, young Joseph next to Clarence, then was Rosie, and to the other side, Hans and Elizabeth.

"I'm glad you're keeping the graves clean," she said to Magnus, who smiled.

"That's all Tillie, Mama. Every Saturday she comes down and cleans. During the dust times, she hauled a bucket from the well down here and sprinkled it over the graves to keep them nice. She brings flowers, too. Theresa helps." He indicated his seven-year-old daughter, who stood shyly by his leg. She waved at Bernadine.

"Thank you, Tillie, Theresa." Bernadine tried but was not quite successful in keeping the tears in her eyes from leaking out.

Tillie smiled. "Mama, they're my kin too, and I'm right down the road. Don't you worry, I'll always keep the graves up." She shook her head. "I can't imagine why Rosie did what she did."

"She didn't mean to," Bernadine cried. "She thought she was in trouble, and she thought she could get herself out. She didn't mean to kill herself, she just …"

"Shhh," John whispered, as a group of townspeople approached.

"Bernadine," Katherine had to use a cane to get around these days, but she was doing better than Mary, who was in a wheelchair. "We heard Rosie was in an accident. We're all so sorry. We wanted to see you again, but not like this."

In an accident, not "had an accident?" Bernadine looked at John, who was studiously picking lint off his black suit.

She hugged her old friends. "I'll try to get back to town soon, maybe for a happier occasion. You know I love you both."

Mary smiled. "You'd better come back. I want one of your pumpkin pies again before I get to heaven, so I'll be able to compare your food to theirs."

Bernadine smiled. It was forced, but Mary didn't seem to notice.

"Do you suppose they really have pumpkin pies in heaven?" Katherine asked.

"If they don't, then I won't go. I'll just stay right here," Mary declared.

It was on the train going back to Templeton, John by her side, and Rita and Ardyth sitting opposite them, that for some reason, Mary's inane remark about pumpkin pies and heaven made Bernadine start laughing. She hadn't laughed or cried since finding Rosie's body, but now that she started laughing, she couldn't stop. Her two daughters looked at her, and at each other, and back at her again, but she didn't care. John stiffened beside her and was looking out the window with fierce determination.

"Mom, are you all right?" Rita asked, and just that fast, Bernadine's laughter turned to great heaving, gulping sobs. John jumped up and left the compartment. Rita and Ardyth rushed to her. Rita pulled her into her arms and began soothing her like a baby, and Ardyth rubbed her back and whispered silliness like "it'll be okay." Bernadine barely heard or felt any of it. She was focused only on God, and how he surely abandoned her.

How long she cried, she had no idea. At one point the conductor stepped in and tried to shush her, but Ardyth grabbed his hand. "What would you do if your daughter bled to death?" she demanded, and the conductor looked embarrassed and ducked back out, shutting the sliding door behind him.

Eventually the sobs quieted, not because she no longer grieved, but because she ran out of energy. Her nose was as red as a fire engine and her face was wet and streaked, but the hurt remained. "Why?" she asked again.

The answer did not come to her. There was no peace.

"Mama," said Rita, "God speaks in a still, small voice, remember? You can't hear him if you're screaming."

Ardyth turned 18 and moved to Des Moines that winter, where she got a job at the Lee Hotel. Finally, Bernadine and John were alone together and any hope she had for peace evaporated as John sank back into his old, domineering ways. Bernadine had enough of it. Now when he criticized her use of time, she replied that if he had nothing better to do than watch what she was doing, then he was the one who was not managing his time wisely. When he wanted to stop heating the bedroom in winter, she moved out to the kitchen again and refused to come back until he heated the room.

Everything changed when Magnus came for an unexpected visit one day, as he drove a truck full of produce to Des Moines. Bernadine noticed that John was polite and courteous to him, and John was even polite and courteous to her. Then she understood John recognized Magnus as an equal, possibly even a superior. There was in John's mind a craving for complete order, not just in his house, but in his relationships. He probably didn't realize he was a bully. He simply regarded himself as superior to Bernadine and therefore felt permitted to order her around. He treated his wife and daughters the same way. Magnus was tall, strong, considerably stronger than John, and the farm he rented and managed was bigger than anything John ever had. That was when the idea came to Bernadine. She wrote to Laurie and Sylvia, and within a few weeks, Laurie wrote back. Smiling, Bernadine went to John.

"John, I know Templeton is your home, and this is a nice little house. We've been comfortable here. We're four miles from town, and even though the rains have returned, the land we're living on isn't as productive as it used to be. The house and land are too small for the price we're charged. Would you consider moving to St. Benedict?"

"Why do we have to be near your home? Why not just move nearer to Templeton?"

Funny to think of St. Benedict as "home," For her, Germany was always home. She gave John a harmless smile.

"I miss my family, especially my grandchildren. If you had grandchildren, I'm sure you would want to be close to them."

John stared blankly at her, and she thought *of course, sending all your daughters to a convent is hardly a good way to get grandchildren.* She had too much sense, though, to say it aloud.

John thought for a minute. "It would have to be a bigger house than this one, a few acres at least. This land never adequately supported us. We'd need more."

She nodded.

"I'd want a couple of cows. Losing that one a few years back was bad, we had no more milk."

"True."

"All right," he said. "I'm open to the idea."

"Well, as it happens, Laurie mentioned casually in her latest letter that there's a little place near her and Ben that's for rent. Would you like to look into it?"

"Why not, we certainly could."

A week later, Ben drove Bernadine and John to the small farm that was near his place. It was only fifteen acres, but that was ample for a couple of cows. There was a small barn and chicken coop, and a garden patch, even strawberry beds. The house was large and spacious. Bernadine barely allowed herself to hope the place would satisfy John's picky nature, but he looked it over and pronounced it satisfactory. He rented the place on the spot. Sylvia, Laurie, and Emma cleaned the place and their husbands prepared the outbuildings while John and Bernadine packed. A month later he and Bernadine were living just outside St. Benedict.

Bernadine chuckled. "I'm so glad to be home." Then she marveled, home. Had St. Benedict really become home for her?

She didn't question it for long. Except for Verena, her children lived in St. Benedict or close by and all welcomed her back. Ella just married ("Finally," John muttered), so there was a new husband to become acquainted with.

Soon Bernadine and John, whether he wanted to or not, were hosting weekly family get-togethers with Bernadine's children, their spouses, and all Bernadine's grandchildren. All spent their Sunday afternoons eating, and for entertainment, playing poker and pinochle. Everyone brought food, so no one went short on supplies, and John became more sociable. Again, whether he wanted to or not.

"I'm so glad to be doing these dinners," Bernadine confided to her girls as they walked through the house the first week. "I've missed those times. The porch, don't you love the big front porch and the large lawn, girls? Come spring we'll put rocking chairs out there, and I can watch my grandkids roll and tumble on the grass."

During the week she worked in the garden. Frequently her grandchildren popped in on their way home from school. All of them knew she would have cookies and milk waiting. Now and then she went to see Mary and Katherine. She always took a pumpkin pie along, saying it was so Mary could put off going to heaven for a little while.

On Sundays, she most often made her famous strawberry shortcake for dessert. Soon she was known all over the county for her strawberry shortcakes, with homegrown strawberries and farm-fresh cream.

Of all the grandchildren she loved, Bernadine could not have a favorite. There was one she was especially close to. Theresa never tired of hearing Bernadine's stories about her life as a child in Germany, and the voyage across the ocean. She thrilled to the tales of Bernadine's early days in Iowa and meeting Joseph. The two spent many hours together in the kitchen and garden while Bernadine taught Theresa to cook and bake.

"Grandma, tell me about Uncle Hans and Aunt Elizabeth. Dad says they were the best."

Bernadine laughed. "I suppose it seemed that way to your Dad when he was little. They were generous bringing gifts for everyone at Christmas. Elizabeth spent a few weeks with us every summer and had new games and puzzles for everyone. Yes, the children loved it when they came."

Bernadine grew quiet. She bit her bottom lip.

Theresa leaned forward to look into Grandma Bernadine's face. "Did you like it when they came?"

"Oh, yes, dear. Elizabeth was a great help to me when I had so many little ones to take care of. But …"

"But what," she wanted to know.

Bernadine shook her head. "It's nothing."

"But something made you sad."

"I get sad when I think how Uncle Hans and Aunt Elizabeth died so suddenly. They would love to have met you and all your cousins." With an effort, Bernadine brightened. "Let's not talk about sad things. Tell me what you're learning in school."

"All right, but I hope you'll tell me more about Uncle Hans and Aunt Elizabeth someday, Grandma. I don't want to make you sad, though."

"You could never make me sad, Theresa. You keep me young and grateful."

France and Great Britain declared war on Germany after the invasion of Poland in September of 1939, and for several months nothing happened. The Germans took over Poland in a matter of days, and Great Britain sat on her hands. In May of 1940—almost a year after Judith's arrival in Belgium—Hitler invaded France.

France spent the majority of the 1930s building a series of fortifications along their eastern border to ensure that Germany could never invade them again. Somehow they forgot that when Germany invaded them during the Great War, they did not go across France but across Belgium. Now, thirty years later, history repeated itself. Germany marched across Belgium and turned the Low Countries—Belgium, Luxembourg, and the Netherlands—upside down.

Reading the newspapers, all Bernadine could think was "Judith and her family were right in the way."

She saw a dog hit by a car once. The dog was oblivious as it trotted across the road, and the driver was going too fast. The car smashed into and over the dog, leaving it splattered across the pavement. Bernadine now realized Judith was just like that little dog, in the wrong place at the wrong time. She was right in the way, with tanks, artillery, and hate-filled Nazis bearing down on her, and there wasn't a thing Bernadine could do.

While most of Europe waged war on one another, and Japan dropped bombs on China, the Western Hemisphere sat peacefully in an isolationist bubble. President Roosevelt signed the Lend-Lease Act into effect in March of 1941, but most people thought that would be the limit of the United States' involvement.

Until December of that same year, the Japanese bombed Pearl Harbor. Hawaii was only a U.S. possession, not a state, and many Americans couldn't have pinpointed it on a map. When most of the United States Navy was destroyed there, it was an outrage to everyone. Men rushed to their nearest recruiters to join the military. The government, foreseeing lean times, began rationing things like sugar and gasoline.

In St. Benedict Bernadine and John faced a different difficulty. Ben and Laurie saved for years to buy a real farm. The little chunk of land they had was barely enough to live on. In March of 1942, they bought a 240-acre farm in Minnesota and moved north. Laurie and Ben were Bernadine's closest neighbors and helped with getting them to church, the grocery store, and John's frequent doctor appointments. Without Ben and Laurie, they could not stay where they were. Sylvia found them a house in town and helped them move into St. Benedict.

"It's only half a mile from Magnus," she told them.

"I don't want to move again," John muttered.

Sylvia, however, was impervious to grumbling. "Then stay here, but I'm moving my mother into town where she can be near people."

John moved.

"There will be room for your rabbits, and there's a chicken coop on the property," Sylvia said, "but you'll have to sell the cow." Before John could protest, she went on. "Magnus has agreed to provide you two with all the milk and cream you need, whenever you need it."

John let out a martyred sigh. "I suppose it's for the best." For someone as controlling as John, it was difficult to take orders from someone else, especially a stepdaughter. Though he hated to admit it, he was getting older and life wasn't getting any easier. Settling into new surroundings took more time than it did in the past. Bernadine resumed her cooking and cleaning while John managed to care for the few remaining rabbits.

"When these few are gone my days of raising rabbits will come to an end," he mumbled. "I'll continue with the chickens, so we'll have fresh eggs."

"When they stop laying," Bernadine declared, "we'll butcher them and use the meat. All these chores are getting to be too much for you."

Although local family members dropped in often, Bernadine and John's home could not accommodate large family gatherings. Those shifted to the homes of Bernadine's children. The food, laughter, and celebrations—birthdays, First Communions, confirmations, graduation parties—continued with Bernadine's grandchildren.

John, however, now found the many gatherings overwhelming. Too much noise. He much preferred prayer times with Bernadine in the peace and quiet of their small home. For Bernadine, though, every time she read the paper and saw the many young boys going overseas to fight, it made her grateful to have family nearby. At least that way she knew they were safe. They also had a telephone now, which John hated, but it was necessary. The children who lived far away, like Ardyth in Des Moines and Laurie and Verena in Minnesota, called, so Bernadine could keep up with them.

The children and grandchildren dropped in when they could. One grandchild who always stopped by was Theresa, still wanting stories of the old days. She and Tillie still went to the graveyard each week to tidy the graves and bring fresh flowers. Bernadine often joined them.

One day in late 1943 Ardyth called. "Mama, there's no easy way to tell you this—I'm pregnant."

She was also unmarried. This sort of thing was happening a lot now with the war going on. People uncertain of tomorrow so often grabbed with both hands at today.

Bernadine gasped. "Ardyth, please, don't do anything foolish."

"You mean like Rosie? No. I wouldn't, I couldn't."

"Will you marry the father?"

"Um no, he's married. I didn't know at the time, but …"

"That's all right. Don't worry about it. Do you want to come home?"

"No, Mama. I love you, but I have no wish to hear what John will say about me. I'm coming back to St. Benedict, though. Emma said I could live with her and Frank. They'll help me."

"Then I'll come and see you when you get back, and I will surely come and help when the baby comes."

"That's sweet, but don't worry about it. Emma and Frank are both great, and we'll be fine."

"Oh, yes … another grandchild to hold. I can hardly wait."

As she hung up the phone, John shook his head. "You should've sent her to the convent."

Bernadine crossed her arms. "At least she calls me. John, when's the last time you heard from your children? The five daughters you forced into the convent—or the two sons I never knew you had until I found their pictures when we moved? We've been married almost twelve years, and not once has one of your children written or visited. My children may make mistakes, but at least they know I love them."

Kenneth, better known as Kenny Rahm was born in 1944. He was only in the news a short time, though, for at the next family gathering, Rita announced her engagement.

"Rita," her mother and sisters all exclaimed, surrounding her for hugs.

"What's his name?" John demanded. "Is he in the army? Does he have a steady job? Why didn't he come with you today?"

Rita took a deep breath and looked John in the eye. "His name is Iver. He is not in the army, but he does have a steady job. He didn't come with me today because of the baseball game."

"Whoa," Magnus hollered. "What kinda guy abandons his girl for a baseball game?"

"He's a bum," John proclaimed.

Rita glared at both of them. "He's not a bum, and he's at work right now."

"I thought you said he was at a baseball game," John said.

"That's his job. He plays for Sioux City."

"Wait, wait," Magnus exclaimed. "Do you mean Iver Fee, of the Redbirds?"

"Yes."

Jaws dropped across the room, children and grandchildren all talking at once.

Darwin, Emma's oldest, crowed, "That is the greatest thing I ever heard in my life."

When Iver did come out to meet the family, eight of Bernadine's grandchildren demanded his autograph, even Magnus shyly requested one.

He looked around at them. "How about we play ball instead? That's lots more fun."

From then on, whether it was playing baseball or cutthroat pinochle, Iver was just one of the family. When outsiders asked they were told Rita had caught a celebrity.

The war dragged on. There was no escaping it. Even in the small-town Iowa newspapers, it was on the front page. Photos barraged the readers of grinning soldiers loading artillery rounds with, "This one's for you, Adolf," chalked on the side.

In January of 1945, Bernadine read of a concentration camp where some three thousand Yugoslavian patriots had been shot. It was the first she heard of "concentration camps." It would not be the last, though, because in April British forces liberated one called Bergen-Belsen. Most of the prisoners there, emaciated, bald, hollow-cheeked ghosts, were Jews.

"Bergen was where Judith used to live," Bernadine whispered, fisting her hands around the newspaper. John would be furious at her for wrinkling it like this, but she couldn't help it.

With the liberation of each subsequent camp, more news came out. "Concentration camp" became a word to fear. Out of 234,000 Jews deported from France, Belgium, the Netherlands, and Norway, fewer than 10,000 returned home," said the Overseas News Agency in August.

This, then, was what probably happened to Judith and her family. The place she always thought of as "home" had done this.

No, it wasn't Germany's fault. Even Jesus said that people were like sheep. They followed any shepherd. The country Bernadine came to had good shepherds. Germany had not. It was Bernadine's own idealized notion of home that kept her rooted in Germany her whole life long. She refused to give up the notion of going "home" even after spending more than fifty years in America. She gave birth to eleven children here and knew the love of her life here. Now her grandchildren spoke English with ease, regarded America as their country, and knew no German at all.

She pushed through the back door. The house they moved to was near the edge of town. She could see the green stalks of the cornfields towering in the distance. This was the view she saw most of her life, but suddenly it was brand new. There in plain view were the azure skies, golden sun, and the life-emanating green of the corn growing in silky rich black soil, the product of glaciers long ago, just as Mr. Leonard said. Why hadn't she seen it back then? Why had it taken so long to appear this way?

BERNADINE, AFTER ALL THESE YEARS, REALIZING IOWA IS
HOME

This was home. Iowa was home.

She turned back to the door. "John," she called.

He grunted an acknowledgment.

"How does one take out citizenship papers, John? I want to be an American."

He looked up from the newspaper and chuckled. "It's about time."

# ᴄᴀ⌢Chapter Seventeen⌢ᴂ

B ernadine Vornhold Rahm Bierl became a US citizen in 1946, not long after the phone call from Ardyth informing her that she was marrying a wonderful man named William Thomason, and that he would be adopting Kenny.

The years after that saw both happiness and loss, Emma and Frank moved to Algona, about ten miles away, and bought a restaurant. "Frank & Em's Café" became a popular hangout both for Algona locals and Rahm family members.

John died in 1959, after a long illness. Bernadine wept, but even in her most honest, vulnerable moments, she was never entirely certain of her feelings for him. In the end, she decided that he at least wanted to be a good man, and if he wasn't always one, neither were most of the people she knew.

Once again Bernadine's family rallied around her. Although John was buried next to his first wife near Templeton, his service was held at the St. Benedict Church. During the fellowship following the funeral, John was remembered as a man who enjoyed his peace and quiet, whether fishing at the river or saying the rosary.

Now in her early 80s, Bernadine faced another major adjustment—living alone. When some of her children nagged her to remarry, she told them, "I tried to make John happy. He tried to be a good husband. In the end, his biggest flaw was that he wasn't Joseph. Any other man I marry now would have that same flaw."

Instead, she countered her loneliness with activity to her family's amazement.

"Don't you ever have aches and pains, Grandma?" Theresa asked one day. "You always walk everywhere. You seem so healthy. How do you do it?"

"I stay active. It seems I'm always on my feet puttering around in my kitchen or outside. I just don't sit still for long periods of time. I think the answer to staying healthy and not having aches and pains is to keep your body active, moving. So, remember that when you get older. Don't just sit around."

"Okay, Grandma. Would you sit long enough to tell me the story again of how you met Grandpa Joseph? I just love that story."

"So do I, Theresa. So do I."

In 1961, Emma died suddenly of a heart attack while visiting Laurie. She was only 49.

Then in 1965, Verena died, also of a heart attack.

And in 1969, Ella died.

Four daughters and one son gone, sometimes Bernadine wondered if God realized just how wrong it was for children to die before their parents.

Maybe this was why she finally agreed to move in with Tillie in 1971. Tillie insisted she wanted to take care of her, but Bernadine—Mother Dena, as many were now calling her—was not interested in anyone taking care of her. She just wanted to stay near her children. Too many died before she did.

But the biggest blow came just a few weeks after she joined Tillie. Grandson, Kenny, joined the army several years before as a combat engineer, planning to make his life in the military. On his second tour in Vietnam, the dream was shattered when his artillery firing position was overrun.

At age ninety, Bernadine stood stiffly, leaning on her cane, watching as the five soldiers in the honor guard pointed their rifles into the air and fired a three-volley salute. She jumped a little with each shot. It sounded so ...final.

The pallbearers, all soldiers as well, removed the flag draped over the coffin and in a series of synchronized movements, folded it into a neat triangle. One of them carried it over to Ardyth and placed it gently in her arms. White-faced and dry-eyed, the already widowed Ardyth accepted the flag and nodded to the soldier, who saluted her.

Posthumously, Kenny was awarded the Silver Star. "For gallantry," they said.

"Pish-tosh," Bernadine muttered. "It doesn't bring him back. What good is it?"

Theresa rang the doorbell. It was a cold day in early October, 1973.

"I'm coming, just a minute," Bernadine called. A moment later the door opened.

Bernadine squinted for a minute. "My goodness, Theresa, here you are, still looking just like that little eight-year-old girl with the gap-toothed grin, the one who always wanted family stories." She smiled. "I thought that Marine of yours dragged you off to some island in the middle of nowhere."

"I came back just for you." Theresa hugged her. "He's back from Vietnam, you know. He got the Legion of Merit."

"That's okay, just so long as he came home all right."

"I called earlier. Tillie didn't tell you? I was going to the cemetery today. She said it was a while since the weeds were pulled."

"Tillie's at work right now, neither sleet nor snow nor whatever. I can never remember that mail-carrying slogan. You know she does that now, right? She's not an emergency medical technician anymore."

"I know that, Gran. We can go over and maybe she'll meet us there."

"Let me get my sweater first. There's a chill in the air. I wouldn't be surprised if it snows tonight."

Theresa picked up the heavy wool sweater for her. "I'll help you."

Bernadine fussed with the sweater for a moment and then slid her arms in. Theresa put her arm through Bernadine's and together they went to the cemetery.

Bernadine sighed, looking around, "So many graves, so many, too many."

"We'll take care of them, Grandma, all of them, Elizabeth and Hans, Grandpa Joseph, Clarence, Emma, Ella, Rosie, Kenny, everyone."

"I know, and soon, me." Bernadine coughed a little.

"Not you. You're gonna live forever."

"I used to think so." She smiled. "Now, not only do I not think so, but I also don't want to. The book of Ecclesiastes says, 'To everything there is a season—a time to be born and a time to die.' I think my time to die is coming, and it's all right, Theresa, it really is. I've lived a long and full life."

Theresa tried to smile back, but it didn't quite take. "How old are you? You never would tell me."

"Would you believe I'm ninety-two? Deep down inside, I still feel like the eleven-year-old child on the boat, coming to America."

She walked slowly over to the plot that housed Elizabeth and Hans, braced her hand on the tombstone, and got down on her knees. She kissed her fingertips and touched them to the stone again.

"These days I think a lot about the people here," Bernadine said, putting on her work gloves and grabbing a handful of weeds. "I want to see them all again."

"Don't be in too big a rush," Theresa said, dropping to her knees on the other side of the grave. "Some of us here love you."

"And I appreciate that."

For a moment, they worked in silence.

"It's all pretty again, Mama." Bernadine smiled as she sat back and looked.

For a moment fear gripped Theresa. As long as she had known Grandma Bernadine, she had a sharp mind and a sharper wit. Was it failing at last?

Bernadine gave Theresa a wink. "I call her that here. It's the only place I can get away with it."

"You call your sister 'Mama'?"

"She's not my sister," Bernadine replied. "She never was."

"What?"

Bernadine went on as if she hadn't spoken. "It was a stupid, stupid secret and I'm tired of keeping it. I should have told it thirty-five years ago, maybe then Rosie would still be alive. I should have told it seventy-five years ago when Joseph asked me to marry him. Maybe he would still be alive. He had so many burdens to carry, and he always knew I was holding something back from him."

She looked intensely at Theresa, her eyes leveled at her, gauging …something.

Theresa stretched out her hand. "Grandma, whatever it is, you can tell me."

"So I will." Bernadine's voice cracked a little. "You're the family historian, aren't you? Yes, Elizabeth was my mother." She gulped. "You've seen her photograph, haven't you, Theresa? You saw how beautiful she was."

"Of course, I did."

"Imagine her at thirteen, just discovering her womanhood. You know what it's like. Nowadays they call it 'hormones.' If there was a word for it then, I never knew it, but you're all confused, wanting to be a good girl, but wanting to attract men, not knowing why."

"I remember," Theresa said with a rueful laugh.

"Well, maybe you can imagine what it was like with her, then. There was a handsome man who lived not far away. He used to see her when he walked past her parents' house. Sometimes he stopped and hung over the fence and talked to her. Bewitching, she said. Nowadays they have a different word. 'Predatory,' I think. She was young and silly and … she had hormones, you know, and she thought she must be in love with him."

"Oh," Theresa thought of her own daughter at that age and shuddered.

"Thirteen years old and pregnant by a married man from down the road, a man with money. Her father confronted the man, but he denied everything and said terrible things about Elizabeth."

Theresa swallowed, when her voice came out, it was harsh. "That's sinful, Grandma."

"He sent her father away. Then he spread rumors through town about Elizabeth that were not true. You can imagine what this did to her reputation, plans for education, to everything."

"Dear God," Theresa whispered.

"Worst of all, her own parents were so ashamed of her they hardly spoke to her. They feared she might go back to him, so they watched her closely and didn't let her out of their sight. Bernadine rose painfully to her feet. "Her parents were never rich, but they had enough to afford a couple of servants and farmhands. Young Elizabeth was so ashamed and lonely, and she had nowhere to turn. Her parents refused to support her. She suffered through a difficult pregnancy, both physically and emotionally. Some mornings she felt so sick that she could hardly get up, yet she was expected to do her share of the work. Her parent's rejection was more painful than the morning sickness or the complications.

Then they sent her to the servants' cottage to have the baby, and they started making arrangements to move the family north. They sold the farm and bought a much smaller place in the Rhineland, far from Bavaria. Elizabeth had the baby—me. I felt she didn't want me, and I grew up thinking this most of my life. She treated me terribly," I thought.

"That's awful." Theresa cried. "How could she be so cruel? It wasn't your fault."

"No, no it wasn't. It wasn't really hers, either, was it? She was still a child, one with a brilliant future at one point. Now the future seemed in tatters, and there I was, very tangible evidence of a serious mistake." Bernadine burst out coughing.

"Grandma, we need to get you home and warm. The graveyard can wait for another day when you feel better."

"I don't want to leave. Now that I finally started talking, I don't think I can stop. Please, let me finish."

When Theresa found her voice, it was doubtful. "All right ..."

"Her parents purchased the farm in the north. Once I was born, she wanted them to take me. I was sure she didn't want me. My grandmother named me Bernadine after her sister. Elizabeth idolized her Aunt Bernadine. So, still in Bavaria, I was baptized Bernadine. When we moved, I was known as their younger daughter. I grew up believing it at first but Elizabeth, God bless her, she could never decide what she wanted. She told me one day that she was my real Mama. I was a small child at the time, but I still remember. She was so serious. 'You can call me Mama when we're alone, but not around other people, all right?' she said to me. She was so beautiful, and I wanted her to love me, so I agreed."

"Oh," Theresa could think of nothing else to say.

"She went away for a while to a teaching school, and then came home again. All that time my grandparents, the people I called Mama and Papa, cultivated the story that I was their daughter. If I slipped up and said 'Mama' to Elizabeth, they told people I was 'slow.'" She chuckled. "Well, I was never as smart as she, maybe, but I was hardly slow."

"You were in an impossible situation," Theresa responded. "You must have been so confused."

"Yes, and then some fellow named Julius, he had been one of Papa's farmhands, came into Coesfeld one day and saw us all. He went to Papa and demanded a large sum of money, threatening to expose Elizabeth if Papa didn't pay up. Well, Papa didn't have much money, and you know how farming is—every dollar you make goes right back into the farm. Papa had a heart attack that very night, and he died the next morning. I guess Julius went home disappointed."

"That must have been terrible for everyone. You can't keep a farm going without a manager."

Bernadine nodded. "That was when my grandmother told Elizabeth she needed to start over. Not long after that, she died. When Elizabeth sold the farm, she took every cent and put it into passage to America. Before we left the country, though, she took me aside and said, 'Now you must never, ever again call me Mama, not even in your dreams. From now on, we are sisters.

We're going to America to start a new life, no more scandal or people looking down on us. I want to meet my true love, marry, and have more children. You must promise me that you will never call me Mama again. We are sisters. I will always care for you as my sister. I will be with you and give you a home as long as you need me. Never, ever call me Mama. Do you understand? You must never tell anyone our secret.'

"Then Mama cried like I'd never seen her cry before and wrapped me in her arms. 'I will always love you as my daughter. From now on, though, I'm your sister Elizabeth. Please, remember that.'

311

"I didn't know what to say. I had never seen my Mama like this before, not even when Grandpa and Grandma died. Here we were leaving everything I knew and going to a country where everything would be new to me, different and strange. I wouldn't have any friends. Now more than ever I needed a mother, and she was asking me never to let anyone know she was my Mama."

"Why," Theresa asked.

"I asked her the same thing. She said if anyone found out, she would be ruined and could never get married." Bernadine shook her head. "Elizabeth was a romantic. She believed in love at first sight. She believed in love forever and that she would marry and have a lot of children that could call her Mama. When she met Hans, she believed in him. I don't know if she ever told him about me, but I do know that for all his promises of having me visit them, I was never once invited to their house." She reached over to Hans's grave and ripped a couple of weeds out. "I said he would come between us and he did. I said she would leave me for him, and she did. Because she loved him, I can't hate him. Does that make sense?"

"Yes, of course," Theresa assured her.

Bernadine continued, "We clung to each other and sobbed. 'I …don't …understand. But I'll do what you say,' I promised. Theresa, I've kept that promise until now. I never told Joseph or John. I've never told anyone in America until now. Before I die I want my family to know the truth about the woman they've always known as Aunt Elizabeth and me."

"I think she really must have loved you, Grandma. The secret was the best way she knew to give you both a fresh start. Even in America, people would think better of two sisters coming to the country than a single mother."

"I know, Theresa. I realized that myself as I grew older. Still, for much of my life, I resented Elizabeth for making me keep her secret. I don't want to go to my grave with that bitterness in my heart. Please tell the rest of the family, and be sure they know that deep down in my heart I felt Elizabeth always loved me like the daughter I was."

"I will tell them, Grandma, I will."

"This was my goal in life—never to tell her secret until my dying day." She sighed. "I know I am dying, and I kept my secret."

"I kept the secret. I hated it. Sometimes I hated her. Every time I went into labor, I called for her. 'Mama, help me …' she never came. Katherine and Mary were with me for the births of all my children. My Mama never came. She never came when Clarence died. She never came when I was hiding in a cellar during a tornado and thought I would die. She came every Christmas and brought all the children lots of expensive presents, so they all loved her. She was jealous of me because I had children, and for some reason, she could never have another one. She kept saying she wanted a child, and I kept thinking, 'You've got one. Is it so bad, even now, that you can't call me what I am?'

"In the Rhineland we lived just outside Coesfeld. My best friend was a Jewish girl named Judith. She knew Elizabeth was my Mama, so did Judith's mother. I told them before Elizabeth made me promise never to call her Mama again. So they knew, but as far as I know, they never told anyone. Judith died in the camps. I got a letter from her daughter years after the war, telling me about it, and how all her life, Judith wished she could leave Germany and come to America. All my life, I wished I could leave America and go back to Germany. I went through life resenting Mama because she loved Hans more than me. You know, a wife should love her husband more than anything. That's how I felt about Joseph. I wasted so much time on silly thoughts, but I want you to know, I'm glad now that I stayed in America." She looked down at Elizabeth's grave. "When I get to heaven, I will call her Mama, and there's not a thing she can do about it. I know God forgave her. I hope she figured it out. He forgives us all, even before we ask."

"Grandma, you look tired. We can finish all this another time. Let's go home and I'll put you to bed."

To her surprise, Bernadine did not resist. They made their way back to Tillie's house, and Theresa put Bernadine to bed like a child.

Looking up at her, Bernadine said, "You'll tell them, my daughters, son, and their families, won't you after I'm gone? I never told Joseph or John. If I had told Rosie—I was going to, but I didn't get the chance. Tell them I'm glad I became an American, and that I was proud of them. I hope Elizabeth was proud of me for keeping her secret."

"I'll tell them, Gran. I promise."

At about three in the morning, the phone rang, and Theresa picked it up and said with a mumbled, groggy voice, "Hello."

"Theresa, it's Tillie. I'm calling everyone in. Mama died in her sleep tonight."

"What?" She sat up, wide-awake.

"I know you were really close to her, but don't cry, Theresa. She looked so peaceful. You'd think an angel came to take her straight to heaven. After all those years of looking worried, she's at peace now."

Theresa looked out over the crowd. It would be a large funeral. They said Grandpa Joseph had one of the biggest funerals ever held in St. Benedict, but Bernadine lived there even longer. She knew so many generations of people and was loved by so many. She only hoped Grandma knew it. Theresa adored her grandmother but now, knowing all she knew, her respect for the dear woman deepened and grew. Theresa's father, Magnus, was a great man, and her mother, Rosalia, a wonderful mother. Theresa always took her parents for granted. She never would again, not after hearing what Bernadine went through.

Once the gathering was over, once all the guests were gone and only family remained, she would tell them. Yes, she would tell them, but just not yet. After all, the secret was kept for almost a century. A couple hours more wouldn't hurt.

# ↶Afterword↷

As Bernadine requested when she knew she was dying, Theresa revealed her grandmother's secret to the rest of the family. Following the funeral luncheon, she gathered the family together.

"You know that I was with Grandma Bernadine at the cemetery the afternoon before she died. What you don't know is what I'm about to tell you and what she asked me to share with you." Theresa retold Bernadine's story including Bernadine's life-long struggle to accept Elizabeth's decision to relinquish her role as a mother and hold her to their secret relationship. Stunned, Bernadine's daughters and son gaped at one another.

Sylvia turned to Magnus. "I had no idea? Did you?"

"None, I had none."

"As I think back," Laurie said, "Aunt Elizabeth … well, Grandma Elizabeth was exceptionally attentive and generous. I always thought it was because she and Uncle Hans …wait …was he our grandfather? Anyway, I thought it was because they didn't have children of their own."

"But we were her grandchildren," Tillie remarked. "No wonder she doted on us."

"It makes our mother's life all the more remarkable," Sylvia said. "She had to be strong from a very early age, and she was. We just didn't know how much she had overcome."

Joseph and Bernadine's greatest legacy is their family who carries on their penchant for hard work, good food, fellowship and faith.

Sylvia, whose musical talent was recognized early in life, attended music school in Dubuque, Iowa for a short time. She played the piano beautifully, almost entirely by ear. Family dinners at Sylvia's house often concluded with everyone singing around the piano and Sylvia accompanying every request. Though none of her family was Irish, "Irish Eyes Are Smiling," was a favorite.

Sylvia lived on a farm with her husband and family. They rented the land as did many other farmers. She kept a large garden and sold some of their garden vegetables and fruits to townspeople who were eager for fresh produce.

Ella had a head for business. In her early twenties, she worked in the bank at St. Benedict with many of Joseph's relatives. In 1930, three men driving a stolen Ford Roadster robbed the bank of $3000. Ella, the assistant cashier, was the only employee in the bank at the time. The men locked her and the two customers in the vault. After the robbers left, Ella found a screwdriver and escaped the vault.

About three weeks later, the bank was robbed again. Only a small amount of money was taken because the time lock on the vault prevented it from being opened. This time the robbers stole a car from pheasant hunters and burned it about two and one-half miles north of a nearby town. Ella and one other person were the only ones in the bank during the second robbery. She thought the bandit said, "Stick 'em up" and immediately she laid face down on the floor. The robber, assuming she was going for a gun, jumped through the cashier's window. Ella was unharmed. Two nineteen-year-olds were sentenced to life imprisonment for this crime.

During WWII, Ella worked in the State of Washington for a defense company contracted by the United States government. Her job required top-secret clearance, and she never talked about it. Ella lived comfortably there for many years and enjoyed showing her family the tourist attractions when they came to visit. She married later in life and lived with her husband, Floyd, in Pennsylvania for some years. After they divorced, Ella moved back to St. Benedict.

Laurie, the grandmotherly type, was relaxed and easygoing. She married a local farmer. They rented farmland near St. Benedict and raised hogs and chickens, milked cows and sold milk and cream.

Sunday dinners at Laurie's home were a favorite with the cousins, especially the young girls. While the boys played games outside, Laurie gave the girls free range in her closet. They tried on her clothes, applied her makeup and nail polish, and adorned themselves with her jewelry and fancied themselves pretty, stylish ladies. Laurie took it all in stride.

Laurie and her husband, Ben helped care for Bernadine and John when they moved from Templeton to the acreage close to where Ben and Laurie farmed. When the opportunity to purchase farmland in Minnesota arose, Laurie and her family moved away. They rarely returned to St. Benedict after that due to the demands of a large dairy herd and milking operation.

Verena attended the local schools and the Immaculate Conception Academy of Dubuque where she took courses in sewing, music, and secretarial training. She married and lived with her husband in Minnesota for a while before moving to Mason City, Iowa where they raised their family.

Verena's husband worked as a mail clerk on the railroad for many years. In his free time he did carpentry work. He oversaw the construction of Bernadine's small home that is still standing on the corner lot in St. Benedict.

The Rahm families often joined Verena, her husband, and their family at Clear Lake for a day or two in the summer. Nearby Mason City was a favorite shopping destination since it usually included a stop at Verena's. And a stop at Verena's always involved food. No matter the time or how many were in your party, Verena made her guests feel welcome.

Magnus, the only surviving son with eight sisters, was only a little spoiled. After Joseph died, Magnus and his wife, Rosalia, rented the farmland from the insurance company that bought the farm. Several years later, the land was sold to a successful professional photography company that bought it as an investment. Magnus and Rosalia helped the overseer hired to manage the farm work out the details of the arrangement, including the profit-sharing agreement and tracking maintenance expenses and area land values.

Magnus and the overseer worked well together, but when farmland increased in value, the company put the farm up for sale. Before it sold, Magnus and Rosalia bought the acreage with the house and outbuildings. A local farmer whose land was adjacent to it purchased the remaining acres.

Magnus and Rosalia opened their home many times for Sunday dinners and special celebrations. Card-playing and low-stakes poker games were favorite adult activities. Snacks and adult beverages were plentiful, and games often went on until the wee hours of the morning.

Emma was happy-go-lucky and ready for a party anytime. She and her husband were regulars at the poker games Magnus hosted. They farmed many acres of rented land where they raised corn, beans, and some livestock. In the summer they often hired nieces and nephews to work the bean fields. This meant chopping out unwanted corn stalks and cockleburs. The youngsters earned decent money for the few weeks the worked lasted. The work was hard and the weather usually hot and humid.

In later years, Emma and her husband, Frank, bought and operated a restaurant in Algona, about ten or twelve miles from St. Benedict. They lived above the restaurant until they passed away.

Good-hearted, Emma helped anyone in need. She loved cooking. Pastries, cakes, pies, cookies, and candies were her specialties, which made their restaurant a favorite spot for many diners.

Tillie lived with Magnus and his wife, Rosalia, after Grandma Bernadine married John and moved to Templeton. When she married, she moved to Algona where she and her husband raised their family.

Like Emma, Tillie was a generous, caring person. She cared for her husband's brother when his health failed, and he had no place to go. He stayed with them until he passed away. Grandma Bernadine also spent her final years with Tillie after she was not able to live alone.

Tillie had an adventurous spirit. She rode motorcycles, long before it became an acceptable activity for women, as well as men. She was always ready to take one for a spin. In her later years, however, she led a quiet, reserved life.

Rita married a professional minor league baseball player, which made him extraordinary in the eyes of the siblings and their families. He, however, shunned the attention and preferred to be treated like one of the family.

The nieces and nephews loved Rita because she brought them treats of gum and candy. They looked forward to her visits for they knew what her large purse contained.

Rita and her husband, Iver, lived about a hundred and fifty miles from St. Benedict. They often visited over Memorial Day and brought flowers to decorate the graves of Grandma Bernadine, Joseph, and other relatives buried in the St. Benedict Cemetery. Iver served his country proudly during WWII and was stationed in Europe during part of the conflict.

Rita and Iver moved to another small town when his baseball career was over. He worked as a sales representative for a company that made barbeque sauce. His salesmanship and popularity as a baseball player helped make Cookies BBQ Sauce a favorite on many Midwest tables.

Ardyth, the youngest, was often called on by her married siblings to babysit her nieces and nephews and she was a favorite. Parents were barely out of the driveway when Ardyth found the pots and pans and started making candy. Homemade fudge was her specialty. She knew the recipe by heart and knew that beating it long and hard was the key. She stirred that candy by hand until it was the right consistency and ready to be put in the pan. It was perfect and delicious each time.

After high school, Ardyth worked as a hotel maid in Des Moines. There she became pregnant by one of the individuals who stayed at the hotel while on a business trip. He was married and had a family. Ardyth did not want to cause problems or embarrassment, so she never asked anything of him.

Emma took her in and helped her through the pregnancy and birth of a healthy boy. Ardyth loved her child and worked hard to support him. She married when Kenneth was a young boy and her husband, W. S. Thomason adopted him.

Kenny enlisted in the military during the Vietnam War. Staff Sergeant Kenneth A. Thomason served his second tour of duty in Vietnam with the US Military Assistance Command, Vietnam (MACV). Because of his combat experience during his first tour, he was assigned to a South Vietnam Army Infantry Battalion as a Military Advisor. On April 3, 1971, his unit was overrun by a large North Vietnam Army unit resulting in a fierce battle and his death. He was awarded the Silver Star for Gallantry and Purple Heart, posthumously. He was twenty-seven years old when he was killed. Survivors included his mother Ardyth, his wife, and a young son. Staff Sergeant Thomason's name is engraved on the Vietnam War Memorial in Washington, D.C. and can be found on Panel 04, Row 103. He gave up his life for his country, and Ardyth was proud of that. He is buried in the St. Benedict Cemetery.

BERNADINE WITH FAMILY – FRONT ROW: VERENA, SYLVIA,
GRANDMA BERNADINE, AND ELLA

BACK ROW: TILLIE, RITA, LAURIE, MAGNUS, EMMA, AND
ARDYTH

St. Benedict, like many Iowa towns that thrived in the late nineteenth and early twentieth centuries with the coming of the railroad, has since died out. The 2017 census identifies it as a Designated Place (no longer an incorporated town) with a population of thirty-nine. The Industrial Revolution that began at the turn of the century, enabling fewer farmers to farm more acres of land, initiated a shift from rural to urban areas that continues today. The population became increasingly mobile venturing on to larger towns and cities with a wider selection of goods and services.

Many of the businesses in St. Benedict were destroyed by fire in the 1920s because there was no firefighting equipment and limited water supply. Some stores were rebuilt.

The bank building survived several fire threats, but the People's Saving Bank of St. Benedict closed its doors in 1931, a victim of the stock market crash and the Great Depression. At the time Joseph's uncle, Martin Rahm, was president. His father, Joseph, Sr., was vice-president. Another uncle, Ed along with Joseph and Bernadine's daughter, Ella, were cashiers.

The school was torn down in 1984 and a Parish Center built on its site. Children from the area are bussed to larger grade schools in Wesley and Algona and to a large high school, the Bishop Garrigan High School in Algona.

The small home where Bernadine enjoyed her last years of independence remains on that corner lot in St. Benedict with a new owner and occupant.

All of Joseph and Bernadine's daughters, son, and spouses are deceased, but some grandchildren and their families still live near St. Benedict.

The 160 acres of land that Joseph lost during the Depression sold eventually to a local St. Benedict farmer who owns them today. Before the sale, however, Magnus and Rosalia bought the acreage with the house and other buildings.

ACREAGE IN THE EARLY DAYS.

They raised six children in the house that Joseph built for Bernadine, and both lived there until their deaths. The acreage has since been sold several times, and the house remains intact and occupied with little change to the exterior.

The 120 acres Joseph and Bernadine bought and lost were sold eventually to Magnus's son, Joe. He owns them today and lives in the house on the place. Two of his sons, Chris and Noel, farm the land.

# ᏭᎳ Author's Note ᏬᏓ

ernadine Vornhold Rahm Bierl was my
paternal grandmother. I always thought I was
one of her favorite granddaughters because
she made me feel that way. I felt special whenever I was with
her.

As a young girl, I spent many summer vacation days
with Grandma Bernadine. Sometimes it was just a few days.
Other times I spent a week or two helping her with housework
and gardening, and whatever else needed to be done. She
sewed clothes for my dolls. We shared secrets, played cards,
prayed together, giggled and laughed. We derived happiness
from being together. Grandma Bernadine generated warmth
and kindness, and I loved being around her.

We remained close even after I married and moved
away. Return visits to my home never failed to include time
with Grandma Bernadine—reminiscing, laughing, and crying
together—sometimes tears of sorrow, but often tears of joy
over some long-forgotten escapade or event.

Bernadine was mentally alert and sharp right to the
end. She kept abreast of all the local and international news
and was well versed on world leaders. She carried on
articulate conversations on nearly any subject, a tribute to her
lifelong love of books and reading and her amazing capacity
to recall much of what she learned.

I knew that Grandma Bernadine had endured much sadness in her life, outliving two husbands and five children. It wasn't until she shared the truth about her relationship with Elizabeth that I came to understand more fully what a remarkable woman my grandmother was. Despite being deprived of the mother-daughter relationship as she entered her formative years, Grandma Bernadine brought positive energy and joy to everyday tasks. Strong and resilient throughout difficulties, she gave generously to others and asked nothing in return. She reminded me often of the importance of spreading laughter and kindness to those around us. Just a smile, she'd say, sometimes lifts burdens.

I was born in the house Joseph built for Bernadine. Magnus and Rosalia were my parents. I attended the grade school that stood where the Parish Center now stands. I was baptized, received my First Holy Communion, was Confirmed, and married in the St. Benedict Church with its beautiful stained-glass windows.

One of those windows had been donated by my great-grandfather Joseph Rahm Sr. and his brother Martin. It depicts St. Wendelin, revered in Germany as the patron saint of country people. In the image, the saint holds a staff and tends a sheep.

BEAUTIFUL STAINED-GLASS WINDOW FROM ST. BENEDICT
CHURCH DONATED BY JOSEPH RAHM, SR. AND BROTHER,
MARTIN

This church building and its faith community played a
central role in my grandmother's and my life. My
grandmother and I often attended Mass together there. We

both found purpose in praying for something in particular and giving thanks when we received it. I like to think my grandmother found comfort in the Rahm stained-glass window, that St.Wendelin portrayed for her the Good Shepherd who had guided her from Germany to a German community in America that loved and cared for her.

Attending the final Mass there before the church closed in 2017 was especially poignant for me. St. Benedict Catholic Church contained generations of memories. Celebrating them and acknowledging the end of an era was bittersweet. More than anything, though, I felt Grandma Bernadine's presence. I sensed her kneeling alongside me and sharing my joy and sorrow. Her spirit joined ours at the Parish Center where we laughed and cried for the friendships and memories we shared in this place.

My hope and prayer in writing Grandma Bernadine's story is that her spirit—her kindness, patience, and love of life—would also be my legacy. My wish is that friends and family find me to be the same kind of positive influence in their lives that my grandmother was in mine. I hope in sharing her story others are inspired to live similar generous, grace-filled lives. I pray I have done her story justice.

## ∾About the Author∾

R aised on a farm in north-central Iowa, Diane Holmes loved the wide-open spaces. She even had a pony named Dolly that she'd ride to the pasture to round up cows for milking in the barn. She cherished her home life with five siblings and loving, caring parents.

When she was just twelve years old, Diane's Mom made a statement to her sister and her about their Grandma Bernadine. From that statement (She can't mention because it'd give the secret away.) Diane knew exactly what the title of a good story could be. She went through many years of mentally writing parts of the story, but in 2014 her New Year's resolution was to put pen to paper and fingers to keyboard and start writing. It took Diane nearly two years to complete, and then it was only a skeleton of a book. After several years of revising and embellishing, she felt it was complete and ready to share with readers. *Two Sisters' Secret* is historical fiction set mostly in the rural community of Diane's childhood and based on the story of her grandmother, Bernadine.

Following high school graduation, Diane left the farm life to attend the American Institute of Business in Des Moines, Iowa, and married high school classmate, Lyell, a career Marine Corps officer who flew helicopters and jets. They made their home in many states, including Hawaii for three years, where Diane even took hula lessons and danced with her group at the Officers' Club for family and guests. She loved the adventure of living in different states and learning about each one and what they had to offer.

Diane Holmes worked seventeen years for a large school district in CA supervising their workers' comp and property/liability insurance programs.

She and her husband raised two daughters and a son, all of whom they are very proud. Although it was difficult at times for her three children to leave their friends, she was relieved to see them adjust quickly, make new friends, and love the excitement of a new place. Even the family dog, Peaches, loved exploring new surroundings.

331

Diane and her husband eventually returned to their roots in Iowa and now make their home near Des Moines. She hopes you enjoy reading *Two Sisters' Secret* as much as she enjoyed writing it.

CPSIA information can be obtained
at www.ICGtesting.com
Printed in the USA
FSHW010718100520
70105FS